An Introduction to PHP

Learn PHP 8 to Create Dynamic Websites

Mark Simon

Apress®

An Introduction to PHP: Learn PHP 8 to Create Dynamic Websites

Mark Simon
Ivanhoe VIC, VIC, Australia

ISBN-13 (pbk): 979-8-8688-0176-1   ISBN-13 (electronic): 979-8-8688-0177-8
https://doi.org/10.1007/979-8-8688-0177-8

Managing Director, Apress Media LLC: Welmoed Spahr
Acquisitions Editor: Smriti Srivastava
Development Editor: Laura Berendson
Coordinating Editor: Shaul Elson

Cover image designed by Freepik (www.freepik.com)

Distributed to the book trade worldwide by Apress Media, LLC, 1 New York Plaza, New York, NY 10004, U.S.A. Phone 1-800-SPRINGER, fax (201) 348-4505, e-mail orders-ny@springer-sbm.com, or visit www.springeronline.com. Apress Media, LLC is a California LLC and the sole member (owner) is Springer Science + Business Media Finance Inc (SSBM Finance Inc). SSBM Finance Inc is a Delaware corporation.

For information on translations, please e-mail booktranslations@springernature.com; for reprint, paperback, or audio rights, please e-mail bookpermissions@springernature.com.

Apress titles may be purchased in bulk for academic, corporate, or promotional use. eBook versions and licenses are also available for most titles. For more information, reference our Print and eBook Bulk Sales web page at http://www.apress.com/bulk-sales.

Any source code or other supplementary material referenced by the author in this book is available to readers on GitHub (https://github.com/Apress). For more detailed information, please visit https://www.apress.com/gp/services/source-code.

Paper in this product is recyclable

To Inge and Maria, who helped me to put things in context.

Table of Contents

About the Author

Mark Simon has been involved in training and education since the beginning of his career. He started as a teacher of mathematics and moved into IT consultancy and training. He has worked with and trained in several programming and coding languages and currently focuses on web development and database languages. When not involved in work, Mark can be found listening to or playing music, reading, or just wandering about.

About the Technical Reviewers

Jeff Friesen is a freelance software developer and educator conversant in multiple operating systems, programming languages, and other technologies. His specialty is Java Standard Edition.

Satej Sahu is a Senior Software Data Architect at the Boeing Company. In his current role, he is responsible for architecting enterprise systems with a focus on system integration, data pipelines, ETL, data architecture, machine learning, large language models, and MLOps. He has worked in both service- and product-based companies in startups and MNCs and has been in the roles of Principal Software/Enterprise Architect at Honeywell and Solution Architect at Adidas previously. He has experience in full-stack development in PHP environments using enterprise frameworks leveraging cloud-native solutions. He is a certified AWS Architect and holds leading industry certifications in a variety of databases, data, architecture, and Linux environments. He has been an active member of the Association for Computing Machinery (ACM) since 2013 and is also the coauthor of the book *PHP 8 Basics: For Programming and Web Development* from Apress.

Acknowledgments

Many of the images used for the sample site come from Wikimedia Commons (`https://commons.wikimedia.org/wiki/Main_Page`), while other photographs are my own and can be used freely for the purpose. The background pattern comes from Pattern Cooler (`https://patterncooler.com/`).

The text, alas, is my own, and I am unable to shift the blame.

Introduction

When the World Wide Web was invented, it was designed for scientists to share information with other scientists, which is to say it wasn't meant to be exciting. Things have, thankfully, come a long way since then.

At the time, pages were statically created—that is, each page was crafted one at a time. Fortunately, the web server was designed to be extensible, and it is possible to interface the server with external software. The standard way to do this is to use the Common Gateway Interface, or CGI to its friends.

In the early 1990s, Rasmussen Lerdorf developed a collection of CGI programs for his Personal Home Page. This grew into what became Personal Home Page Tools (PHP Tools, for short), version 1. Others began to get involved, and this grew into version 2.

In the late 1990s, Zeev Suraski and Andi Gutmans rewrote things and developed version 3, renaming it to PHP: Hypertext Preprocessor. This, in turn, grew into PHP 4, based on the new Zend Engine, named after Zeev and Andi. PHP 4 is the earliest version mentioned on the official website, http://php.net.

Since then, things have moved on. PHP 5 improved on the syntax, overhauled support for Object-Oriented Programming, and introduced PHP Data Objects, PDO, to access the database. PHP has always been able to work with databases, but PDO does it in a much more organized way.

PHP 6 was supposed to add a number of new features, in particular better Unicode support, but it was taking so long that the improvements were gradually added to PHP 5, and PHP 6 was absorbed into it.

All of this is, hopefully, ancient history. PHP 5 has long been retired, as has PHP 7, which vastly improved performance, including a new JIT (Just in Time) compiler, and added significant improvements to the syntax.

The current version of PHP is version 8 point something, and PHP 7 and below are regarded as old. The main differences you'll see include improved performance, more improvements to the syntax, and significant steps toward better consistency in the language.

This book, of course, works with PHP 8. Unfortunately, a significant number of web hosts, quite possibly including yours, are slow to make the move from a previous version, since that risks breaking some sites which rely on older features. We'll allow for that by showing alternative code to work with older versions.

PHP was never originally meant to be a programming language, and it shows. Coming from a mixed environment results in some features which are more like other programming languages and some features which are more like working with a Unix-like shell. Functions have inconsistent naming and usage, and the whole appears to be a growing collection of ideas rather than a planned and organized language.

Things are getting better, but it will still drive many experienced programmers to distraction. Nevertheless, it all makes some sort of sense, and it's not hard to get into the spirit of things.

What's in the Book

This book is all about developing for the Web. At some point, you're expected to have access to a web server and, for the data, a database. You won't want to experiment with a live server, so Chapter 1 focuses on setting up your own development server as well as the tools you'll need to write and work with your code.

To get to know the ideas better, we'll be working on a sample site, the files for which you'll download and install. They have the basic outline, layout, and styles ready to go, and it will be your job to finish the site with the PHP you'll be learning.

You'll then start writing the code. Chapter 2 looks at how you actually write PHP and how you can organize your code. In the chapter, you'll get the basic principles of PHP programming. Chapter 3 puts the coding into practice and looks at working with a form and sending an email. Forms will be a fundamental technique working with PHP, as they will enable you to send data and maintain it on the web server.

Chapter 4 will concentrate on uploading files to the web server. These will include image files. The images will eventually be used in an image gallery, so you'll also look at manipulating these images to get them ready.

A core part of the website is about the data. In Chapter 5, you'll look at connecting to the database and getting the database ready for the back end of the site. From there, you'll learn how to add data safely in Chapter 6.

In Chapter 7, you'll look at working with ZIP files and processing CSV files. This will enable you to do a bulk upload of data and images for the image gallery.

The image gallery itself is developed in Chapter 8. You'll develop skills in reading the database, fetching images, and preparing HTML content from the database data.

In Chapter 9, you'll learn about maintaining the data. Not only will you be inserting and reading data, you'll also be editing and deleting some of it. This gives you complete control over the content of the database.

In Chapter 10, the focus is on security. You'll learn about how PHP maintains continuity for individual users and how we manage passwords and logging in. Chapter 11, on the other hand, focuses on configuring the site and develops a configuration page which manipulates a configuration file.

In Chapter 12, you do it all again—well, much of it, anyway, but with some improvements. The goal of the chapter is to develop a simple blogging system which allows you to add and maintain articles and links them to new or existing images. It's a project to consolidate what you've learned in the book.

The blog articles are simple text articles, but you can extend the blogging system using markdown to produce richer formatting. This is covered in Appendix A.

The appendixes also cover some of the other techniques used to enhance the site, as well as some details of the differences in PHP versions. Finally, there's a discussion of some of the additional custom functions used in the book.

You may have come into this with some existing knowledge of programming, such as with JavaScript or some other language not connected to web development. On the other hand, you may have had no programming experience whatsoever. We won't assume that you have programming skills, but you will develop them through the book. You'll learn not only the specifics of PHP programming but the principles of programming in general, so you'll be in a good position to develop your skills further.

CHAPTER 1

Introduction and Setting Up

Before you get started with learning PHP, you will need to have a working development environment. Ultimately, PHP will be running from your web server, either on the Internet or on an intranet. However, for development (and training) purposes, it makes sense to set up a local web server. This can be any machine on your network, but it's very easy to set up everything you need on your own desktop or laptop computer.

The good thing about web development is that it is culturally agnostic. It doesn't matter whether you develop on Macintosh, Windows, or even Linux: the product will be the same. What does matter is that you have all the right software in the right place.

For the impatient:

If you're anxious to get going, you can ignore all of this and skip over to the "Web Server Setup" section. It's very important and will make the rest of the book much easier to work with.

© Mark Simon 2024
M. Simon, *An Introduction to PHP*, https://doi.org/10.1007/979-8-8688-0177-8_1

How the Web Works

When you open a page in your web browser, typically there's a lot of activity before you actually see anything. The process is something like this:

- You enter a URL in your browser's address bar.

  Modern browsers will hide part of the URL—notably the `https://` protocol. However, it's all there when you highlight it and copy it.

- The **domain name** needs to be **resolved** to an **IP address**.

  The domain name is something like `sample.example.com`. That could be anywhere, so the browser needs to search for it in the following locations.

- The **hosts** file is on the browser's computer and has a hard-coded list of domain names and IP addresses. The one you're looking for is almost certainly not there, but it doesn't hurt to look.

- If the hosts file doesn't have the domain name, the browser then looks in a distributed database called the **Domain Name System** (**DNS** to its friends).

  Presumably, it's found a matching IP address. If it hasn't, you'll get an error message.

- The browser then makes a connection to the server at the IP address.

  The server may well have many services to run, and each has been assigned a **port** number to identify which service you want.

For a live web server, the port number is almost always port 80, so that's the default. That may be included in the URL, but you probably won't see that. For a testing or development server, it's often a different number, which will need to be specified.

- The web server typically manages multiple sites at the same IP address in various directories. It then uses the domain name to choose which directory has what you want.

  The multiple domains on a single server are referred to as **virtual hosts**.

- If a page (or some other resource) has been specified, the server will try to satisfy your request. If it hasn't, the server will assume that you want a default page, typically called index.php or index.html.

  Of course, if it can't be found, you'll get a response telling you as much.

- If the request is for a PHP page, which is the whole point of this book, then the server will pass the file on to the PHP processor for further processing. You'll see more of this later.

  The result, with or without additional PHP processing, will be sent back to your computer, where it's up to the browser to work out what to do with it.

For learning and development purposes, we can create a simplified environment which works the same way, but stays on your own machine. You'll see this in the setup section.

The Sample Project

For learning purposes, we'll work on a sample site about Australia, because why not? You can see what the site will eventually look like here:

```
https://down-under.net
```

When you've finished the job, it should look like Figure 1-1.

Figure 1-1. *The Sample Project Site: Australia Down Under*

The sample project is what you might call a "brochure site." If you can imagine what a color glossy brochure would look like if it was implemented on the Web, it would be something like this.

Here are some of the things you would expect of a brochure site:

- An introduction to whatever it is the brochure is about

- A contact form to allow visitors to get in touch

- A collection of photos

- A collection of articles

Not much else. We're not trying to sell anything—managing online commerce is a tricky and risky business and left to another book. We're not starting discussions—that would also involve managing and registering users as well as moderating user content. Again, best left to another book.

You can quite easily adapt the site to any other context. It could be your amateur theater group, or hobby group, or advertising your flower shop or some sort of club. You'll probably need to put some work into the CSS to give it a more suitable appearance, of course, but any decent designer can do that for you.

The point is that you'll have the skills to generate and maintain the content of the site in any way you want.

The Tools

Presumably, you've already got a computer. It doesn't matter what the operating system is, as long as you can install whatever software you need.

The main tools you'll need are

- A working web server, which is described in the next section.

- A web browser. Almost any current web browser will do, but it's probably a good idea in web development to test your results in more than one browser. For PHP development, we won't stretch the browser features too far.

- A good coding editor.

You'll also need a copy of the sample project, as we'll describe in the Web Server Setup section.

A Coding Editor

Most of the files for a website are text files. There are also images and the database, but all of your actual coding will involve text.

That means you can edit these files with any old text editor. More realistically, you'll want to use a text editor designed for writing code. Here are the features you'll want:

- There is a view of the project folder, making it easy to switch between files.

- The coding editor supports **syntax highlighting**, which recognizes the type of document you're editing (HTML, CSS, JavaScript, etc.) and highlights the parts of the language.

You may already have your preferred coding editor. If you don't, you can try one of these:

- **Pulsar**: https://pulsar-edit.dev/

  This is the successor to the Atom Text Editor.

- **VSCodium**: https://vscodium.com/

  This is the open source of Microsoft's Visual Studio Code (https://code.visualstudio.com/), without Microsoft's specific telemetry and proprietary features.

Both are free, cross-platform, and open source. They also have additional extension packages available to customize your editor.

If you have another coding editor already, that will do as well.

Web Server Setup

If you're going to work with PHP, you'll need to have a web server running PHP and a database. If you're doing this on Linux, you'll probably have that already, though there's still going to be some setting up to do.

If you're doing this on Macintosh or Windows, you'll need to download and install a web server for development. Fortunately, it's easy to install.

If you are doing this on Linux, you may prefer not to use the preinstalled web server and database for learning or development. One of the following recommended packages also has a version for Linux.

To begin with, you'll need to download a few things:

- Download and install a web server package. We recommend XAMPP or MAMP, and the following instructions presume that you're using one of these.

  You can download a package from the following locations:

  - **XAMPP**: `www.apachefriends.org/download.html`. Download and install the latest version for your operating system.

  - **MAMP**: `www.mamp.info/en/downloads/`. You won't need the MAMP Pro version for anything in this book.

- Download the sample site from `https://github.com/Apress/Introduction_to_PHP`. Unzip it and put it in a convenient location. For example (depending on your username, of course):

  `/Users/fred/Documents/australia`

  `C:\Users\fred\Documents\australia`

  Wherever you put the folder, your convenient location should not include spaces in the path name. The Apache Web Server really doesn't like spaces, so you may have issues if you use them.

- Download the **Virtual Hosts** application from `https://github.com/manngo/virtual-hosts/releases/latest`.

You'll use the Virtual Hosts application to set up the virtual site. It also includes a PHP runner to test sample PHP code.

You can set up everything without the Virtual Hosts application, of course, but it will involve hunting around for the files and editing them yourself.

One of the problems with editing these files is that you may need to have administrative permissions. The Virtual Hosts application will ask you.

For this book, we're going to set up a virtual host called australia. example.com. The example.com (as well as example.net and example.org) domains are reserved for testing and training and will never be used in live websites. That makes them ideal for this sort of thing.

Using the Virtual Hosts application (or not, if you prefer), you'll go through the following steps:

- Select your installed web server.

- Edit the hosts file to add the sample domain name.

- Edit the server's httpd.conf file to allow virtual hosts. You'll also need to change the user and group if you're on a Macintosh.

- Add the virtual host details for your sample.

- Edit the server's php.ini file to enable a fake mail server and to enable working with graphics.

Some of the files, particularly the hosts file, are in protected areas, so you may be asked for your admin password when saving your changes.

Using the Virtual Hosts Applications

The Virtual Hosts application will run without any special installation, so you can use it immediately.

The first step is to set up for your installed web server (Figure 1-2):

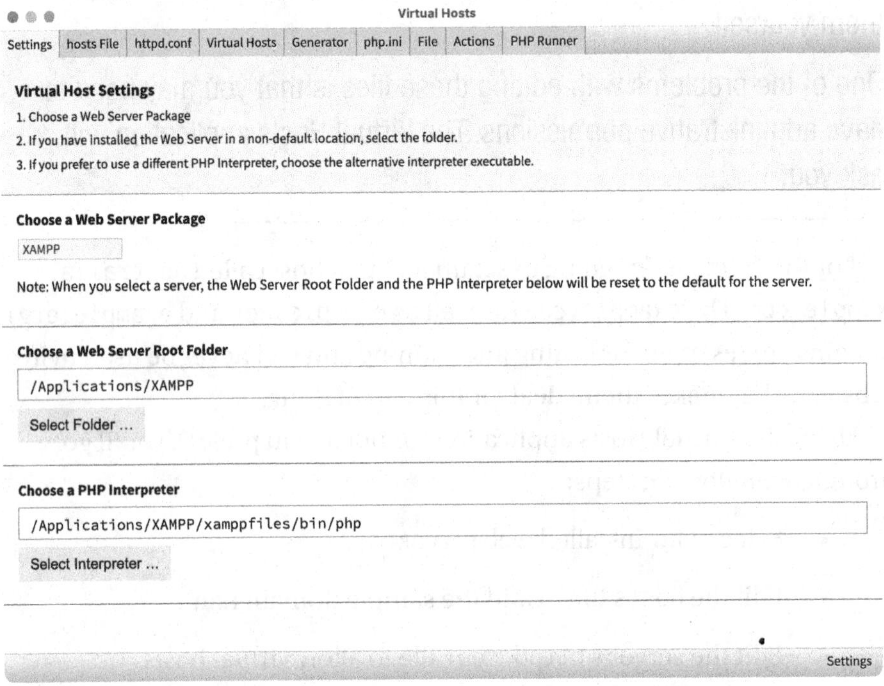

Figure 1-2. *Virtual Host Settings*

- Choose your web server software.

  It will prefill the Root Folder and PHP Interpreter values.

- If you have installed your web server other than in the default location, choose the location for your **Web Server Root Folder**.

- If you have a preferred PHP interpreter you want to use for testing code samples, choose the executable file for your **PHP Interpreter**.

  Changing this PHP interpreter is purely for the PHP Runner tab. For the website, the web server will still use the standard built-in PHP interpreter.

Save these settings for next time. They will be saved in a file called .virtual-hosts.json in your home directory.

Adding the Domain Name

The hosts file is where the browser will look first when resolving a domain name. The location of the hosts file is

- Macintosh and Linux: /etc/hosts

- Windows: C:\Windows\System32\drivers\etc\hosts

This is independent of the installed web server software. It's used by all interested applications.

The hosts file is in a protected area, so you may have trouble editing it yourself.

Using Virtual Hosts, select the **hosts File** tab (Figure 1-3).

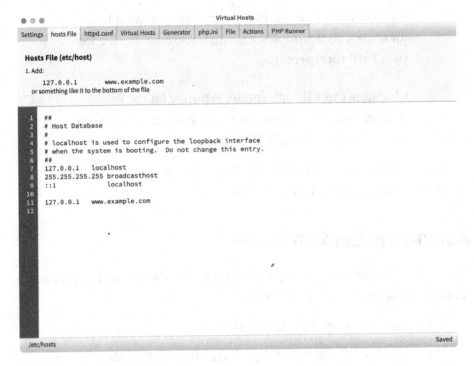

Figure 1-3. *Hosts File*

Add the following to the end:

```
127.0.0.1    australia.example.com
```

The IP address 127.0.0.1 is the virtual IP address for your own computer. It means that australia.example.com will resolve to your own computer which is where your development server (probably) is.

For future projects, you can have as many additional domain names as you like, and they can all resolve to 127.0.0.1. It's up to the web server to associate each name to a different web directory.

Don't forget to save the file and, if requested, enter your password.

Editing the httpd.conf File

The Apache Web Server uses the `httpd.conf` for its main settings. It's normally located in

- **XAMPP (macOS)**: `/Applications/XAMPP/etc/httpd.conf`

- **XAMPP (Windows)**: `C:\xampp\apache\conf\httpd.conf`

- **MAMP (macOS)**: `/Applications/MAMP/conf/apache/httpd.conf`

- **MAMP (Windows)**: `C:\MAMP\conf\apache\httpd.conf`

Using Virtual Hosts, select the **httpd.conf** tab (Figure 1-4).

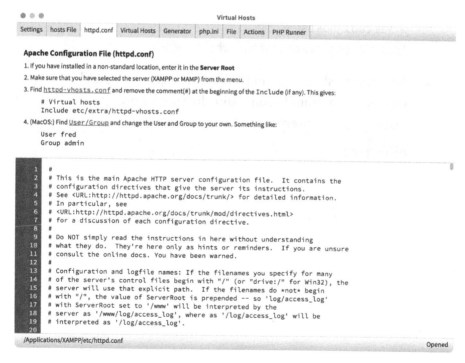

Figure 1-4. `httpd.conf` *File*

The instruction section at the top of the page includes shortcut links to some sections you'll need to find.

- Find the comment line which says # Virtual Hosts. There's a shortcut by clicking the httpd-vhosts.conf link in the instruction section.

  Remove the comment (#), if any, at the beginning of the Include ... line below it. Don't change the actual Include statement. Depending on your operating system, you should have something like

  ```
  # Virtual hosts
  Include etc/extra/httpd-vhosts.conf
  ```

  or

  ```
  # Virtual hosts
  Include conf/extra/httpd-vhosts.conf
  ```

- For Macintosh users, find the User/Group section, and change the settings to something like the following, using your own username, of course:

  ```
  User fred
  ```

  ```
  Group admin
  ```

- Don't forget to save the file and, if requested, enter your password.

Adding a Virtual Host

The actual Virtual Hosts file is where you give the details of your virtual host and where the directory is located. It can be found at the following locations:

- **XAMPP (macOS)**: `/Applications/XAMPP/xamppfiles/etc/extra/httpd-vhosts.conf`

- **XAMPP (Windows)**: `C:\xampp\apache\conf\extra\httpd-vhosts.conf`

- **MAMP (macOS)**: `/Applications/MAMP/conf/apache/extra/httpd-vhosts.conf`

- **MAMP (Windows)**: `C:\MAMP\bin\apache\conf\extra\httpd-vhosts.conf`

The web server won't bother looking for virtual hosts unless it has been set in the `httpd.conf` file, which is what you did in the previous step.

Setting up the virtual host will involve changing some data in the **Virtual Hosts** tab, using data from the **Generator** tab.

Using the Virtual Hosts application, select the **Virtual Hosts** tab (Figure 1-5).

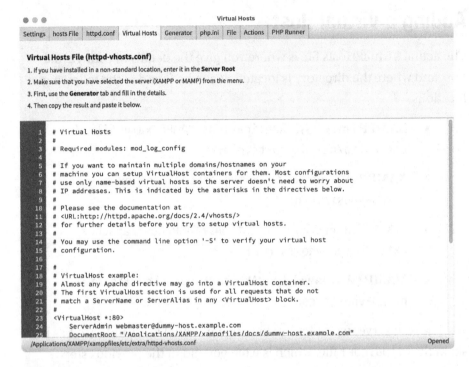

Figure 1-5. *Virtual Hosts*

There may be some commented instructions as well as some default settings. You can safely delete all of this and replace it with the data from the Generator tab in the Virtual Hosts application.

After clearing out the old contents, select the **Generator** tab (Figure 1-6).

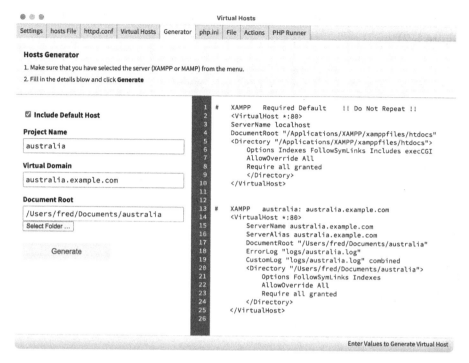

Figure 1-6. *Generator Tab*

- If this is your first (or only) virtual host, be sure to select `Include Default Host` if available. You'll probably need this for XAMPP but not for MAMP.

- Select a Project Name. You can call it anything you like, but it's best to use a simple lower case name without spaces, such as `australia`.

- Enter the Virtual Domain that you added to the `hosts` file earlier.

- Select the folder of your sample project.

You can then click the **Generate** button (or just click in the text area on the right).

Copy the generated text and paste it into the Virtual Hosts tab (Figure 1-7).

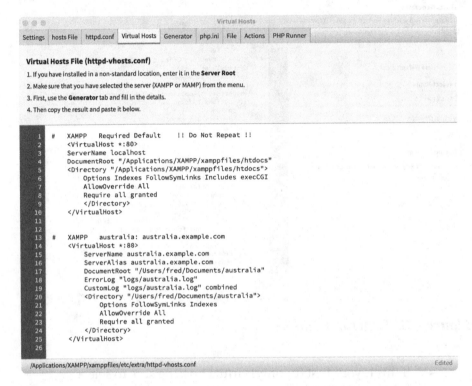

Figure 1-7. *Virtual Hosts Copied*

For additional projects, you can repeat the process (with different names and directories, of course), but you shouldn't repeat the Do Not Repeat section.

Don't forget to save the file and, if requested, enter your password.

Fixing the php.ini File

The php.ini file contains default settings for how PHP works. Many of these settings can be changed later, and we'll look at doing that later. However, there are two settings which need to be configured before PHP starts up.

The `php.ini` file can be found at

- **XAMPP (macOS)**: `/Applications/XAMPP/xamppfiles/etc/php.ini`

- **XAMPP (Windows)**: `C:\xampp\php\php.ini`

- **MAMP (macOS)**: `/Applications/MAMP/bin/php/php{version}/conf/php.ini`

- **MAMP (Windows)**: `C:\MAMP\conf\php{version}\php.ini`

Note that in MAMP, there are several versions of PHP and so several locations for the `php.ini` file. The default will be the latest version.

Using the Virtual Hosts application, select the **php.ini** tab (Figure 1-8).

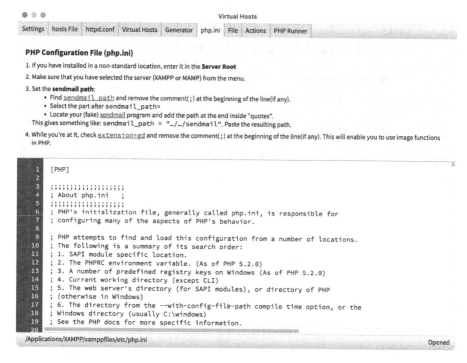

Figure 1-8. `php.ini` File

19

The instruction section at the top of the page includes shortcut links to some sections you'll need to find.

One of the things we'll be doing involves email. PHP doesn't actually send the email, but passes it on to a separate email server. In a live server, there would be a proper email server to do the job, but in this case, we'll work with a fake mail server. The fake mail server will accept whatever is passed to it as an email, but will save it into a file instead of sending it on.

- Find the `sendmail_path`, and remove the comment semicolon (;) before it.

- Click the **locate (fake) sendmail** link and locate the fake sendmail file. You'll get a file dialog where you can choose a fake mail program.

  There's one in the `resources` directory in your sample project. For macOS, you should use `fakemail.sh`, while for Windows, you should use `fakemail.bat`.

  Once you have selected the file, paste it at the end. The result should be something like this:

  `sendmail_path = ...`

The other thing you'll need to fix is a reference to the **gd** library. This library is used by PHP to manipulate images.

- Find the reference to `extension=gd` (it might be something like `extension=php_gd2.dll`).

- Remove the comment semicolon (;) before it. It should look something like this:

  ```
  extension=php_gd2.dll
  ;   or, maybe this:
  extension=gd
  ```

  The actual library name will depend on your server version.

If you're on a Macintosh, you may find the only reference to GD is a
.dll file. If so, don't bother enabling it—DLLs are for Windows only.
GD is probably enabled anyway.

Configuring PHP

PHP allows you to configure its behavior in many useful respects.
Here, we'll discuss just a few which may be of most use to you as a web
developer.

At its most fundamental level, you can reconfigure PHP by compiling it
with different options or by including different libraries to supplement its
behavior. However, the following three techniques are used for a working
implementation of PHP:

- php.ini

  PHP uses settings from the php.ini file when it starts up.
  These settings affect all PHP scripts on the server, so
  changes to this file are global.

  Generally, php.ini is inaccessible if you are not using
  your own personal server, such as a hosted or corporate
  server. If you do make changes to this file, then you will
  need to restart your web server to reload these settings.

- .htaccess

  If you are running PHP as a module under the Apache
  Web Server, such as with XAMPP or WAMP, then you
  may be able to use the .htaccess file to adjust your
  configuration. (The dot at the beginning of its name
  tends to hide it from view on Unix-type servers such as
  Linux and is common for configuration files.)

21

The `.htaccess` file should be placed in a directory where you want the changes to be made. It will be applicable to the current directory as well as all of the subdirectories. You can have different `.htaccess` files in different directories: the current settings will always override the settings of parent directories.

Apache will apply the settings when it loads a file. This means that changes are instantaneous, and you will not have to restart your server. It also means there is a slight overhead of additional file handling when you load pages.

The `.htaccess` file may also contain some settings for the web server other than for PHP. In fact, that's its main purpose—to customize the web server.

There is a `.htaccess` file in the root directory of the sample project.

- `.user.ini`

This is an alternative settings file for PHP, but it only applies when PHP is not running as an Apache Module. Even if this is the case, there may be some additional settings in the `.htaccess` file for the web server alone.

There is a .user.ini file in the root directory of the sample project.

- PHP ini_set() functions

  PHP will also allow you to reconfigure some settings
  using PHP functions. This is most suitable if you want
  to make changes for a single script at a time. It is also an
  option if your server cannot support .htaccess files or
  if it deliberately ignores them.

  Not all PHP settings can be changed this way. In
  particular, 'some changes will be made too late, since
  they may be required if there are problems with
  processing the script altogether.

The supplied .htaccess and .user.ini files have the default or most
useful settings for the current project. In the next section, we'll discuss
these particular settings; in later chapters, we'll also revisit some of these
settings in context.

Setting PHP Options

Generally, each setting has a name and a value. In the php.ini or .user.
ini file, the format is

```
setting_name = value
```

For .htaccess files, which may include other non-php settings, the
format is

```
php_value setting-name value
```

For a PHP function, you use the function ini_set(name, value).
In this function, both parameters are supposed to be strings, though the
second parameter (value) may be a number:

```
ini_set(name, value);
```

Some Useful Configuration Options

The following are some PHP configuration options which you may find useful for individual scripts or projects.

PHP Execution

The following settings may be useful for some scripts with unusually large processing requirements:

```
max_execution_time = 30
memory_limit = 16M
```

This is the default timeout and memory limit for a single task. If you have a particularly long or memory-intensive task, you may need to increase these. Note that you can't afford to have too much of this going on on a single server.

File Uploads

Two settings are useful when uploading files, such as image files:

```
upload_max_filesize = 2M
post_max_size = 8M
```

Again, these are the defaults. It means that we'll accept a maximum of 2Mb for a single file and 8Mb for the total upload for a single submit. If you're uploading video files or some image files, you may need to change these.

Legacy Settings

PHP originally used some settings to make scripting easier. Unfortunately, they also backfired and so should be disabled. In modern versions, they are removed altogether, or at least disabled by default, in which case these settings will be ignored. If, however, you're stuck on a very old web server, these settings may still need to be turned off:

```
register_globals = Off
magic_quotes_gpc = Off
```

The register_globals setting was to do with how PHP automatically accepted incoming form data, which can be risky. The magic_quotes_gpc was associated with modifying incoming data for the database, which was messy and unreliable.

Modern techniques are safer and more reliable.

Sessions

PHP sessions allow you to keep track of user-related data between pages. We'll be working with sessions later.

```
session.gc_maxlifetime = 1400

session.gc_probability = 1
session.gc_divisor = 100
```

The session.gc_maxlifetime setting is an idle time, in seconds, for session data, after which the data can be expired.

The session.gc_probability and session.gc_divisor settings combine to determine how often expired data is actually deleted.

These settings may well be adjusted for your particular application. They may also be adjusted between the development and final deployment versions of your site.

Error Reporting

PHP will normally report on errors, either on the screen or in a log file. Error reporting can be set to different levels, and you may choose whether PHP will display only serious errors or less serious errors from which PHP can continue.

```
error_reporting = E_ALL
display_errors = On
log_errors = On
```

The `error_reporting` setting determines how much you want to report; this includes minor warnings to fatal errors. For development, you'll want to set it to maximum.

The `display_errors` setting is whether you want errors displayed on the screen—for development, yes; for deployment, probably not. The `log_errors` setting is whether you want the errors logged to a file.

Other Settings

The following settings are purely a matter of choice, but suggested anyway:

```
php_value date.timezone Australia/Melbourne
```

If you're working with dates in PHP, and you will in this project, you will need to have your time zone set. It may already have been set in your `php.ini` file, but it may not be to your liking. We'll look at using this setting in Chapter 2.

```
php_value mail.log /var/log/phpmail.log
php_flag mail.add_x_header Off
```

We'll be sending email in Chapter 3. These settings determine where any log files are stored and whether PHP should add its own custom header to the email:

```
php_flag output_buffering Off
```

When working with cookies and session data, we'll encounter issues with outputting data before the cookies have been set, which is fatal. Output buffering helps in solving these issues, so it's actually convenient to have this setting turned to **On**. However, it's turned off here, so that we can experience the issues and learn how to fix the code.

Starting Up

When everything is set, you can start up your web server and database. How you do this depends on your software and operating system. Open the application control panel:

- For **XAMPP** on macOS, select the **Manage Servers** tab and start both the **MySQL Database** and the **Apache Web Server**.

- For **XAMPP** on Windows, select the **Start** button for both **Apache** and **MySQL**.

- For **MAMP** on macOS, select the **Start** button, which will start both the web server and the database server.

- For **MAMP** on Windows, select the **Start Servers** button, which will start both the web server and the database server.

You should now be ready to view your project site.

The Project Configuration Files

The sample project includes both .htaccess and .user.ini files, and you can see the preceding settings as described. The syntax for the .user.ini file is different from the syntax in the .htaccess file, but the intention is clear enough.

If you're running XAMPP or MAMP, or indeed many other web server packages, you'll be running PHP as a **module**, which means that PHP will be an extension of the Apache (or other) web server. In that case, the .htaccess file will be used, and the .user.ini file will be totally ignored.

It's not so simple if you're running PHP as a separate process.

If you're not sure, both XAMPP and MAMP have a link to phpinfo, which will dump a lot of information about PHP and its setup.

27

Somewhere near the top (thankfully) is a setting for the **Server API**:

- If its value is **Apache 2.0 Handler**, then Apache is running as a module.

- If the value is something like **CGI/FastCGI** or **FPM/FastCGI**, then it's running as a separate process.

The reason why this is important is that if PHP is running as a separate process, and not as a module, then any PHP settings in the .htaccess file will cause errors, as they won't be recognized. For that reason, you'll see the PHP settings inside a conditional block:

```
<IfModule php_module>
    ...
</IfModule>
```

This is supposed to include the PHP settings only if the PHP module is running.

Unfortunately, the PHP module isn't always called php_module, so the test may not work.

If you're sure that PHP is running as a module, and you're sure that the preceding block isn't working, you can try commenting out the conditional lines:

```
#<IfModule php_module>
    ...
#</IfModule>
```

The # at the beginning of the line treats the rest of the line as a comment, and the whole line will be ignored. The settings between will then be loaded as expected.

Finishing Up

If all is working, you can enter the following URL:

`australia.example.com`

When you do, you should see the page shown in Figure 1-9.

Figure 1-9. *Australia Down Under Home Page (Incomplete)*

It's not as complete as the live sample, and if you click any of the menu items, it will all fall apart.

That's the whole point of this book. We are going to look at how to write the code that will complete the rest of the site.

To begin with, we'll look at how we actually write PHP in Chapter 2.

CHAPTER 2

Working with PHP

PHP has a rather confusing beginning—it was not originally intended to be a programming language. Instead, it was a collection of tools to be mixed in with HTML.

Things have moved on since then, and there is quite a lot of programming in PHP, and we'll certainly be doing quite a lot of it ourselves. However, PHP on the Web is still designed to be mixed in with HTML, and you'll especially see that when you include the results of your PHP coding in your output page.

As a result of this hybrid nature, you'll see two particular features in PHP coding:

- All PHP code will be in files with the `.php` extension. This causes the web server to send the code to a separate PHP processor.

  As you'll see later, PHP files can include other files. Those included files don't technically need to have the `.php` extension, because they'll be regarded as part of the original PHP file.

- All PHP code needs to be enclosed in special PHP blocks enclosed in PHP tags. Anything not included in the PHP tags will be simply passed through.

© Mark Simon 2024
M. Simon, *An Introduction to PHP*, https://doi.org/10.1007/979-8-8688-0177-8_2

For a normal web page, any text not inside a PHP block is presumably HTML. It doesn't matter—PHP will just leave it alone and let the browser deal with it. On the other hand, code in PHP blocks *may* also add to the output to be included with the rest of the text.

In this chapter, we'll look at setting up our pages to work with PHP. This includes renaming pages to have the correct extension, adding PHP blocks to do any processing that needs to be done, and including special blocks to output any processed results.

We'll also look at delegating some of the code to separate files to make your code management easier.

In the process, we'll start to learn about how to write PHP statements and storing data in simple and complex variables. We'll also learn a little about some of PHP's built-in functions.

Finally, we'll look at *not* writing code, that is, how to put additional comments into our PHP code.

Before We Start

Programming is a matter of stating things precisely. For this reason, we will also need to be clear about our terminology.

Grouping: Brackets and Friends

There are three sets of symbols used to group items:

Symbol	Name	Use
( )	Parentheses	Functions and function dataCalculations
{ }	Braces	Blocks of code
[ ]	[Square] Brackets	Array values and keys

Note that the proper name for the [ ] symbol is simply **brackets**. However, to avoid confusion, we will stick to calling them **square brackets**. However, we will also stick to the proper names for the other symbols and never call them brackets.

Sometimes, you'll see braces referred to as "curly braces," but not in this book.

Data Types

PHP, like most programming languages, works with different types of values. We'll look at more complex types later, but there are three simple types:

- **Numbers** are stored in a binary format and are used whenever you need to count something. They are normally written plain, though there are some special formats.

- **Strings** are strings of characters. This may be interpreted as text, but can contain non-text characters.

- **Boolean** values are special values for true and false, so-called after the mathematician George Boole. They are very often used indirectly, such as when comparing values, such as a < b.

There are other special values, such as null, which we'll see more later. When you write the value in code, it is called a **literal**. For example:

- 23 is a numeric literal.

- "hello" and 'goodbye' are both string literals. String literals are normally written in single or double quotes, depending on how you're going to use them.

- The values true and false are the only boolean literals.

You can store values in **variables**, which are named placeholders for values.

33

How PHP Processes Files

The web server is responsible for fetching and sending all requested files back to the user's browser. With PHP installed, the web server will send the file first to the PHP processor, but, to save wasted effort, this happens only if the file has .php extension.

Often, there will be another step. Many sites, including this sample project, maintain much of the data in a database. Here, PHP will be used to send requests to the database server and to process the results.

Figure 2-1 illustrates the process.

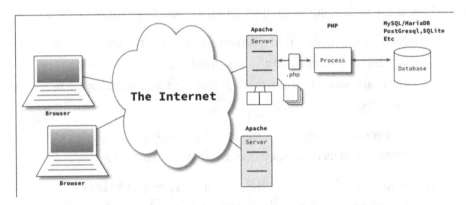

Figure 2-1. *Serving Web Pages with PHP*

In a PHP page, the PHP process will only process code which is inside PHP blocks (<?php ... ?>). The content of these blocks will be replaced by their output, if any, or removed. All text outside the PHP blocks will be left as normal. When the web server gets the file back from PHP, the entire document will be PHP free. This is illustrated in Figure 2-2.

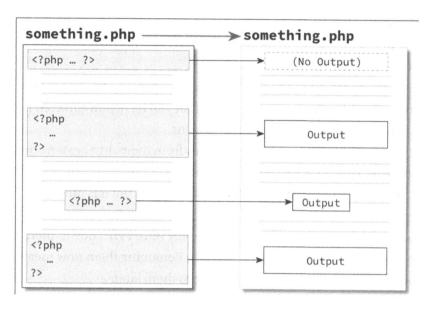

Figure 2-2. *PHP Processing*

In the example, some of the blocks might include some sort of output statement; the first one doesn't. Anything outside the PHP blocks is output.

The point is that the finished product bears no sign of PHP's involvement, and, presuming that you haven't made a mess in the PHP itself, the browser will just get what appears to be an ordinary HTML page.

Renaming the Files

To begin with, we'll rename the index.html file to index.php. If you reload the sample site, you won't see any difference.

For your convenience, web servers will allow you to omit a page in the URL. If you do, they'll look for a default page. In the httpd.conf file, there is a directive listing what the default page will be. For example:

```
DirectoryIndex index.html index.php default.html index.php4
```

The list may be quite long and is in order of preference—if the first page doesn't exist, it will try the next. Only if it can't find any in the list will you get the dreaded 404 missing file error.

Since you've renamed index.html to index.php, you've only moved it down the list. What's more important is that you have now directed the server to pass the file to PHP for preprocessing.

Later, we can rename the rest of the files from their .html extension to a .php extension. This can be wasteful of server processing power if the files have no actual PHP script blocks to process, but it is otherwise harmless.

In our project, all of the files will eventually have PHP code in them, so the .php extension will be required anyway. Renaming them now means that you won't have to worry about linking to them later.

PHP Scripts

In a very real sense, every PHP document is a single PHP script. This script generally has a mixture of processing and output.

A PHP processing block is contained within PHP tags:

```
<?php
    doSomething();
    doSomethingElse();
?>
```

The spacing of the tags is not important, as long as there is some sort of spacing after the opening tag. For example, you may include simple processing in a single line:

```
<?php doSomething(); ?>
```

What is important is that the tags are not themselves interrupted by space and that they are separated from the actual processing by space. The start of the block has six characters: <?php plus a space, tab, or line break. The following are both common errors:

```
<? php dosomething(); ?>
<?phpdosomething(); ?>
```

Any text not inside PHP processing tags will simply be output. PHP processing statements may also include additional output commands, but text outside of the PHP processing tags is always output.

PHP tags have one surprising feature: any space or line break after the closing tag will be removed. That may seem an odd thing to do, but it allows you to put one PHP block below another without adding extra line breaks.

If you're wondering why you want to avoid extra line breaks, some PHP code will cause problems if you (accidentally) output something before the rest of the code is finished. We'll see more on that in later chapters when we discuss HTTP headers.

A PHP script can have multiple PHP processing blocks. These separate blocks are regarded as part of the same script. Logically, you would normally not break up processing into separate blocks, but you can. Generally, you would do this if you have a lot of intervening output which would be more convenient if placed outside the PHP blocks.

Experimenting

From time to time, you might want to experiment with a little PHP to try out a new concept or to see how something works.

37

The Virtual Hosts application has a **PHP Runner** tab to allow you to try things out (Figure 2-3).

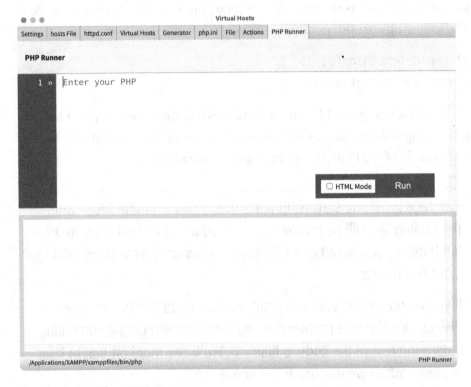

Figure 2-3. *The PHP Runner*

This uses the PHP interpreter which comes with your web server, unless you have gone to the trouble of selecting another. It runs in two modes:

- In non-HTML mode, you write pure PHP *without* PHP tags.

- In HTML mode, you need to include the PHP tags. This allows you to test PHP mixed in with HTML.

Adding Dynamic Data to the Page

Much of the data will come from a database, but PHP is also capable of generating its own data. One example is to display the current date and time in the footer.

It is always good practice to separate the main PHP processing from the HTML output. This can be done entirely in a separate file, but should at least be done by putting your main processing before the HTML part of the file.

Having some PHP processing in the HTML is practically unavoidable, since it will be required when you want to display the data previously processed and also when you need to select different sections of HTML. However, it should be kept to a minimum.

Although PHP was designed to be mixed in with HTML, you really should resist getting carried away. You'll find some code out there in the wild which constantly switches between PHP and HTML code, making the whole a very messy collection of fragments.

We recommend that all of the actual logic and processing code should be written in PHP blocks at the beginning, or even in separate files. That's certainly the approach taken in the book.

The PHP in the rest of the file—where the HTML is—will be mostly limited to using results of the PHP processing gone on before.

To display the date and time, we'll do it in two steps:

- At the beginning, we'll use PHP to generate the date and time.

- In the footer, we'll use PHP to display it.

We'll start by adding a PHP block at the beginning of the file:

```
<!-- Begin head.inc.php -->
<?php

?>
<!DOCTYPE html>
...
```

(The HTML comment `<!-- Begin head.inc.php -->` at the very beginning is for a task we'll be doing later in the chapter.)

PHP has a `date()` function which returns a formatted date, using special formatting codes. This formatted date can be saved for later or displayed using the PHP print statement. The date function takes one or two values:

```
date(format, time)
```

If the time is omitted, the time used will be the current date and time.

The format is a string with some counterintuitive letters. We will use the string:

```
<?php
    $date = date('l, jS F Y g:i a');
?>
```

which means

```
[Day Name], [Day Number][Ordinal] [Month Name][Year]
```

For example:

```
Sunday, 20th July 1969 8:17 pm
```

which is when the Lunar Module first landed on the Moon.

The result of the date() function is saved in the variable $date. A variable is a named reference to a value. In PHP, the variable *always* has a dollar sign ($) at the beginning to indicate that it's a variable. The $ isn't actually part of the name—it's an indicator.

Variable names are case sensitive: it doesn't matter whether you use upper or lower case as long as you remember. In PHP, it's traditional to use lower case names.

Each PHP statement ends with a semicolon (;). Technically, you can omit the semicolon for the very last statement of the script, but that's risky and not something we'll encourage.

Note that this is the date and time on the *server*, where, obviously, PHP is doing the work. To make this clear, you might want to read the server's time zone into another variable:

```php
<?php
    $date = date('l, jS F Y g:i a');
    $timezone = date_default_timezone_get();
?>
```

You can get more information on the date() and date_default_timezone_get() functions here:

- www.php.net/manual/en/function.date.php

- www.php.net/manual/en/function.date-default-timezone-get.php

The date and time are, of course, dependent on the time zone. Although the real server may be in one part of the world, it's possible to set its time zone to another. This has already been set in the special file .htaccess and in .user.ini, which are configuration files for the web server.

You can open .htaccess and .user.ini and change the time zone to your preferred zone. You can get a large list of supported time zones from www.php.net/manual/en/timezones.php.

We now need to display it.

Displaying Data

In the footer, we can display the contents of the two variables set up at the top. Currently, the footer has something like the following:

```
<!-- begin footer.inc.php -->
    <footer>
        Copyright © Down Under
    </footer>
<!-- end footer.inc.php -->
```

To print data in PHP, you can do something like this:

```
<?php
    ...
    print ... ;
    ...
?>
```

However, if that's all you're doing in a simple block, you can use a simpler version:

```
<?= ... >
```

The expression will be completely replaced with the output.

Apart from the short PHP output tags (`<?= ... ?>`), PHP has two common output statements, `print` and `echo`. They are *nearly* the same, but not quite. The `print` statement can be used in more complex statements, while `echo` can't. On the other hand, `echo` can output multiple expressions while `print` can't.

Since we won't be pushing either feature very hard, for the most part, it really doesn't matter which one you use.

Most PHP developers end up using the first one they learned about. In this book, we'll use `print`, for the same reason.

We can add this to the footer as follows:

```
<footer>
    Copyright © Down Under<br><?= "$date ($timezone)" ?>
</footer>
```

An expression with double quotes (" ... ") is called a **string**. In PHP, you can use single or double quotes, but the double quotes are needed if you want to include variables or some special characters in the string.

A single-quoted string doesn't interpret variables, so it's actually safer (and, technically, less time-consuming). For most of the strings in this book, we'll use single-quoted strings, unless we need variables or special characters. When you use double-quoted strings with variable names, we say that the values are **interpolated** into the string.

43

If you reload the page now, you will see the date and time, together with the time zone (at the server).

PHP has no way of knowing the time server at the browser end. If it's really important, you can use some JavaScript to set the browser time zone in a cookie.

We'll look at using cookies later.

Next, we'll look at splitting up the page.

Including Files

Much of the page includes content which will be duplicated on other pages. This would include things like the banner and menu, as well as the footer. There's nothing technically wrong with that, but it will be harder to manage if you need to make a small change to this duplicate content. For that reason, we're going to move the content into separate files to be included in this and other pages.

PHP has four variations on a statement to include external content:

- `include` will include a file if it's available; if it's not, well, it will try to cope.

- `include_once` will also include a file if it's available; if it's already been included before, it will just ignore this one.

- `require` will include a file if it's available, but if it's not, the script will grind to a halt with an error.

- `require_once` will include a file if it's available unless it's already been included.

Generally, the `require_once` is probably appropriate: if the file isn't available, you have a serious problem. If the file has already been included, you probably don't want it again. However, we'll still casually refer to this as "include," which is what it's doing.

In our code, there will be five sections which we will extract into includable files:

- The head section comprising the `DOCTYPE` and the head element.

- The header section which contains the `header` element.

- The navigation block which is a collection of links in a `nav` element.

- The aside which will contain a random photograph in an `aside` element. It won't appear on all pages.

- The footer section which has the `footer` element, which we have just modified.

If you find the difference between "head" and "header" confusing, you can blame HTML itself. The `head` element contains information about the page, including the title and CSS links. The `header` is one of the newer structural elements added to HTML later along with other structural elements such as `nav`, `aside`, and `footer`. Basically, it contains content you'd expect to see at the top of a page.

We'll now split off these sections and reattach them to the page.

Preparing and Implementing Include

To modify our page, we will need to do the following:

- Cut the existing section of code from the page, and paste it in a new document.

- Save the new document in a suitable location.

- Replace the cut code with a require_once statement to include it again.

The actual name and location of an included file is entirely up to you, but the following is recommended:

- Have a special folder for your included files. This will simplify your file management.

- Always use the .php extension for your includable files.

PHP does not require this at all, which is why some people ignore this recommendation. However, if, somehow, a user locates and displays an included file without the .php extension, they will see the raw unprocessed PHP code since it won't have gone through the PHP processor. This may include code or data which you don't wish to share with the world at large. This is not good.

The project already has a folder called includes, which we can use for locating our included files. Open the file index.php, and locate the part of the head section between the comments:

```
<!--    begin head.inc.php -->
<?php
    $date = date('l, jS F Y g:i a');
    $timezone = date_default_timezone_get();
?>
<!DOCTYPE html>

    ...

<!--    end head.inc.php -->
```

Cut the content between the comments and paste it into a new file and save the file as head.inc.php inside the includes folder.

Replace the cut contents with the following code:

```
<!--    begin head.inc.php -->
<?php require_once 'includes/head.inc.php'; ?>
<!--    end head.inc.php -->
```

You can also delete the comments which are only there as markers.

The name head.inc.php is arbitrary. You can call it anything you like, though we recommend the .php extension as before. The name follows a simple pattern: the name of the block with .inc attached. It's only to make the purpose of the file easier to see.

Sometimes, you'll see a file with just the .inc extension. That may or may not work as intended. Certainly, you can include it with any extension you like, but you may not get the protection of running it through the PHP processor.

By default, .inc files are not treated as PHP files. However, the following line in either the httpd.conf file or the .htaccess files will fix that:

```
AddHandler application/x-httpd-php .inc
```

If you reload the page now, hopefully, you'll see nothing different. If you view the page source in the browser, you'll still see nothing different. That means it's working, and PHP has replaced the statement with the output, which is the included file.

Repeat the process for the following files:

- header.inc.php

- nav.inc.php

- footer.inc.php

- aside.inc.php

and test your page.

47

Apart from typing errors, the most common mistake you're likely to make is to forget to save your file before testing changes. Don't forget to save your file before testing changes.

When you've finished, the code should look like this:

```
<?php require_once 'includes/head.inc.php'; ?>
<?php require_once 'includes/header.inc.php'; ?>
<body>
<?php require_once 'includes/nav.inc.php'; ?>
    <main>
        <article id="index">
            ...
        </article>
<?php require_once 'includes/aside.inc.php'; ?>
    </main>
<?php require_once 'includes/footer.inc.php'; ?>
</body>
</html>
```

The remaining PHP pages already have the include statements, so you won't need to worry about them.

Headings and Titles

The problem with including content is that it's all the same. That includes the headings and titles for each of the pages.

If you're wondering about the difference between headings and titles:

- The title element appears in the head element and is information about the page. You won't see it on the page itself, but it will appear on the browser window title bar (if there is one), the tab name, and on the bookmark if you bookmark the page.

- The various headings appear in the body element. In particular, the h1 element is the main heading of the page and, in this case, appears in the header section.

To make this work dynamically, we'll include variables in the head.inc.php and header.inc.php files to display the content. Then, we'll assign to those variables in the various pages.

Including Variables in the Include Files

We're going to use the following variables for the content:

- The page title will be in the $pagetitle variable.

- The page heading will be in the $pageheading variable. It will end up in an h1 element.

For the title element, we'll need to make a change to the head.inc.php file. Currently, the content includes the following:

```
<title>Australia Down Under<!-- page title --></title>
```

As you see, the comment anticipates a dynamic heading. Modify it as follows:

```
<title>Australia Down Under
    <?php if(isset($pagetitle)) print " - $pagetitle"; ?>
</title>
```

(The new content doesn't need to go an additional line—it just fits better on this page.)

- The if() conditional statement tests whether a condition is true. If it is, the following code will run.

- The isset() construct tests whether a variable has been set. Here, we're testing whether the variable $pagetitle has been set.

- If the variable has been set, we can use it in the print statement. Again, the print statement prints a double-quoted string, which includes the value of the variable.

For the page heading, we'll modify the header.inc.php file. Currently, the h1 element is hard-coded:

```
<h1>Australia Down Under</h1>
```

We'll also use a conditional statement, but it will be used to replace the whole of the content:

```
<h1><?= isset($pageheading) ? $pageheading : 'Australia Down
Under'; ?></h1>
```

- The conditional operator (test ? planA : planB) results in one of two values, depending on the test at the beginning. It's also known as the **ternary** operator, because it has three parts.

- Here, the test is whether the variable $pageheading has been set. If so, we'll use its value (*plan A*); otherwise, we'll use the hard-coded value (*plan B*).

Now that we've modified the included files, we can set the values to be used.

Setting the Title and Heading

You won't yet see anything until you set these variables. You'll have to do that for every page, unless you're happy with the default values earlier.

In the index.php file, add the following code with the include:

```php
<?php

        $pagetitle = 'Home';
        $pageheading = 'Australia Down Under';

        require_once 'includes/head.inc.php';
?>
...
```

We've reformatted the include block, since it's no longer a single statement.

For your convenience, this has been added to every other page in the project. However, it's not fatal if it's been left out, since the included files have allowed for missing variables.

The Navigation Block

Currently, the navigation block is a hard-coded collection of anchors:

```html
<ul>
    <li><a href="index.php">Home</a></li>
    <li><a href="about.php">About Oz</a></li>
    <li><a href="contact.php">Contact Us</a></li>
    <li><a href="blog.php">Oz Blog</a></li>
    <li><a href="gallery.php">Animals</a></li>
    <li><a href="admin.php">Administration</a></li>
</ul>
```

To highlight one of the pages, one of those anchors will be replaced with a span element, using CSS to give the appearance of an inactive link:

```
<ul>
    <li><a href="index.php">Home</a></li>
    <li><a href="about.php">About Oz</a></li>
    <li><span>Contact Us</span></li>     <!-- current (no
    anchor) -->
    <li><a href="blog.php">Oz Blog</a></li>
    <li><a href="gallery.php">Animals</a></li>
    <li><a href="admin.php">Administration</a></li>
</ul>
```

A span element is one of the miscellaneous elements available in HTML. The other is the div element. The difference between the two is that span is an *inline* element, while div is a *block* element, which affects where you can use them and how they appear by default.

By default, the span has no special appearance at all. However, if you identify a span, either with an id or class attribute or through its container, you can use CSS to make it look any way you want. In this case, we make it look like an inactive link.

What we'll do is use PHP to generate the collection dynamically. This way, we can decide whether each link should be a real anchor or a span element.

To do this, we'll follow this process:

- Create a collection of links.

- Determine the current page.

- Convert the collection into a collection of either link elements or, if the page is current, a span element.

We will begin by creating the array and converting it into a collection of links. Afterward, we will include the logic for the current page.

The Links Array

A PHP **array** is a collection of keys and values. In many languages, it's always a numbered collection, and the keys are all consecutive integers. Arrays with strings as keys are often called **associative arrays**. In PHP, keys can be numbers or strings, in any order, and you can even have a mix.

To create an array with string keys, we can use the following construction:

```
$array = [
    'key' => 'value',
    'key' => 'value'
];
```

You can, of course, write the statement on one line or as many lines as you need to make it readable.

- The square bracket ([...]) notation is used both to define an array and to specify one of the members of the array.

- The => operator has nothing to do with either the = or the > operators. It's supposed to be a sort of arrow, suggesting that the key points to a value. When we need to give it a name, we'll call it a **thick arrow**; later, you see a **thin arrow** (->) which, of course, has a completely unrelated meaning.

- The array elements are separated by a comma (,). It's OK to have an extra comma at the end of the list, and it's often done. It has no effect on the collection.

For now, the links array will be derived from the existing unordered list. It will follow the pattern:

```
text => href
```

The associative array will have the link text for the key and the href for the value. We will call the array $links. Ultimately, the value will be the href for the anchors.

Add the following PHP block at the beginning of nav.php:

```php
<?php
    $links = [
        'Home' => 'index.php',
        'About Oz' => 'about.php',
        'Contact Us' => 'contact.php',
        'Oz Blog' => 'blog.php',
        'Animals' => 'gallery.php',
        'Administration' => 'admin.php'
    ];
?>
<nav>
    ...
</nav>
```

Creating the List of Links

The next step will be to convert the links into an unordered list (<ul>). Each list item (except the current page) will have a link in the following form:

```
<li><a href="contact.php">Contact Us</a></li>
```

This will come directly from the contents of the array.

To do this, we will

- Create an empty array of list items

- Iterate through the links array

- Copy the array keys and values into strings for the list items

- Print the item string in the page

To create an empty array of list items is a matter of creating a new empty array:

```php
<?php
    $links = [
        ...
    ];
    $ul = [];
?>
```

Before we iterate through the array, we'll prepare template strings for the anchors and span.

In PHP, there's a function called sprintf(), which you can pronounce as "s-print-f." It's supposed to print formatted data into a string, but it's easier to think of it as putting values into a template string. It looks like this:

```php
sprintf($template, value, value, ...)
```

The template string itself is just a string, but it includes special placeholder codes which will be replaced by the values which follow. Typically, the code is %s which means a string.

In our case, we'll use the following template strings:

```php
<?php
    $links = [
        ...
    ];
```

```php
    $a = '<li><a href="/%s">%s</a></li>';
    $span = '<li><span>%s</span></li>';

    $ul = [];
?>
```

Notice that the $a string has two placeholders, while the $span string has one. We'll need to remember that when we apply them since sprintf() requires the number of placeholders to match the number of values.

To iterate through an array, PHP has the foreach(...) statement:

```php
foreach($array as $key => $value) {
    ...
}
```

You can use foreach on other types of collections, such as data which we'll get later from the database. You don't always want the key, and, in some non-array collections, there won't actually be a key. If you want just the values, you can use

```php
foreach($collection as $value) {
    ...
}
```

In this case, our foreach() looks like this:

```php
<?php
    ...
    $ul = [];

    foreach($links as $text => $href) {

    }
?>
```

Within the iteration, we can take the data, run it through the template string, and add the result to the $ul array:

```php
<?php
    ...
    $ul = [];

    foreach($links as $text => $href) {
        $ul[] = sprintf($a, $href, $text);
    }
?>
```

A statement starting with $ul[] = means to add the following to the $ul array. The technical term is to push the value on to the array. There's a PHP function called array_push() to do that, but there's no point.

When using a statement like

```
$ul[] = something;
```

the biggest mistake you're likely to make is to forget the square brackets and write something like

```
$ul = something;
```

That will end up replacing the variable with a simple string, and you'll have lost your array.

Note that the $href variable appears before the $text variable: that's the order they are to be used in the $a string.

We haven't used the $span string yet, but first we'll use the newly generated navigation block.

Displaying the Links

The actual HTML for the navigation block appears as

```
<nav>
    <ul>
        <li> ... </li>
        <li> ... </li>
        <li> ... </li>
    </ul>
</nav>
```

We'll replace the contents of the unordered list with our new array:

```
<nav>
    <ul>
        <?= $ul ?>
    </ul>
</nav>
```

This won't work yet. PHP really hates printing arrays, and you would get a message to that effect if you tried. To print the array, you'll have to join the array items into a single string. You can do that with the implode() function:

```
<?php
    ...
    foreach($links as $text => $href) {
        $ul[] = sprintf($a, $href, $text);
    }
    $ul = implode($ul);
?>
```

The `implode()` function takes an optional *first* value which is a string to put between the joined values. In this case, we've left it out, meaning that they'll be joined with nothing in between. The odd thing here is that normally if a function has an optional value, it comes *after* the other values; here, it comes *before*.

`implode()`? Normally, such a function would be called `join()`, and PHP does have `join()` as an alias of `implode()`. In the past, there was a function called `split()`, which would split a string into an array. However, its implementation proved to be problematic, so it was removed in favor of `explode()` which did a better job.

The `implode()` function is just the opposite of `explode()`.

You can now test the page. Once again, it's all working if you see nothing new.

Highlighting the Current Page

So far, you've gone through a lot of effort just to get something you already had. Now we're going to get PHP to dynamically highlight the current page.

First, we need to know something about PHP's so-called superglobals. These are built-in arrays of special data. There are nine of them:

- `$_GET`, `$_POST`, `$_COOKIE`, and `$_REQUEST` all contain data sent from the browser to the server. We'll be using these when uploading data and storing current values.

- `$_FILES` contains data about files which are uploaded to the server. We'll also use this when uploading files.

- `$_SERVER` has information about the web server and what's happening with the server. This will be very helpful when we need to know about the current page.

- $_ENV has information about the running server environment. We won't use this much.

- $_SESSION is used to store information between pages. It's particularly useful when managing user logins.

- $GLOBALS is a collection of variables.

If you think calling these arrays "superglobals" is a little strange, it's because it's not a very informative name. When you start writing functions, you'll learn more about global variables and why these are "superglobal." For now, just think of them as "magic" arrays.

In PHP, all variable names are case sensitive, and the superglobal names are all defined in upper case. Don't try your luck with variables such as $_Post or $_post, as they definitely won't work. This also applies to the keys in the arrays.

In particular, the value of $_SERVER['SCRIPT_FILENAME'] gives us the path of the currently running script.

The value includes the full path, relative to the machine root. That's going to be a problem later, when we want the path relative to the site root. For now, we'll need to extract only the file name, without the rest of the path, using the basename() function.

At the beginning of the code, add

```php
<?php
    $current = basename($_SERVER['SCRIPT_FILENAME']);

    ...
?>
```

To use this value, we will need to incorporate a test in the code which develops the link: if the $href matches the current page, we will use a span element instead of the anchor. Otherwise, we will use the anchor element as before.

For the test, we can use the conditional operator. The test is something like this:

```
href is current ? use span : use anchor
```

In our case, the code is

```
$ul[] = $href == $current
    ? sprintf($span, $text)
    : sprintf($a, $href, $text);
```

- The test $href == $current (double equals) compares whether the two variables have the same value. It's a *very* common mistake to use $href = $current (single equals). In PHP, that would assign a new value to the $href variable.

- Note that we've written the code on three lines to fit better. That's OK with PHP. We've also indented the subsequent lines to make it clear that they're a continuation.

We can add the following code:

```
<?php
    $current=basename($_SERVER['SCRIPT_FILENAME']);

    ...
    foreach($links as $text => $href) {
        $ul[] = $href == $current
            ? sprintf($span, $text)
```

```
                : sprintf($a, $href, $text);
    }

    $ul = implode($ul);
?>
```

Comments

No, not comments about this chapter, but how to use **comments** in PHP. There are many times when you need to add notes to your PHP code. These notes should be for the benefit of the human reader only and ignored by the PHP processor.

In PHP, there are three ways to write comments. They can be mixed with ordinary PHP code. For example:

```
<?php
    /*  This is a comment block. */
    //  Single line comment
    #   Another single line comment
?>
```

The comment block starts with /* and ends with */. The block can span multiple lines. Note that comment blocks can't be nested.

The single-line comments start with either // or # and end at the end of the line. From PHP's perspective, it doesn't matter which type you use. We're going to take advantage of that and use the different type for two different purposes.

Some of the things you would use comments for include

- Explain something in your code that's not immediately obvious. You'll need some discernment in how you define what's "obvious."

- Act as headings for sections of code.

- Disable sections of code for testing or troubleshooting. Because we can, we'll use the # for troubleshooting comments; there's no technical reason, but it helps to distinguish what's meant to be temporary.

You must resist the urge to over-comment or explain what should be obvious. Over-commenting just clutters up your code and makes it harder to work with and, frankly, is an insult to whomever is supposed to read your code.

Of course, deciding what is or isn't obvious is a matter of judgment and experience.

We'll use all of these comments as we write PHP code, but for now, we'll just add one comment to illustrate the point. In the PHP block at the beginning of your index.php page, add the following comment:

```php
<?php
    // Page Title and Heading
        $pagetitle = 'Home';
        $pageheading = 'Australia Down Under';

    require_once 'includes/head.inc.php';
?>
```

Note that the two statements setting variables have been indented to make it clear that the heading comment applies to them. Using the tab key helps to keep everything neat and tidy.

In the rest of the book, we'll be using comments extensively to help document the code.

If you're familiar with other coding languages, you'll probably find that they all have some form of comments. Of course, they're slightly different. Here are the comment styles you're likely to encounter in your web development:

Context	Comment Style
PHP	`/* block comment *//// line comment# line comment`
HTML	`<!-- block comment -->`
CSS	`/* block comment */`
JavaScript	`/* block comment *//// line comment`
SQL	`/* block comment */-- line comment`
ini Files	`; line comment`
config Files	`# line comment`

It's very easy to get lost in the comment styles when you're working with multiple languages, as with typical web development.

Summary

This chapter focused on the basics of writing PHP and introduced a few of the basic concepts.

PHP was designed to be mixed in with HTML. In order to reduce wasting time and energy, only files with the `.php` extension will be sent to the PHP processor.

PHP code is written in PHP blocks which are contained between PHP tags. This is even if there is no other HTML in the file. Code which is not inside a PHP block will be passed through, effectively becoming output of the script.

There are also output statements, such as `print` and `echo`, when you need to output something from the block itself. PHP has a special output block (`<?= ... ?>`) which allows outputting simple data in the HTML code.

A lot of processing involves managing data, which is stored in variables. Although there are different types of data, PHP variables are flexible enough to store any type.

There are simple and complex types of data. Simple types include numbers, strings, and boolean values. Complex types include arrays, which are collections of data.

A larger project may need to be split into smaller parts, and PHP is capable of including code in separate files. This can be to make the code more manageable, but also to allow some code to be used in multiple places.

You can use PHP to generate content for HTML. This can be simple content, such as the content of a paragraph or heading, but it can also be entire HTML structures, such as a list of links for a menu. Much of what we'll be doing later in the book will culminate in generated HTML output.

Coming Up

In the next chapters, we're going to write some more serious code, with complex programming structures, and we'll manage and manipulate data.

To begin with, in Chapter 3, we're going to look at how PHP handles incoming data from a web form. We'll look at checking and manipulating the data and then sending it out as an email.

CHAPTER 3

Email and Form Processing

One thing you'll often do in PHP is use it to process data from the user. Later, we'll be sending data in the form of images and text to be stored in a database. In this chapter, we'll send data to be sent on as an email.

In the past, websites included links to email addresses, and some still do. However, that proved to be an invitation to spammers who were always on the lookout for legitimate email addresses. It also made it more difficult to control what sort of email was being sent.

In this contact form, we're going to accept data from a web form, check over it, and, if it's acceptable, send it off as an email to the website administrator.

There is a downside to doing things this way in that the user won't be using their regular email client, so they won't have access to regular features of email. In particular, they won't have a copy of the email. So, we'll make sure, at least, that they get a copy as a courtesy.

In this chapter, we're going to learn how data is sent from a web form to the web server and how it is processed by PHP. We'll see how PHP perceives the uploaded data and how it can examine and manipulate it.

When dealing with user-submitted data, it's very important first to test it—not only for errors but also for attempts to intrude into the system. We'll look at how to preprocess and check data and to report on potential errors.

© Mark Simon 2024
M. Simon, *An Introduction to PHP*, https://doi.org/10.1007/979-8-8688-0177-8_3

We'll then look at how to send email from PHP to an external mail process. This includes preparing the rest of the data for email.

Once we've successfully sent the email, we'll look at how to toggle different parts of the page using conditional PHP blocks. This allows us to have a single page with multiple sections.

Finally, we'll look at how to reorganize the code to make it easier to modify and maintain.

Preparation

The end product will be an email. This is not actually done in PHP, but is delegated to an external program.

In your development environment, you probably don't have a suitable program to generate real email, but you can still test the process using a substitute as detailed in Chapter 1.

The Contact Form

A form is an HTML container element. Inside the form element, you can place a number of form elements to gather or organize input data, as well as a number of non-form elements, such as paragraphs, for display.

The HTML for the contact form is essentially as follows:

```
<form method="post" action="" novalidate>
    <p><label for="name">Name:</label>
        <input name="name" id="name" type="text" value=""
            required>
    </p>
    <p><label for="email">Email:</label>
        <input name="email" id="email" type="email" value=""
            required>
```

```
</p>
<p><label for="subject">Subject:</label>
    <input name="subject" id="subject" type="text" value=""
        required>
</p>
<p><label for="message">Message:</label>
    <textarea name="comments" id="comments" required>
    </textarea>
</p>

<p><button type="submit" name="send">Send Message</
button></p>
</form>
```

In the browser, it looks like Figure 3-1.

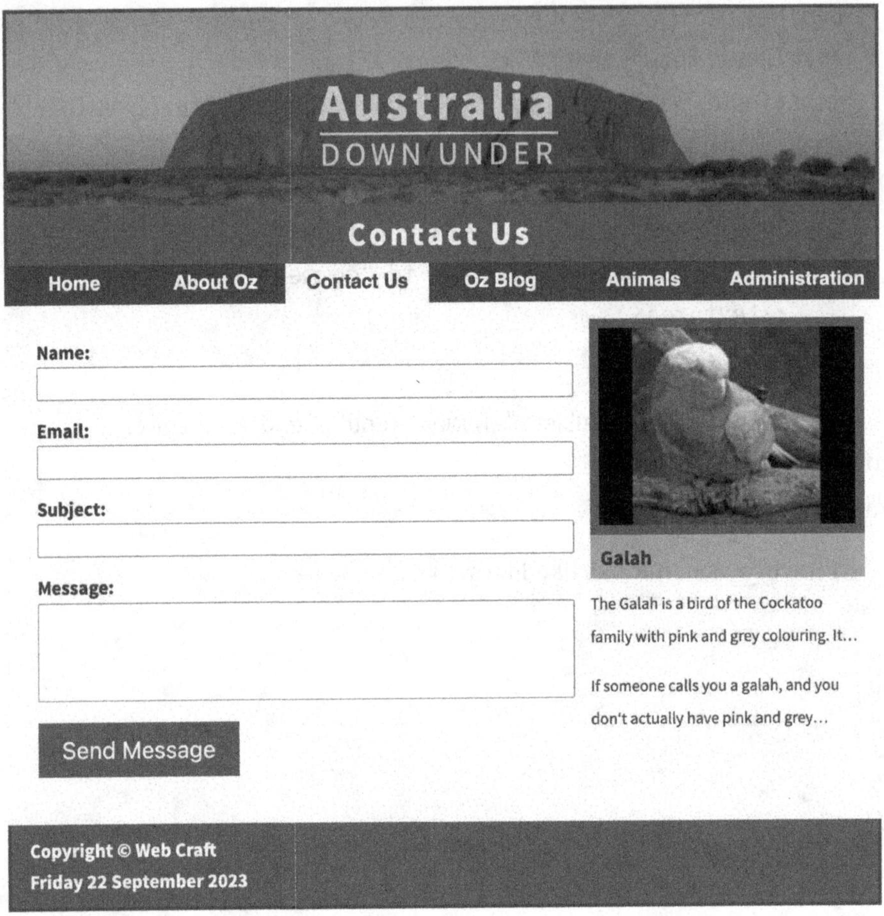

Figure 3-1. *The Contact Form*

Our PHP code will process the text from three text fields and one text area.

The form has two important attributes and one temporary attribute:

- The action attribute has the URL where the data should be submitted. The fact that it's empty doesn't mean that it's going nowhere; it means to submit it to the *current* URL (contact.php).

- The method attribute is how the data will be sent. Using get means the data should be attached to the URL as a query string; using post means that the data should be sent inside the HTTP body.

- The novalidate attribute prevents the web browser from validating the form.

In real life, you should allow the web browser to perform its own form validation, so the novalidate attribute shouldn't be used. It's used here so that we can send invalid data for further testing in PHP.

You can test this form by replacing the action to

```
<form method="..." action="/resources/testform.php">
```

with both method="get" and method="post". Fill in some values and you can see the sort of data that PHP will be getting.

When you've finished, remember to restore the attributes:

```
<form method="post" action="">
```

When you clear out the action attribute, the form data will be sent back to the contact.php script. This is called **reentrant** form processing: the script is used to both collect and process the data. The process looks like Figure 3-2.

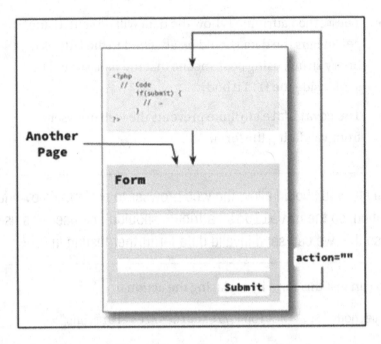

Figure 3-2. *Reentrant Form Processing*

You can send the data to a different script if you prefer, but it's often easier with a reentrant script, since you can retain values and you have fewer script files to manage.

The Plan of Attack

Now that we know how the form works, we'll need to plan what we're going to do with it. Generally, processing form data will go through the following steps:

- Read the form data.

- Check for errors.

- If no errors, use the data.

- Else, report errors.

There'll be a little more to this, of course, but at least now we have a plan.

Reading the Form Data

When the form is submitted, the PHP script at the receiving end will receive the data in the $_POST array, as you've specified the POST method in the form. The keys will correspond to the names of the form fields. Among other things, this means that if the form field doesn't have a name attribute, that field will not be submitted.

The submitted form data can then be read as follows:

```
$value = $_POST['key'];
```

The array has one key for each named form element, including the submit button. When processing the data, we'll test for the submit button and then work with the values from the text fields.

Since the page is sending data to itself, the page will start off simply displaying an empty form. After a submit, the page then needs to process any data coming in on reentry.

To begin, we'll add a PHP block at the beginning of the script:

```
<?php

?>
<?php
    // Page Title and Heading
        $pagetitle = 'Contact';
        $pageheading = 'Contact Us';

    require_once 'includes/head.php';
?>
```

In principle, having one PHP block immediately after another is unnecessary—you could have put the code in the same block. However, writing the code this way helps to separate the form processing code from the preliminary code for the page.

The first step in the script is to check whether the page is supposed to process incoming data. The technique is to check whether the Submit button has been used:

```php
<?php

// Process Submitted Form
if(isset($_POST['send'])) {

}

?>
```

- The if() statement tests whether something is true—in this case, whether there's something in the $_POST array.

- The isset() function tests whether a variable has been set or, in this case, whether an array has a value of that key. Technically, isset() is not a real function, but a **language construct**. They are similar, but there are some differences in what you can do with them.

- The braces ({ ... }) after the if() contain a block of code. If the test succeeds, the whole block will be run.

- We've added a heading comment and indented the if() to make it clear what this part of the code will do. There's also some space above the code since we're going to add more code later.

Although we'll be using isset(), many developers prefer to use the array_key_exists() function. The technical difference is that isset() will fail if there is a value which is *like* false, which will not be the case in our forms.

To use the array_key_exists() function, you would write

```php
php if(array_key_exists('send', $_POST)) ...
```

From here, we will do all of our processing inside the if() block.

Outlining the Plan

It is always a good idea to write down your plan for any process, and placing it in comments keeps everything where you can see it.

In your contact.php form, add the following comments in the processing block:

```
if(isset($_POST['send'])) {
    //  Read Data
    //  Check Data
    //  If no errors, Send Email
    //  Else, Report Errors
}
```

When you have finished developing the process, you may keep some of the comments to annotate your code. You may, however, end up rearranging your code or comments, and some comments may be entirely supplanted by a line of code which is just as, if not more, readable.

Reading the Form Data

Each form field will appear in the $_POST array. For convenience, we will copy the data into local variables:

$name = $_POST['name'];

Of course, the variable name doesn't have to be the same as the name in the original form. However, it is convenient, as long as the form names are suitable.

There was a time when PHP did this automatically, with data from the $_POST, $_GET, $_COOKIE, and $_REQUEST arrays all copied into variables. This is called registering global variables. This is a very bad idea since this gives evil users the opportunity to sneak in a few variables of their own. Fortunately, this is unavailable in modern versions of PHP.

In your contact.php file, add the following code to read the data:

```
if(isset($_POST['send'])) {
    //  Read Data
        $name = $_POST['name'];
        $email = $_POST['email'];
        $subject = $_POST['subject'];
        $message = $_POST['message'];

    //  Check Data

    //  If no errors, Send Email

    //  Else, Report Errors

}
```

These variables will hold the four values from the text fields of the form. Of course, they may be empty, and they may be unsuitable. For that, we've got some more processing and checking to do.

Preparing the Data

The data from the form may have been entered carelessly. In this case, we can clean it up a little by removing extraneous spaces.

The trim() function removes extra spaces at the beginning and end of a string and returns the result:

```
$newString = trim($oldString);
```

Much of the time, you simply want to replace the original string without generating a new string:

```
$string = trim($string);
```

We will modify the data gathering part of our code to include the trim() function:

```
if(isset($_POST['send'])) {
    // Read Data
        $name = trim($_POST['name']);
        $email = trim($_POST['email']);
        $subject = trim($_POST['subject']);
        $message = trim($_POST['message']);
    ...
}
```

This cleans up the data, but now we'll need to check it for suitability. Before we do, we'll have a look at reusing these variables.

Persisting Fields

It is infuriating to have to reenter a whole form just because of a simple error in one of the fields. We will print the old values back into the form:

- In the case of input fields, we'll print them back into the value attribute.

- In the case of the textarea field, we'll print the old value between the tags.

In the contact form, you'll see placeholders in the text fields, as well as one for the errors. We'll handle the errors later.

```
<form ...>
    [errors]
    ...
    <input ... value="[name]">
    ...
    <textarea ...>[message]</textarea>
</form>
```

We've left out most of the details here, but you can see that the placeholder is just a name in square brackets. That won't actually do anything useful until we replace them with PHP output tags.

Here's a simplified version of what we need:

```
<form ...>
    <?= $errors ?>
    <p><label ...>Name:</label>
        <input name="name" ... value="<?= $name ?>">
    </p>
    <p><label for="email">Email:</label>
        <input name="email" ... value="<?= $email ?>">
    </p>
```

```
<p><label for="subject">Subject:</label>
    <input name="subject" ... value="<?= $subject ?>">
</p>
<p><label for="message">Message:</label>
    <textarea name="message" ...><?= $message ?></textarea>
<p><button ... name="send">Send Message</button></p>
</form>
```

The trap with a reentrant form is that it is possible to attempt to print a variable without it being defined yet. In our example, the variables $name, $email, $subject, and $message would only be defined inside the if() block, only if the page is processing submitted data, and the $errors variable will be defined later. If you are loading the page for the first time as an empty form, the variables would not be defined, and you will get a PHP warning.

The solution is to define and initialize these variables at the beginning of the script:

```
<?php
    // Initialise
    $name = $email = $subject = $message = '';
    $errors = '';

    // Process Submitted Form
        ...
?>
```

PHP allows you to chain an assignment into multiple variables, which is useful for initializing variables. We could have included the $errors variable in the chain, but it's on a separate statement to reinforce the idea that it's there for a different job.

Form Validation

It's always important to check the incoming form data. Generally, you will be on the lookout for the following:

- **Errors**: A user may have omitted a required field or filled in some data incorrectly.

- **Adjustments**: Sometimes, the data may not be in the correct format or of the correct type, but you may be able to fix this in your script.

- **Security**: A carefully crafted piece of data may be used to try to break into your server or your database. This can happen by accident, but is also a real threat.

Checking your data for the preceding list is referred to as data **validation**.

JavaScript and HTML5 Validation

JavaScript can also be used to validate data before it is sent to the server. This is very convenient for the user and should be considered wherever possible.

HTML5 also incorporates a measure of data validation directly in forms. This includes testing for required data and matching patterns.

However, browser validation can never be 100% relied upon as it can be bypassed. If you have a choice between validating on the browser and validating on the server with PHP, it's no choice: *always validate incoming data on the server*.

You should always check your incoming data in PHP, regardless of what JavaScript or HTML5 you have in place to pre-check the data. In this case, we haven't included any JavaScript validation and we've turned off HTML5 validation, so that we can test everything in PHP.

Planning for Validation

In our contact form, there'll be three types of error to look for:

- **Missing data**: We'll assume all fields are required, so anything missing will be an error.

- **Email address**: The email address must at least look like an email address.

- **Header injection**: We need to check whether some malefactor is attempting to use our contact for some nefarious purpose.

For maximum helpfulness, we will report on all of the individual errors. We'll also repopulate the form with old values if the data does not completely pass validation, so that the user does not have to type it all again.

First, we'll create an array to contain all of our error messages. Using an array is a convenient way of accumulating data. When we have completed our error checking, we will convert the array to a string for printing.

To create an empty array, we use the [ ] operator and assign the resulting empty array to a variable, which we will call $errors:

```
if(isset($_POST['send'])) {
    //  Read Data
        ...

    //  Check Data
        $errors = [];

    ...
}
```

There is an older construct called `array()` which can be used exactly the same way:

```
$errors = array();
```

As you saw in Chapter 2, you can also create an array with existing values.

Required Fields

In the contact.php form, *all* fields are required, so if they're empty, you should include them in the errors.

All submitted text fields from a form have a value; if the field is empty, the value is an empty string (' '). For our purposes, an empty string in this case would be an error.

There are a few ways to test for an empty string. For example:

```
$test = '';

if($test = '') print 'empty';
if(empty($test)) print 'empty';

if(!$test) print 'empty';
```

The last test (`!$test`) is the simplest, but will need a little explaining. Normally, the `if()` statement includes a test which evaluates to `true` or `false`:

```
$a = 3;
$b = 4;
if($a < $b) print 'smaller';
```

However, it can also be used to test whether a value is a nonzero number or a non-empty string:

```
//  Number
    $a = 3;
    if($a) print 'something';

//  String
    $a = 'hello';
    if($a) print 'something';
```

In this simpler version, you can think of if() as meaning "if ... is something."

You can test the opposite using the **not** operator !:

```
//  Number
    $a = 3;
    if(!$a) print 'nothing';

//  String
    $a = 'hello';
    if(!$a) print 'nothing';
```

This is the common way to test for empty values, and we'll use it to test for empty form data.

Add the following code in the processing block:

```
if(isset($_POST['send'])) {

    ...

    //  Check Data
        $errors = [];
```

```
        if(!$name) $errors[] = 'Missing Name';
        if(!$email) $errors[] = 'Missing Email Address';
        if(!$subject) $errors[] = 'Missing Subject';
        if(!$message) $errors[] = 'Missing Message';
}
```

Remember, the expression $errors[] = means to add the value to the array—also known as pushing a value.

Checking an Email Address

Just because a user submitted a value, it doesn't mean that it's suitable. Next, we will check the email address.

The most complete way of testing an email address is to send an email and wait for the reply. This is one reason many registration forms require responding to an email to complete the process.

At this stage, we cannot check whether the email address is correct, but we can check whether it follows a pattern.

PHP includes a function to test a string against various patterns:

```
filter_var(variable, filter)
```

There are many filters available, collected in types. The one we will use from the validate type is FILTER_VALIDATE_EMAIL, which checks whether the string looks like an email address. If it does, the result is true; otherwise, it is false.

To check whether a value **doesn't** pass, we use the not (!) operator. In this case, we'll test the $email variable against the FILTER_VALIDATE_ EMAIL filter:

```
if(!filter_var($email, FILTER_VALIDATE_EMAIL)
    $errors[] = 'Invalid Email Address';
```

We've written the second part on another line simply because it doesn't fit on this page. You can leave it on the same line if you wish. If you do write it on a second line, it's helpful to indent the second line to make it clear that it's a continuation. It's not necessary, but helps to make your code more readable.

We have previously checked and reported on a possible empty field. An empty field would also fail the preceding validation test, but it would be pointless to report it as another error.

For this reason, the email pattern test should only be the *alternative* to an empty field address. This we can do with an elseif(). In PHP, this is a single word:

```
// Check Data
    ...

if(!$name) $errors[] = 'Missing Name';
if(!$email) $errors[] = 'Missing Email Address';
elseif(!filter_var($email, FILTER_VALIDATE_EMAIL))
    $errors[] = 'Invalid Email Address';
if(!$subject) $errors[] = 'Missing Subject';
if(!$message) $errors[] = 'Missing Message';
```

Using elseif() makes it possible to have alternative tests.

Email Injection

Internet email has been around for a very long time and uses a simple format which is *very* easy to exploit.

Basically, all emails are sent as a simple text. The text has two parts: the headers, which have information about the email, and the message body itself. The two parts are separated by an empty line.

For example:

```
Message-ID: <4DB3FF7A.70602@example.net>
Date: Sun, 24 Apr 2011 20:46:18 +1000
From: Wilma Bloggs <wilma@example.net>
To: Fred Nurke <fred@example.net>
Subject: This is a very long subject header which
    wraps to another line.

This is a message.
```

The headers appear on new lines. They are a header name, a colon, and the header content. If the header is too long to fit on one line, such as a very long subject, it can continue on the next line, as long as subsequent lines are indented.

The headers control what happens to the email, such as where it's sent, and also contain additional information such as the date.

As soon as you have an empty line, the message begins, and any further content that *looks* like a header is just more text.

Modern emails can also contain images, attachments, and HTML code. If you look at the source of the email, however, you'll find that all of that has been encoded as text in special sections.

We won't write any of this by hand, as PHP has a function to do this. However, if we're not careful, we might accidentally include additional headers that shouldn't be there.

For example, suppose, somehow, the user has managed to put this in the subject line:

```
Test Email
Bcc: everyone@etc.com
```

You can't do that in a normal web form, but miscreants have other means of sending data to the server, so it's a very distinct possibility. If we naively add the preceding subject to our email, the Bcc will cause a copy to be sent elsewhere. That's the sort of thing we want to avoid.

Fortunately, it's *very* easy to nip this in the bud. Remember, each additional header starts on a new line. If we look out for line breaks, we'll intercept any fake headers. None of the fields should include line breaks, except the message, where it's too late for additional headers.

Unfortunately, PHP has no simple filter for checking line breaks, so we'll have to search the string ourselves.

The most flexible function for searching a string is called preg_match(). This odd looking name can be pronounced as "p-reg-match" and is short for something like "perl regular expression match"—PERL is a programming language noted for its powerful regular expressions. A regular expression is a pattern to be matched.

Regular expression patterns can be pretty cryptic. The one we'll use here is

/\r|\n/

- The / ... / forward slashes contain a regular expression, similar to how quotes contain a string.

- The \r and \n expressions represent the carriage return (CR) and line feed (LF), two codes which can be used to break lines.

- The pipe (|) between them means "or."

Here, the regular expression represents a carriage return or line feed character. Of course, there may be more than one, but one is sufficient to reject the value as an attempt at header injection. *None* of the headers can legitimately have a line break.

We'll test the subject and name variables, but only if they're non-empty, just like the email variable:

```
// Check Data
    ...
    if(!$name) $errors[] = 'Missing Name';
    elseif(preg_match('/\r\|\n/', $name))
        $errors[] = 'Invalid Name';
    ...
    if(!$subject) $errors[] = 'Missing Subject';
    elseif(preg_match('/\r\|\n/', $subject))
        $errors[] = 'Invalid Subject';
    ...
```

In principle, the same would apply to the email address. However, the FILTER_VALIDATE_EMAIL test would pick up any invalid characters in the email address, and this already includes a line break, so we don't need to bother with that.

The testing code should now look like this:

```
// Check Data
    $errors = [];

    if(!$name) $errors[] = 'Missing Name';
    elseif(preg_match('/\r\|\n/', $name))
        $errors[] = 'Invalid Name';

    if(!$email) $errors[] = 'Missing Email Address';
    elseif (!filter_var($email, FILTER_VALIDATE_EMAIL))
        $errors[] = 'Invalid Email Address';

    if(!$subject) $errors[] = 'Missing Subject';
    elseif(preg_match('/\r\|\n/', $subject))
        $errors[] = 'Invalid Subject';

    if(!$message) $errors[] = 'Missing Message';
```

We can now look at deciding what to do with the errors.

Handling the Errors

Up to this point, we have been putting possible errors into the $errors array. If all goes well, this array will be empty, as it was when it was created. If it is empty, we can proceed to send the email.

We can test for an empty array by using the fact that PHP treats an empty array as false for testing purposes. This gives us the test of if($errors) for a populated array or if(!$errors) for an empty array:

```
if(!$errors) {        // If no errors, Send Email

}
else {                //  Else, Report Errors

}
```

Note that we've moved the comments to the right of the if ... else ... statements.

Displaying the Errors

If the $errors array is not empty, we'll need to report it, using the values in the array. PHP will not print an array as such, so we'll combine these messages into a string using the implode() function.

The combined string will find its way into a paragraph and output in the HTML part of the page. That part has already been prepared when we added the <?= $errors ?> code.

The implode() function takes two parameters: the "glue" and the array.

```
implode(glue, array.php);
```

The "glue" is the string which will be joined between the values. Often, it is an empty string (''), in which case you can leave it out, but in this instance, we will use the HTML line break ('<br>').

The result of implode() is a string: the original array is left intact. However, in our case, we will place the result into the same variable:

```
if(!$errors) {        // If no errors, Send Email

}
else {                //  Else, Report Errors
    $errors = implode('<br>', $errors);
}
```

It's perfectly legitimate to replace a variable with any value of any type of data. However, we will use the following principles:

- Don't introduce too many new variables: recycle them if it's practical.

- Only reuse a variable if it is being used for the same purpose as the original.

- In this case, we're replacing the $errors array with a string. It is still being used to contain our error messages.

The Errors Paragraph

You can print out the $errors string as it is, but it's better if we put the string inside an HTML paragraph using the errors class so that CSS can style it.

The paragraph looks like this:

```
<p class="errors">%s</p>
```

where the %s is a placeholder for the contents of the $errors variable. You can populate the contents of the paragraph using the sprintf() function:

```
if(!$errors) {          // If no errors, Send Email

}
else {                  //  Else, Report Errors
    $errors = implode('<br>', $errors);
    $errors = sprintf('<p class="errors">%s</p>', $errors);
}
```

Note that the string literal uses single quotes, as is our practice, and has double quotes inside. Sometimes, the choice of using single or double quotes for string literals is simply a matter of whether the string itself has the other type of quote.

You can combine the two steps:

```
if(!$errors) {          // If no errors, Send Email

}
else {                  //  Else, Report Errors
    $errors = sprintf('<p class="errors">%s</p>',
        implode('<br>', $errors));
}
```

You can now test your code, making sure that you leave something out or have an invalid email address.

Printing Empty Arrays

If you test the script at this point, you will find that you either get

- A generated error message if there are errors

- The word "Array" and a possible PHP warning if there are no errors

The second case is because you will still have an empty error array if everything is OK. PHP doesn't like printing arrays, so it will complain.

91

Don't panic. This is undesirable, but OK at this point. It will not occur when we have finished our script, as the final step will be to show an alternative message.

Sending Email with the mail() Function

PHP has the functionality to send an email message, using the mail() function.

PHP does not actually handle the sending, but passes it off to an external program, such as sendmail on Linux.

The main function to send mail is

```
mail(to, subject, message, headers)
```

The parameters are the to: address, the subject, and the actual message body. The headers parameter is a string containing all of the remaining mail headers. It seems strange that the mail() function treats the remaining headers so lightly and that you'll need to construct them by hand.

We'll set all of these values in variables ready to send off. In the code, add the following:

```
if(!$errors) {        // If no errors, Send Email

    mail($to, $subject, $message, $headers);
}
else {                // Else, Report Errors
    ...
}
```

After this, we need to set the variables, one by one.

The Main Email Variables

The To: header is where the email will be sent. In this case, it's the owner of the website, which we'll call info@australia.example.net.

You can use a raw email address:

```
$to = 'info@australia.example.net';
```

However, there's a richer email address format which includes the name:

```
$to = 'Support <info@australia.example.net>';
```

In the code, we can add

```
if(!$errors) {       // If no errors, Send Email
    $to = 'Support <info@australia.example.net>';

    mail($to, $subject, $message, $headers);
}
else {               // Else, Report Errors
    ...
}
```

If you're testing this on a live email server in Windows, you may have trouble with the richer form of the email addresses. If the mail server doesn't like your email addresses, you should try the simpler form such as $to = 'info@australia.example.net'; instead.

The next variable is the $subject variable. At this point, there's nothing more to do, so we'll just put in a comment to say that it's ready to go:

```
if(!$errors) {       // If no errors, Send Email
    $to = 'Support <info@australia.example.net>';
    // $subject already set
```

```
    mail($to, $subject, $message, $headers);
}
else {                    //  Else, Report Errors
    ...
}
```

The $message variable is nearly ready to go. However, there's a sort of limit to the line length. The Email Standards require that all long text be hard wrapped to something under 80 characters:

> *There are two limits that this standard places on the number of characters in a line. Each line of characters MUST be no more than 998 characters, and SHOULD be no more than 78 characters, excluding the CRLF. RFC 2822* www.rfc-editor.org/rfc/rfc2822.txt

Hard wrapping is accomplished by adding a line break at a suitable point (such as where there would have been a space) before the line length limit. For safety, as well as readability, we'll wrap our long lines at around 70 characters.

PHP has a function which will insert hard line breaks before a specified line length:

```
wordwrap(text, width, break)
```

For email, we will use a width of 70 and break of \r\n:

```
if(!$errors) {        // If no errors, Send Email
    $to = 'Support <info@australia.example.net>';
    //  $subject already set
    $message = wordwrap($message, 70, "\r\n");

    mail($to, $subject, $message, $headers);
}
else {                    //  Else, Report Errors
    ...
}
```

One of the differences between single and double quote strings is how special characters are interpreted. Double quote strings would see the expression \r\n as line break characters, while single quote strings would see it as four ordinary characters.

The next step is to work on the email headers.

The Email Headers

There are many standard headers, and individual email programs, intervening hosts, and spam filters may also add their own.

Here are some of the most common email headers.

Type	Header	Use
Supplied	To:	Receiver's address
	Subject:	Message subject
Automatic	Date:	Date of email
	Message-ID:	Unique ID of message
Additional	From:	Sender's address
	Cc:	Carbon copy
	Bcc:	Blind (secret) Cc
	Content-Type:	Usually automatically set for text messages. May be set for non-text message
	Reply-To:	Address to reply to, if not to the From: address
	Sender:	Real address of sender, if not the From: address

For our contact email, we'll use the following email headers:

Header	Source
To:	Hard-coded
Subject:	From the form
Date:	Automatic, but we'll supply it ourselves
From:	From the form
Cc:	Same as From: to send a copy to the user

You can set the additional headers string in a single array:

```
$headers = [
    'To' => ...,
    'Subject' => ...,
    'Date' => ...,
    'From' => ...,
    'Cc' => ...
];
```

Older versions of php, before version 7.2, require a string instead of an array. You can see how to do that in Appendix C.

We'll build the headers in the next step.

The Header Data

We'll start with an array of empty strings for the headers:

```
if(!$errors) {        // If no errors, Send Email
    $to = 'Support <info@australia.example.net>';
    //  $subject already set
```

```php
$message = wordwrap($message, 70, "\r\n");

$headers = [
    'Date' => '',
    'From' => '',
    'Cc' => ''
];

mail($to, $subject, $message, $headers);
}
```

The To: and Subject: headers have already been set and are the first two parameters in the mail() function, so they don't need to be added to the $headers array. For the others, they're set to null simply to complete the statement.

The Date: may be added by the mail program, but we can add it here instead. The date needs to follow a specific format for emails, but, fortunately, there's a shortcut for that:

```php
date('r')
```

This produces a formatted date and time using the **RFC 2822 / 5322** specifications, which define the data formats for email. We can add it to our array:

```php
if(!$errors) {        // If no errors, Send Email
    ...

    $headers = [
        'Date' => date('r'),
        'From' => null,
        'Cc' => null
    ];

    mail($to, $subject, $message, $headers);
}
```

The From header is the email address of the user. We'll also send them a copy, so it will be the same as the Cc header.

To get the full email address, we'll combine the name and the email address by interpolating them into a string:

```
"$name <$email>"
```

We can add them to the $headers array:

```
if(!$errors) {         // If no errors, Send Email
    ...

    $headers = [
        'Date' => date('r'),
        'From' => "$name <$email>",
        'Cc' => "$name <$email>"
    ];
    mail($to, $subject, $message, $headers);
}
```

This should work well enough for testing.

As we noted before, if you're trying this on Windows with a live email server, you may get better results if you use the shorter form of the email address, such as 'From' => $email, 'Cc' => $email.

If you used the fakemail file for your email, your email will appear in the file mail.txt by default. It should look something like this:

```
=================================================
Fri Sep 29 09:41:49 AEST 2023
-------------------------------------------------
To: Support <info@australia.example.net>
```

```
Subject: Test
X-PHP-Originating-Script: 501:contact.php
Date: Fri, 29 Sep 2023 01:41:49 +0200
From: Fred Nurke <fred@example.net>
Cc: Fred Nurke <fred@example.net>

This is a test ...
-------------------------------------------------
```

If it's worked successfully, you'll see the word `Array` above the form, where the error messages should be, possibly with a warning about printing arrays. That's because the `$errors` variable was already created as an empty array, and this part of the code left it alone, since there are no errors. You'll also see the data in the form, since we've done nothing about clearing it.

We'll fix that in the next section.

After Sending the Message

If everything has been sent successfully, we will see the word Array where the error message should be. This is because we still have the empty `$errors` array. It doesn't matter, because if the message has been sent, we want to see a different message anyway.

Alternative Parts

A useful technique, which we will use again later, is to include additional parts of a page and let PHP decide which part to let through. This involves using an if block.

When mixing PHP in with HTML, you can spread your PHP code over multiple PHP blocks. For example:

```php
<?php
    $test = true;
?>
<?php if($test) { ?>
    Plan A
<?php } else { ?>
    Plan B
<?php } ?>
```

Remember whatever's not inside a PHP block is simply output. This is equivalent to

```php
<?php
    $test = true;
    if($test) {
        print 'Plan A';
    } else {
        print 'Plan B';
    }
?>
```

The previous form is more convenient if you have a lot of HTML to output.

PHP has an obscure alternative way of writing an if() block:

```php
<?php
    $test = true;
    if($test):
        print 'Plan A';
```

```
    else:
        print 'Plan B';
    endif;
?>
```

Here, the braces are replaced with a colon (:); the final brace is replaced with an endif keyword. You won't normally see this in standard PHP code, but we're going to take advantage of this syntax when mixing in with HTML:

```
<?php
    $test = true;
?>
<?php if($test): ?>
    Plan A
<?php else: ?>
    Plan A
<?php endif; ?>
```

It works exactly the same way, but we'll use this form because it looks more natural among the HTML. For normal PHP code, we'll still write it the standard way.

The two parts will consist of a Thank You message if the message has been sent and the Form if it has not:

```
<?php if(...): ?>
    <!-- Form -->
<?php else: ?>
    <!-- Thank You Message -->
<?php endif; ?>
```

For this, we need to write the if() block and set up a variable to decide which to output.

Writing the Conditional Blocks

In the contact.php form, you'll see something like the following code:

```
<!-- if not sent: -->
    <form id="contact-form" method="post" action="" novalidate>
        ...
    </form>
<!-- else:
    <p>Thank you for your message.</p>
    <p>Now, <a href="/">go away ...</a>.</p>
endif -->
```

There are two commented sections:

- The comment at the beginning marks where we'll test whether an email has *not* been sent.

- The comment at the end marks the alternative.

We'll convert these comments to real code, but first we'll create a new variable, $sent, to decide which part to show:

```
<?php
    // Initialise
    $name = $email = $subject = $message = '';
    $errors = '';
    $sent = false;

    ...
?>
```

The $sent variable will indicate whether an email has been sent, and, to begin with, it hasn't.

Next, we'll set it if the message has been sent:

```php
if(!$errors) { // $errors is empty => no error
    ...
    mail($to, $subject, $message, $headers);
    $sent = true;
}
```

We can now use the variable as a condition:

```php
<?php if(!$sent): ?>
    <form id="contact-form" method="post" action="" novalidate>
        ...
    </form>
<?php else: ?>
    <p>Thank you for your message.</p>
    <p>Now, <a href="/">go away ...</a>.</p>
<?php endif; ?>
```

Note that we've used the negative test (!$sent), since we're testing whether an email *hasn't* been sent yet.

When you test it now, you should see the following:

Thank you for your message.Now, go away ....

The link is simply a link to the home page (/). Of course, you can probably think of a better message, but the point is made.

As you see from the actual HTML, the link reference is href="/", which refers to the **root** of the site.

One reason why the setup procedure puts so much effort into setting up a virtual host is because of the links. By default, the XAMPP and MAMP site root is the management package, and you're expected to put your additional sites within the main directory. Using / would link you back to management instead of your site.

103

Using a virtual host allows you to use your links more realistically.

Reorganizing the Code

Too many developers write code only for the moment, without giving much thought for maintenance. Here, we'll make a few small changes which will help.

First, we'll move the To: address to a configuration section at the beginning. This value has no effect on the logic of the code, and its value should be easily set if necessary.

Second, we'll move the code into a separate file, which allows us to separate the logic from the physical appearance of the page.

Configuration

In a typical project, there may be some values which aren't crucial to the logic and might be easily changed with impunity if only we can locate it. In the contact page, probably the only arbitrary value is the address where the email is being sent.

At the beginning of the code, add the following:

```php
<?php
    // Configuration
        $CONFIG['contact']['to'] =
            'Support <info@australia.example.com>';

    // Initialise
        ...
```

We've put the configurable data in a nested array, which might look a little like overengineering for such a simple value. Obviously, there's a plan here to do this with other code later, where the data will be more complex.

In the code which sends the email, we can modify it to use the configured value:

```
if(!$errors) {        // If no errors, Send Email
    $to = $CONFIG['contact']['to'];
    ...
}
else {                //  Else, Report Errors
    ...
}
```

This should give the same result, but now it's easier to locate and change the To: address.

Moving the Code

All the code we added to the page is beginning to push out the page content. It's still there, but obscured by the PHP programming.

In this case, there's not so much that we can't manage, but in general it would be better to separate the code out to another file, so that the contact.php file can focus on its main job of supplying the content.

The simplest solution is to cut the PHP block out and put it into another file, being sure to include it back in the original.

- First, select the code block we've been working with, cut it, and put it into a new file. This is one reason it made sense to keep it in a separate block to begin with.

- Second, save the file as includes/contact.code.php. Of course, the actual name doesn't really matter, as long as you know what it is.

- Finally, replace the code block with an include statement.

The final code should look something like this:

```php
<?php require_once 'includes/contact.code.php'; ?>
<?php
    // Page Title and Heading
    $pagetitle = 'Contact';
    $pageheading = 'Contact Us';

    require_once 'includes/head.inc.php';
?>
```

There's one more important task. In the new file, contact.code.php, *remove* the closing PHP tag (?>).

PHP will automatically close any PHP blocks at the end of a script, so, if all you have is one big PHP block, the closing tag is unnecessary. That's not why we removed it, however.

When you include a file, you also include any text which is *outside* the block. In this case, it would be a possible line break and possible empty lines. If the file is included at the beginning of your code, you run the risk of including additional (invisible) text at the beginning.

That's not a problem, yet. However, it can be a problem if your PHP needs to write additional HTTP headers, as it will when we start using cookies. If it attempts to do that after other text has been written, you'll end up with an error.

It's always a good idea to minimize unwanted text with included files.

Summary

In this chapter, we worked on processing incoming form data. This will be an important part of the rest of the project as we'll be using forms to interact with the database and the rest of the site.

Another important part of the rest of the project is the process we went through in developing the code: using comments to outline the plan, incrementally improving the code, and reorganizing the code to improve it.

Data from an uploaded form appears in one or other of the superglobal arrays, which are populated with the form data. In this case, the array was the $_POST array which has data from a post method form. Processing the data started with reading it into variables and performing some preliminary cleaning up.

The contact page was designed to be reentrant: the page has the form to collect and submit the data, as well as the code to process it after it's submitted. To manage that, we needed to put the processing code in a conditional block which tests for an upload.

We saw how to return the processed data back into the form in case the form needs to be resubmitted. This required setting initial values prior to reentry and putting PHP output statements in the form fields.

All user-supplied data has the potential to cause problems, especially if it's data from unverified outsiders. To protect ourselves from errors and malicious attacks, we had work on validating the submitted data. Although it's possible to do some data validation on the browser end, this can be bypassed, so it's important to do a thorough job on the server.

In this case, we needed to check for simple errors such as missing data or badly formatted email addresses, but we also had to check against email header injection by testing for code which could be misconstrued as additional unwanted headers.

Checking for errors involved building an array of error messages. After checking for errors, if the array is empty, we can proceed to send the email. Otherwise, we report the error in an error paragraph. To print the error, we needed to convert the array into a printable string.

To send an email, we use the PHP mail() function, giving the function the data from the form as well as additional data for the email. PHP doesn't send the email itself—instead, it sends the data to an external mail program. For testing purposes, we can take advantage of a virtual email program which simply saves the data in a text file.

If the message has been sent successfully, we saw how to display an alternative section of the contact page. This involved setting a suitable variable and using a PHP conditional statement to select which section to output.

Once we had the code working, we worked on improving the code for maintainability. This involved setting up a configuration section with arbitrary data, such as the To: address, and moving the whole of the code to a separate file to be included in the page.

Coming Up

Having now gotten some experience in planning and organizing code, we're going to work with another form. In this case, it's a form to upload data to be saved and used later.

In Chapter 4, we'll reiterate some of what we've done in this chapter, but the goal won't be to send it on. Instead, we'll ultimately save some of it to a database, and we'll have a look at how to check and save uploaded files.

CHAPTER 4

Uploading Data and Files

In Chapter 3, we used a form to collect data to send on as an email. Forms can be used not only to send text data but also to upload a binary file, such as an image or a PDF file.

In this chapter, we'll begin the process of maintaining an image library. This will involve setting up a form for data entry and the script which will process the data. The data will include text, as with the contact form, but also a binary file—in this case, an image file.

Processing the text data will be similar to processing the contact form, so some of the code from that can be adapted to this form. However, processing the image file will be a whole new task and will involve learning more about how binary data is uploaded.

In this chapter, we'll learn about how forms are encoded for binary data, how the binary data is sent to the server, and how PHP handles the data. We'll see how to check the uploaded file for suitability and to save it to a permanent location.

We'll also start looking at preparing the data for use in the database and in an image gallery, both of which will be completed in later chapters.

The Upload Form

The form will be in the uploadimage.php file and looks like Figure 4-1.

© Mark Simon 2024
M. Simon, *An Introduction to PHP*, https://doi.org/10.1007/979-8-8688-0177-8_4

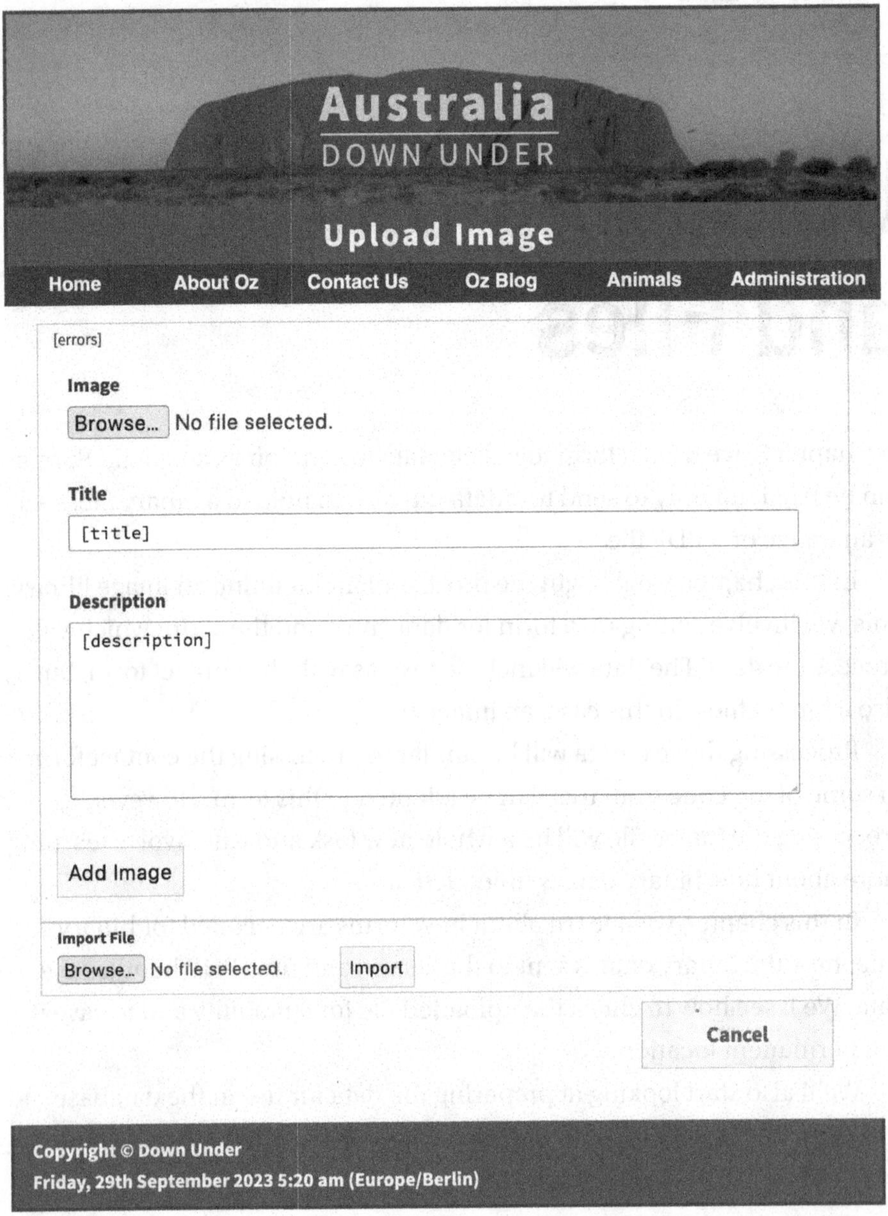

Figure 4-1. *Upload Image Page*

On the inside, this page also includes the additional form elements to allow us to edit existing image data, but we'll look at that later.

At this stage, there is no link to this page. Later, you'll access it through an administration page—for now, you'll have to open it as this way:

`http://australia.example.com/uploadimage.php`

The basic upload form looks something like this:

```
<form method="post" action="" enctype="multipart/form-
data" id="...">
    <input type="hidden" name="id" value="[id]">
    [errors]
    <fieldset [disabled]>
        <p ...><label>Image<br>
            <input name="image" type="file"></label>
            <img id="preview">
        </p>
        <p><label>Title<br>
            <input ... name="title" value="[title]"></label>
        </p>
        <p><label>Description<br>
            <textarea name="description">[description]
            </textarea>
        </label></p>
    </fieldset>

    <p>
        <button type="submit" name="insert">Add Image</button>
    </p>
</form>
```

Information such as id and class, as well as all the code hidden in comments, have been omitted to allow us to focus on the important parts of the form.

This form has text inputs for a title and description and a single file input for uploading an image file, as well as a submit button—more than one submit button, actually. The other submit buttons, currently commented out, will allow the form to be used for editing and deleting rows as well.

The appearance of the file input will vary between browsers and operating systems. You can't change it very much in CSS—that's so that you can't disguise it as something else.

In order to allow file uploads

- The form *must* use the POST method, not the GET method.

- The enctype attribute must be set to multipart/form-data. This allows the attached file to be encoded into a separate part of the http message.

- There must be an input of type file, obviously.

All binary data will need to be encoded for the trip over HTTP using MIME encoding. The encoding and decoding are handled automatically using the form's encoding type.

You'll have noticed another form at the bottom of the page. That's to enable a bulk upload, which is something we'll be doing later.

The File Input

The file input element has a special appearance and behavior in the browser:

- There is always a button to select a file to be uploaded.

- With some browsers, on some systems, there may also be an attached text box. This text box may or may not allow you to type in data, but it will always show you the name of the attached file, once selected.

- You cannot change the appearance of this button very much. This is a security feature to prevent evil developers from disguising upload elements.

You can, of course, have multiple file inputs. They can have individual names or be part of a collection.

Settings

Before proceeding with file uploads, we need to check a few settings. PHP generally allows you to accept uploaded files, but some installations disable it for various reasons. This is usually up to the web administrator to manage.

Two other settings, however, may be available to you. In the .htaccess file, you'll find the following:

```
#   Uploads
    php_value   post_max_size 8M
    php_value   upload_max_filesize 2M
```

and in the .user.ini file, the equivalent settings are

```
#   Uploads
    post_max_size=8M
    upload_max_filesize=2M
```

In the preceding standard settings, you are limited to 2Mb per individual file, and 8Mb total, including all the uploaded files and any other data sent through the form. If you plan on uploading large files, such as TIFF images, you may wish to reconsider these values. You can also upload ZIP files with multiple images, in which case, you will also need larger sizes.

You'll need to change these settings later, but they'll do for now.

Preliminary Coding

Much of the work to begin with will be similar to what we did for the contact form: set some variables, check for incoming data, and read and validate the data.

You'll notice that there's a commented out include at the beginning of the file. It references a nonexistent file in the `includes` folder. We'll honor that promise now.

Create the file `includes/manage-images.code.inc`, and remove the comment hash (#) before the `require_once` statement.

The name of the included file alludes to the fact that we'll do more than just upload images, but that's later.

In the new file, add the following PHP block:

```
<?php
```

Remember, since this is a PHP block and nothing else, it's better to leave off the closing PHP tag.

The Data Variables

As with the contact form, we'll use some variables to store the incoming and error data, and we'll display current values in the form. You'll find the following placeholders:

- [id]: This will be used later when editing existing data.

- [errors]: The error messages, if any.

114

- [disabled]: This will also be used later when editing.

- [title], [description]: The title and description for
  the images we'll be uploading.

We'll use some of these later, but for now, we can turn them into
variables, as we did for the contact form.

In the form, replace the placeholders with PHP output statements and
variables:

```
<form ...>
    <input name="id" value="<?= $id ?>">
    <?= $errors ?>
    <fieldset  <?= $disabled ?>>
    ...
    <input ... name="title" value="<?= $title ?>">
    ...
    <textarea name="description" ...><?= $description ?>
    </textarea>
    ...
</form>
```

Watch for those closing tags. For example, there are *two* greater than
signs (>) on the fieldset: one to end the PHP output and another to end
the fieldset tag.

We'll also set up the preliminary variables in manage-images.code.php:

```
<?php
    // Initialise
    $id = 0;
    $title = $description = '';
    $errors = '';
    $disabled = '';
```

115

The $title, $description, and $errors variables are similar to what we did in the contact form. The others we'll explain later.

You should reload your page now to make sure you don't have any errors.

Processing POSTed Data and Preliminary Validation

As with the contact form, we'll read in the text fields and do some preliminary cleaning up prior to checking them. All of this, of course, will be inside an if() block to test whether the data has been submitted:

```php
<?php
    ...

    //  Upload Image
        if(isset($_POST['insert'])) {

        }
```

This time, the submit button is called insert. Later, we'll add this data to a database table, and INSERT is what the operation is called in SQL, the database coding language.

Again, using our experience with the contact form, we can start on reading the data:

```php
<?php
    ...
    //  Upload Image
        if(isset($_POST['insert'])) {
            $title = trim($_POST['title']);
            $description=trim($_POST['description']);
        }
```

We can then test for missing data:

```
//  Upload Image
    if(isset($_POST['insert'])) {
        $title = trim($_POST['title']);
        $description=trim($_POST['description']);

        $errors = [];

        //  Check Text

            if(!$title) $errors[] = 'Missing Title';
            if(!$description) $errors[] = 'Missing
            Description';
    }
```

We can also outline the code to process the data or report on the errors:

```
if(isset($_POST['insert'])) {
    ...
    //  Process
        if(!$errors) {  //  proceed

        }
        else {              //  handle error
            $errors = sprintf('<p class="errors">%s</p>',
                implode('<br>', $errors));
        }
}
```

You can test your form now and try submitting it without any data to see the error messages.

Image Validation

There are two possible issues with the uploaded image file:

- The file may be missing.

- The file may be present, but not suitable for our application.

In this page, we're expecting an attached image file—that's the whole point of the page. In other projects, an image may be optional, so a missing file is not a problem. However, we still need to check whether the uploaded file is suitable.

The $_POST array does not contain anything about uploaded files. Instead, this information is in the $_FILES array, another superglobal.

The $_FILES Array

The $_FILES array is an array of arrays: each uploaded file has one entry, whose key is the name attribute of the file button. This, in turn, is an array of data about the file. In our case, we only have one upload, but it is still wrapped inside an array.

Each nested array has five pieces of data. For our upload button, whose name is image, we have

Key	Purpose
$_FILES['image']['error']	An error code
$_FILES['image']['name']	The original file name
$_FILES['image']['size']	The size in bytes
$_FILES['image']['type']	The MIME type
$_FILES['image']['tmp_name']	The path where the file is waiting

Normally, PHP will get something in the $_FILES['image'] array even if a file hasn't been attached—we would need to check the value in $_FILES['image']['error'] to see whether it's missing. However, some mobile devices don't send anything at all for the $_FILES array, so we'll first need to check whether there is anything at all. If not, we'll regard it as an error.

Using File Data

In our code, we can add

```
if(isset($_POST['insert'])) {
    ...
    //  Check Text
    ...

    //  Check File
        if(!isset($_FILES['image'])) $errors[] = 'Missing File';

    // Process
}
```

If the $_FILES[] array is present, the next step is to check the $_FILES array for an error code. The error codes are simple numbers:

Code	Name	Meaning
0	UPLOAD_ERR_OK	No error
1	UPLOAD_ERR_INI_SIZE	The file exceeds the upload_max_filesize
2	UPLOAD_ERR_FORM_SIZE	The file exceeds the MAX_FILE_SIZE
3	UPLOAD_ERR_PARTIAL	The file was only partially uploaded
4	UPLOAD_ERR_NO_FILE	No file was uploaded
6	UPLOAD_ERR_NO_TMP_DIR	No temporary folder
7	UPLOAD_ERR_CANT_WRITE	Failed to write disk

Each code number has a name which you can use instead.

- Error code 0 means that the file was uploaded successfully, but we'll still need to check the file itself for its suitability.

- The error codes 1 and 2 both indicate that the file is too big, for different reasons. The first exceeds the value we set earlier and is a hard limit; the second is a less reliable limit you can set in the form itself and can easily be circumvented. We'll give them both the same error message.

- Error code 4 may not necessarily be an error in other contexts, since the file may not be required. Here, it is.

- The other codes, including 3, indicate a more serious problem that the user can't do anything about. We'll bundle them together as a miscellaneous upload error.

Handling the error is best done using a switch() block:

```
// Check File
    if(!isset($_FILES['image'])) $errors[] = 'Missing File';
    else switch($_FILES['image']['error']) {
        case UPLOAD_ERR_OK:

            break;
        case UPLOAD_ERR_INI_SIZE:
        case UPLOAD_ERR_FORM_SIZE:

            break;
        case UPLOAD_ERR_NO_FILE:

            break;
        default:

    }
```

The switch block is a way of testing one expression against a number of possible values. We could have used an if ... elseif ... else block to do the same job, but the switch block makes the purpose clearer.

We've used the code names, but we could just as readily have used the code numbers. The technical name for the code name is a **constant**; once it's been set, you can't change its value. Like variable names, the name is case sensitive; it's a strong tradition to use upper case, but it's not required. Note that unlike variable names, there's no special character prefix.

One thing to be careful of is that each case is a starting point for processing, but not an exit point. Processing will continue through the rest of the block until either the end of the block is reached, or the processing is deliberately terminated. The break statement is used to exit the block when we've handled the case.

We can now add some more error messages:

```
// Check File
   if(!isset($_FILES['image'])) $errors[] = 'Missing File';
   else switch($_FILES['image']['error']) {
      case UPLOAD_ERR_OK:
         // No Error with file, need to check the file later
         break;
      case UPLOAD_ERR_INI_SIZE:
      case UPLOAD_ERR_FORM_SIZE:
         $errors[] = 'File too big';
         break;
      case UPLOAD_ERR_NO_FILE:
         $errors[] = 'Missing File';
         break;
      default:
         $errors[] = 'Problem with file upload';
   }
```

We'll now check the file itself to see whether it's suitable.

Checking an Image File

There are two things you might not like about an uploaded file.

First, it might be too big. The error code UPLOAD_ERR_INI_SIZE would indicate that it's exceeded the settings size, and so the file won't be accepted at all. However, you might like to impose a lower limit yourself.

You'll get the uploaded file size in $_FILES['image']['size'], which you can check yourself:

```
case UPLOAD_ERR_OK:
    //  if($_FILES['image']['size'] > 0x100000)
    //      $errors[] = 'File too big';
    break;
```

The expression 0x100000 is how you write 1 megabyte (1024576) in hexadecimal. We won't actually use this limit in this project, so we've commented it out in case we want it later.

The other thing is that the file may not actually be an appropriate image type.

When a file is sent from the browser to the server, one of the accompanying pieces of information is the **MIME** type. This is a description of the type of file. Some useful MIME types include

Broad Group	MIME Type	File Type
	text/plain	Generic text file
	application/octet-stream	Generic binary file
Images		
	image/png	PNG image
	image/jpeg	JPEG image
	image/gif	GIF image
	image/webp	WEBP image

Broad Group	MIME Type	File Type
Other media		
	`audio/mpeg`	MP3 audio
	`video/mp4`	MP4 video
	`video/webm`	WEBM video
Web files		
	`text/html`	HTML file
	`text/css`	CSS file
	`text/javascript`	JavaScript file
	`application/json`	JSON file
	`application/xmltext/xml`	XML file
Others		
	`text/csv`	CSV file
	`application/zip`	ZIP archive

There are, of course, many others. You can get a more complete list from `www.iana.org/assignments/media-types/media-types.xhtml`.

In our case, we're only interested in some of the image types.

Note that the MIME type is *not* the same as the file extension, though there is often a resemblance. In particular, the JPEG file can have the extension `.jpeg`, but often uses `.jpg` for historical reasons. However, the MIME type is still `image/jpeg`.

The simplest way to check whether the MIME type is one of the types you want is to begin with an array:

```
$imagetypes = ['image/gif', 'image/jpeg', 'image/png',
'image/webp'];
```

In the past, you would have had to accommodate a certain legacy browser which had its own variations on two of these types. If you fall through a time warp and find yourself burdened with Internet Explorer, you may need to add image/pjpeg and image/x-png to your collection.

It's best to put this array before the rest of the code so that it's easy to locate and modify if you need to:

```
//  Check File
    $imagetypes = ['image/gif', 'image/jpeg', 'image/png',
        'image/webp'];

    if(!isset($_FILES['image'])) $errors[] = 'Missing File';
    else switch($_FILES['image']['error']) {
        ...
    }
```

To see whether the uploaded MIME type is one of these, we can use the in_array() function. This function tests whether a value is in an array:

```
if(in_array(value, array)) ... ;
```

In this case, we'll check whether the value is *not* in the array:

```
//  Check File
    $imagetypes = ['image/gif', 'image/jpeg', 'image/png',
        'image/webp'];
```

```
if(!isset($_FILES['image'])) $errors[] = 'Missing File';
else switch($_FILES['image']['error']) {
    case UPLOAD_ERR_OK:
        //  if($_FILES['image']['size'] > 0x100000)
        //      $errors[] = '...';
        if(!in_array($_FILES['image']['type'],
        $imagetypes))
            $errors[] = 'Not a suitable image file';
        break;
    ...
}
```

If the image file exists, is within size limits, and is of a suitable type, we can then proceed to keep the image and store the rest of the data.

Keeping the File

Having established that you have data and an image to keep, it's time to keep it.

Unfortunately, we can't finish the job yet.

Keeping the file and data will involve three steps:

- Add the data to the database.

- Move the original file to a permanent location.

- Make smaller copies of the file for use on the site.

At this stage, we can perform the middle step only, since we haven't yet set up the database. However, we can outline our plan in comments:

```
if(!$errors) {  //  proceed
    // Get Name

    // Add to the Database
```

```
    // Keep Original

    // Resize Copies

    // Finish Up

}
else {              //  handle error
    $errors = sprintf('<p class="errors">%s</p>',
        implode('<br>',$errors));
}
```

We get the name of the image first, because it will be involved in the rest of the code.

When you upload a file to the server, it's kept in a temporary location until we decide to keep it or not. The location of the file is stored in $_FILES['image']['tmp_name']. Where that is isn't important: we'll either move it to a permanent place or leave it where it is, in which case it will be purged when the script is completed.

PHP has a function called move_uploaded_file(), which will not only move the file but also check to see whether the file is a genuine uploaded file, and not a crafty way of moving around other files:

```
move_uploaded_file(temporary, permanent);
```

Before we proceed with this, however, we will need to look at the file name to be used in its new location. It will also be used when recording the file name in a database table later.

The File Name

The original file name can be found in $_FILES['image']['name'], as provided by the upload.

To begin with, we'll copy this into a PHP variable. That way, we can do whatever we want with it.

```
if(!$errors) {  //  proceed
    // Get Name
        $name = $_FILES['image']['name'];

    ...
}
else {              //  handle error
    ...
}
```

There are some possible issues with using this file name as is:

- The file name may not suit your own naming rules or your operating system.

- The file name may not be unique. This means you can't distinguish different versions of the file name, and you may overwrite an existing file since you can't have two files with the same name.

As a result, you'll probably want to make some changes to the name before you use it. We'll make two changes to the file name here. First, we'll change it to lower case just in case; second, we'll replace spaces with hyphens, just in case.

Modern operating systems will handle mixed case and spaces well enough, but they can still be inconvenient, which is why we'll make the changes.

Later, we will be making one more change to make it unique. That will involve our work with the database.

Lower Case

To convert a string to lower case, you can use strtolower(). This returns a copy of the string in lower case:

```
if(!$errors) {  //  proceed
    // Get Name
        $name = $_FILES['image']['name'];
        $name = strtolower($name);

    ...

}
else {           //  handle error

    ...

}
```

PHP also has the functions strtoupper() to convert a string to upper case, ucfirst() to convert the first letter only to upper case, and ucwords() to do this to every word in the string.

Replacing Spaces

We can use str_replace() to replace one substring with another inside the string. This function has three parameter values:

```
str_replace(oldpart, newpart, string);
```

In our file name, we'll use this to replace the space ' ' with the hyphen '-':

```
if(!$errors) {  //  proceed
    // Get Name
        $name = $_FILES['image']['name'];
        $name = strtolower($name);
```

```
        $name = str_replace(' ', '-', $name);
    ...
}
else {            // handle error
    ...
}
```

PHP also has str_ireplace() if you want to replace alphabetic characters, and you don't care about whether it's upper or lower case.

Now that we have a working file name, we can move the file from its temporary location to a permanent location.

Defining the Location

As with the contact code, we should define a configurable value for the location of the image. First, however, we'll need to work with a logistic problem in PHP: that of finding the **root** directory of your site.

The **root** folder refers to the main directory which contains all others.

At the browser end of your code, as in the HTML, JavaScript, and CSS, you can refer to the root folder by starting off with a slash:

```
<a src="/styles/banner.jpg">
```

PHP doesn't see things the same way. Since it's operating at the server end, it's not restricted to an individual site directory, and the forward slash refers to the root of the *operating system*. The actual site root may be several directories further in.

The $_SERVER['DOCUMENT_ROOT'] superglobal value is supposed to help with this, but it's not 100% reliable, especially where virtual hosts are involved. You'll get a more reliable result by calculating the root directory yourself:

```
$root = str_replace($_SERVER['SCRIPT_NAME'], '',
    $_SERVER['SCRIPT_FILENAME']);
```

129

You can take this on faith, of course, but if you want to understand what it's doing:

- $_SERVER['SCRIPT_FILENAME'] is the *full path* of the current file.

- $_SERVER['SCRIPT_NAME'] is the path of the current file, relative to the site root directory.

- You've already seen the str_replace(). Here, it will replace the relative path with an empty string. In other words, it will remove all but the site root directory.

We can set that up in a configuration section:

```php
<?php
    // Configuration
    $root = str_replace($_SERVER['SCRIPT_NAME'], '',
        $_SERVER['SCRIPT_FILENAME']);
```

The next part is to configure the directory where the images will be stored:

```php
<?php
    // Configuration
    $root = str_replace($_SERVER['SCRIPT_NAME'], '',
        $_SERVER['SCRIPT_FILENAME']);
    $CONFIG['images']['directory'] = 'images';
```

Using the two together will be slightly complicated. The plan is to use an expression with the root directory, the images directory, and the image file name.

Within the images directory, there's another directory called originals, where the uploaded image files will be stored. Later, we'll make scaled copies in the other image directories.

We should be able to do this in a double-quoted string:

```
"$root/{$CONFIG['images']['directory']}/originals/$name"
```

Note the braces round the images directory value. In PHP, simple variables can be interpolated as they are. However, there are times when variables can be misinterpreted, such as when you want to include a plural:

```
$fruit = 'apple';
print "I have 3 $fruits";   // error: no variable
called $fruits
```

The solution is to wrap the interpolated variable inside braces:

```
$fruit = 'apple';
print "I have 3 {$fruit}s"; // error: no variable
called $fruits
```

PHP refers to this as "complex notation," not because it's tricky, but because it allows more complex expressions. The other place where you'll need it is when the variable is an array with a string key. If you leave out the braces, you'll end up with a T_ENCAPSED_AND_WHITESPACE error, and nobody's quite sure what it means.

You can put all of your interpolated variables into braces if you like:

```
"{$root}/{$CONFIG['images']['directory']}/originals/{$name}"
```

Here, we won't do that, but you may prefer it that way.

Moving the File

We can now move the image file to a more permanent location, using move_uploaded_file():

```
// Add to the Database
    // nothing yet

//  Keep Original
    move_uploaded_file($_FILES['image']['tmp_name'],
     "$root/{$CONFIG['images']['directory']}/originals/$name");
```

You can now test this. When you do, you'll find a copy of the file in the images/originals directory, within your web root directory.

When you test this successfully, you'll also find a warning message:

```
Warning: Array to string conversion ...
```

This is the same problem as with the contact page: you have an empty array in the $errors variable which PHP doesn't like printing. We'll fix that soon.

As for the title and description, that's going nowhere as yet. However, we still need them to pass the form validation. Later, we'll add them to the database.

Creating Additional Copies

So far, we've uploaded the original image, but it's not necessarily suitable for displaying when the time comes:

- The image may be too large for our gallery.

- The image shape may not suit.

For this, we'll make a number of resized copies and save them to be used later:

- A display copy, in the images/display directory

- A thumbnail copy, to be displayed in the image gallery, saved in the images/display directory

- An icon copy, to be displayed in a list for maintenance, saved in the images/icons directory

- Another scaled copy for use in image pop-ups, saved in the images/scaled directory

In principle, you could use a single image copy and get the browser to resize them with the img tag's width and height attributes. However, that could be squandering resources as you download a larger file just to reduce the size on the page. In some cases, the browser may not do such a good job by simply squeezing the image into a smaller space.

Modern HTML also includes additional elements and attributes to allow the browser to decide which version of an image to download, depending on the environment, so multiple image sizes can also be used there.

In the includes folder, you'll find a file called default-library.php, which we can include at the beginning:

```php
<?php
    require_once 'includes/default-library.php';

    ...
```

Appendix D explains in detail how this function is developed, but, for now, we'll use it as it is:

```
resizeImage($source, $destination=null, $size='160x120',
$options=[])
```

This function requires one or more values:

- $source is required and is the path of the original file.

- $destination is the path where you want the resized copy to be saved. If you don't specify it, the copy will be saved in the original location, with the original file name with the size appended to it.

- $size is a string with the dimensions (width x height) of the resized copy. If you leave it out, the default size is 160 x 120.

- There are additional options, which you can read about in Appendix D.

In our case, we'll specify the first three values for the first three image copies; for the fourth, we'll also include one of the options.

Resized Image Configuration

As with the location of the images directory, the actual dimensions of the resized copies are arbitrary. We can set up some values in the configuration section:

```
// Configuration
   $root = str_replace($_SERVER['SCRIPT_NAME'], '',
      $_SERVER['SCRIPT_FILENAME']);

   $CONFIG['images']['directory'] = 'images';
   $CONFIG['images']['display-size'] = '480 x 360';
   $CONFIG['images']['thumbnail-size'] = '240 x 180';
   $CONFIG['images']['icon-size'] = '40 x 30';
   $CONFIG['images']['scaled'] = '50';
```

You can see that we're grouping the settings in the same nested array.

Generating the Resized Copies

For the resized copies, they'll go into four directories called display, thumbnails, icons, and scaled, in the images directory.

Using the same logic as for storing the original images, the resized copies will be saved into

```
"$root/{$CONFIG['images']['directory']}/display/$name"
"$root/{$CONFIG['images']['directory']}/thumbnails/$name"
"$root/{$CONFIG['images']['directory']}/icons/$name"
"$root/{$CONFIG['images']['directory']}/scaled/$name"
```

We can now use the function to make the resized copies:

```
//  Keep Original
    move_uploaded_file($_FILES['image']['tmp_name'],
      "$root/{$CONFIG['images']['directory']}/originals/$name");

//  Resize Copies
    resizeImage(
      "$root/{$CONFIG['images']['directory']}/originals/$name",
      "$root/{$CONFIG['images']['directory']}/display/$name",
      $CONFIG['images']['display-size']
    );
    resizeImage(
      "$root/{$CONFIG['images']['directory']}/originals/$name",
      "$root/{$CONFIG['images']['directory']}/thumbnails/$name",
      $CONFIG['images']['thumbnail-size']
    );
    resizeImage(
      "$root/{$CONFIG['images']['directory']}/originals/$name",
      "$root/{$CONFIG['images']['directory']}/icons/$name",
      $CONFIG['images']['icon-size']
    );
```

```
resizeImage(
  "$root/{$CONFIG['images']['directory']}/originals/$name",
  "$root/{$CONFIG['images']['directory']}/scaled/$name",
  $CONFIG['images']['scaled'], ['method'=>'scale']
);
```

It's important here that we've used exactly the same name for the different versions of the file, using the directories to distinguish between them. Later, we'll store that name in the database, and we don't want to bog down in recording the different versions and the images directory.

Tidying Up

Unlike the contact form, this form will be part of a bigger picture.

For now, we'll stay on the form for further testing, but later we'll redirect to another page.

If we're going to stay on the page, you won't want the old values or empty $errors array.

Clearing the Error Array

Remember, the $errors variable has an empty array, which PHP doesn't like to print. To clear the error array, we can simply set it to an empty string, so nothing will be printed:

```
if(!$errors) {  // proceed

  ...

  // Finish Up
  $errors = '';
}
```

```
else {            //  handle error
   ...
}
```

Later, we'll redirect to another page, so this won't be necessary, but it's helpful for now.

Clearing the Old Values

Unless you want old titles and descriptions to be the default for the next image, it's better to clear their old values too. (It's not necessary to clear the old value of the file input since it can't retain old values anyway.)

In the Finish Up section, add the following code:

```
if(!$errors) {)
   ...
   //  Finish Up
      $errors = '';
      $title = $description = '';
}
```

Again, this won't be necessary when we redirect to another page.

Summary

In this chapter, we worked with binary and text data uploaded from a web form. This involved working with a file input on the form and possibly modifying the settings in the PHP configuration files.

Part of the processing of the form involves checking the text data just as with the contact form, so some of the processing starts off the same way.

Unlike text input, uploaded files are not collected in the $_POST array. Instead, they're referenced in the $_FILES array, which is an array of arrays for each uploaded file.

The $_FILES array has information about the uploaded file which can be checked. This includes checking whether a file has indeed been uploaded, its size, and whether it's of a suitable type. If everything's OK, we can copy the file from its temporary location to a more permanent location.

Managing uploaded files include storing the file in a suitable location with a suitable file name. The upload form data includes a file name, but we may need to make some changes to suit our own needs.

Because the overall destiny of the file is for display, we can make resized copies to be displayed later. This uses a specially written function which incorporates a number of PHP's image manipulation functions. To work with this, we have a configuration section at the beginning to set various properties of the resized images.

This isn't the end of the job, as we'll need to add some data to the database. However, for now, we've done what we can so far.

Coming Up

The uploaded images and text will be used later in an image gallery. To get that working, we'll need to add some data to the database, so that it can be fetched when the time comes.

In Chapter 5, we'll begin the process by setting up the database. We'll need to learn a little about how databases work and how to create a database, user, and tables to store the data.

We'll also need to learn about how to get PHP to talk to the database.

Working with a Database

Although PHP is a very capable programming language in its own right, much of what you'll be doing involves interacting with a database. The database is used to store and later retrieve information which will eventually be part of the website.

The database is usually, though not necessarily, a separate process. On the Web, the most common database software is MySQL, or its spin-off, MariaDB, although there are many others available, such as PostgreSQL or, with additional software drivers, Microsoft SQL or Oracle. Typically, they run as a separate server on the same host machine.

The main exception to this model is if you're using another database package, SQLite. SQLite is not managed by a separate server but by PHP itself, using additional modules which are normally supplied with PHP. SQLite is suitable for light-duty databases, as the name says.

Working with databases involves working with two languages. PHP is used to work the login and to prepare and process the database data. SQL is used to communicate with the database itself.

© Mark Simon 2024

M. Simon, *An Introduction to PHP*, https://doi.org/10.1007/979-8-8688-0177-8_5

Whenever we need to communicate with the database, we'll go through the following steps:

- Prepare a connection to the database in PHP.

- Prepare an SQL statement. From PHP's perspective, the SQL statement is a string. Of course, what's in the string is important.

- Much of the SQL work will involve additional data. This may be included in the SQL string, but is often in a separate array of values.

- Send the string, and possibly data, to the database software for processing. This involves special functions which interface with the database.

- The SQL may return some data. If so, PHP will fetch the data.

From there, of course, PHP does whatever needs to be done with the results.

In this book, we can only cover some of the fundamentals of a database and SQL.

If you want to learn more about SQL and databases, you might want to look at the book *Getting Started with SQL and Databases* (`https://link.springer.com/book/10.1007/978-1-4842-9493-2`) by the same author.

As a PHP developer, you don't necessarily need to know how to design and create a database (this has typically been done already). However, you should know how a database is constructed, so that you'll be able to understand what it is you're working with.

You'll also need to know the SQL statements which read and write data. They are few and simple, but have a precise syntax you will need to appreciate. It's also important to know some of the dangers in manipulating a database when it involves data which has been carelessly or maliciously constructed.

Finally, you'll need to know how to communicate with the database using PHP. This will involve establishing a connection to the database, sending it commands, and reading the results. Of course, there may be errors in the process, and we'll need to know how to handle those.

Something About Databases

In order to make sure that we have an idea of what's going on, we need to understand a little about what we mean by a database.

In practical terms, a **database** is a collection of one or more distinct **tables**. Each table holds a different set of data. In our simple project, we will have a table of images, a table of users, and a table of blog articles.

Software which manages a database is referred to as a **Database Management System**, or **DBMS** for short. There are many DBMSs available, but the one you're more likely to use on a website is **MySQL**, or its alternative **MariaDB**.

A table is made up of **rows** and **columns**. Each row is one instance of the data, and each column is a detail. For example, in our images table, each image is a new row. Each detail, such as the image title and file name, is in a column. For example:

id	title	name	src	description	gallery
1	Kangaroo	kangaroo.jpg	kangaroo.jpg	Notes on Kangaroos	true
3	Wattle	wattle.jpg	wattle.jpg	About Wattles	true
4	Emu	emu.jpg	emu.jpg	Something about Emus	false
6	Koala	koala.jpg	koala.jpg	Information about Koalas	true

There's an old tradition to use the terms **records** for rows and **fields** for columns. They are not exactly the same, and it's certainly not the language of SQL, but it's easy enough to understand the meaning. However, we'll stick to the more correct names rows and columns.

Most DBMSs are meant to accommodate multiple users, so access to various parts is restricted to particular users, identified by their username and password. These databases generally have a super user, called **root**, who has complete access to everything. It's common practice to create additional users with access restricted to their roles. Each user will need to present their credentials when a connection to the database is made.

There are many DBMSs available. In particular, the following are commonly used on the Web:

- **MySQL** and **MariaDB**: These are by far the most popular on the Web. MariaDB is a modern spin-off of MySQL and masquerades as MySQL for the purpose of programming.

- **SQLite** is actually a single-user database, which is OK since PHP will be regarded as that single user. It saves its data in a single file. It is not well suited to heavy-duty use, especially writing, but is certainly suitable for many web projects.

- **PostgreSQL** is the most advanced of these, but is not so popular for historical reasons. Unlike MySQL/MariaDB and SQLite, you may need to turn on PostgreSQL support in PHP.

Support for all three of the preceding databases is standard with PHP. PHP can also work with other database products, such as **Oracle** and **Microsoft SQL Server**, as well as other ODBC databases, but this generally requires additional software support.

Many modern web servers use MariaDB instead of MySQL for their DBMS. MariaDB is a drop-in replacement for MySQL and identifies itself as MySQL for software purposes. They are 95% compatible and certainly compatible enough for our purposes.

Currently, XAMPP uses MariaDB, and MAMP uses MySQL. If you're working on a different setup, you might be using either. However, the SQL code will be exactly the same, and the built-in tools will work with either.

From here on, we'll just refer to MySQL, even though it may well be referring to MariaDB.

In a typical project, you'll see two meanings of the word user:

- A **database user** is known to the DBMS and has a username and password registered there. The database user will have certain privileges assigned which may or may not give them the ability to read, create, or edit data in particular tables.

- An **application user** is known to the application. It's not really a proper term, because there isn't really a proper term. The user would be a visitor to the site who would presumably have logged in.

  In reality, the application user's details will be stored in one of the database tables. The application (our PHP project) can check against this table whether the user should be doing something.

In our project, there will be one database user. In fact, it will be PHP itself connecting to the database as a user. There will be a separate application user, who will be expected to log in when the time comes.

143

Running SQL

Running SQL consists of sending commands to the server. Ultimately, they are in the form of SQL statements, though there are many GUI client applications to hide that from you.

Since MySQL is so popular in web applications, you will generally find a MySQL client is included with your server. The web client is normally **PHPMyAdmin**, though others may be available. The PHPMyAdmin client is graphical, though it is sometimes more efficient to ignore the GUI and enter commands directly using its Run SQL feature.

You can also get desktop GUI applications for MySQL and other DBMSs.

In the sample project, we recommend using SQL commands directly, via the PHPMyAdmin interface.

Having said that, the sample project will, in fact, be developing a graphical tool of sorts. When we've finished, an authorized user will be able to add, delete, and edit data using web forms, and we'll be fetching data from the data constantly.

MySQL and PHPMyAdmin

If you are running a server package, such as XAMPP or MAMP, you will find that it includes a web control panel page and includes PHPMyAdmin.

The control panel can be accessed through

```
http://localhost
```

This page gives you access to a number of tools.

Although other client programs may offer a smoother experience, they are generally limited to databases on the local network. Using PHPMyAdmin has the advantage of being a web application, so you can control your database from anywhere in the world. It's usually included with remote hosting services.

You can launch PHPMyAdmin directly using the following URL:

- **XAMPP**: http://localhost/phpmyadmin/

- **MAMP**: http://localhost/phpMyAdmin/

Make sure that you have both Apache and MySQL running. In XAMPP, they are started separately.

You can use PHPMyAdmin to run your SQL commands directly:

- From the server control panel page, select PHPMyAdmin.

- Select the SQL tab. You will see something like Figure 5-1.

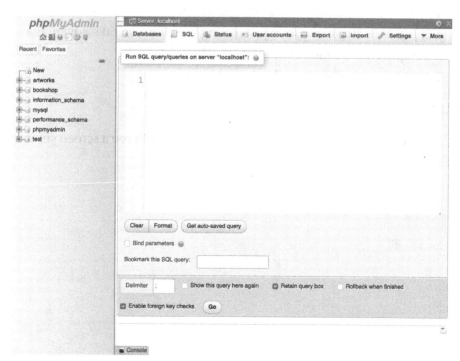

Figure 5-1. *PHPMyAdmin Run Tab*

Make sure that you check ☑ **Retain query box** so that it doesn't disappear after you do something or make an error.

Shortly, we'll use this to create the database, user, and tables.

Browsing

Once you create the database and add one or more tables, they should appear in the navigation panel on the left. You may need to refresh the panel.

When we start adding data to the tables, you can click the table in the navigation panel to see the contents.

The Setup Page

If you are not interested in maintaining the database, or you want to catch up with previous steps, or you're just feeling lazy, you can take advantage of the setup scripts included with the sample.

To enter setup, enter the following address:

```
http://australia.example.com/setup
```

(or whatever domain name you are using). You will see a screen similar to Figure 5-2.

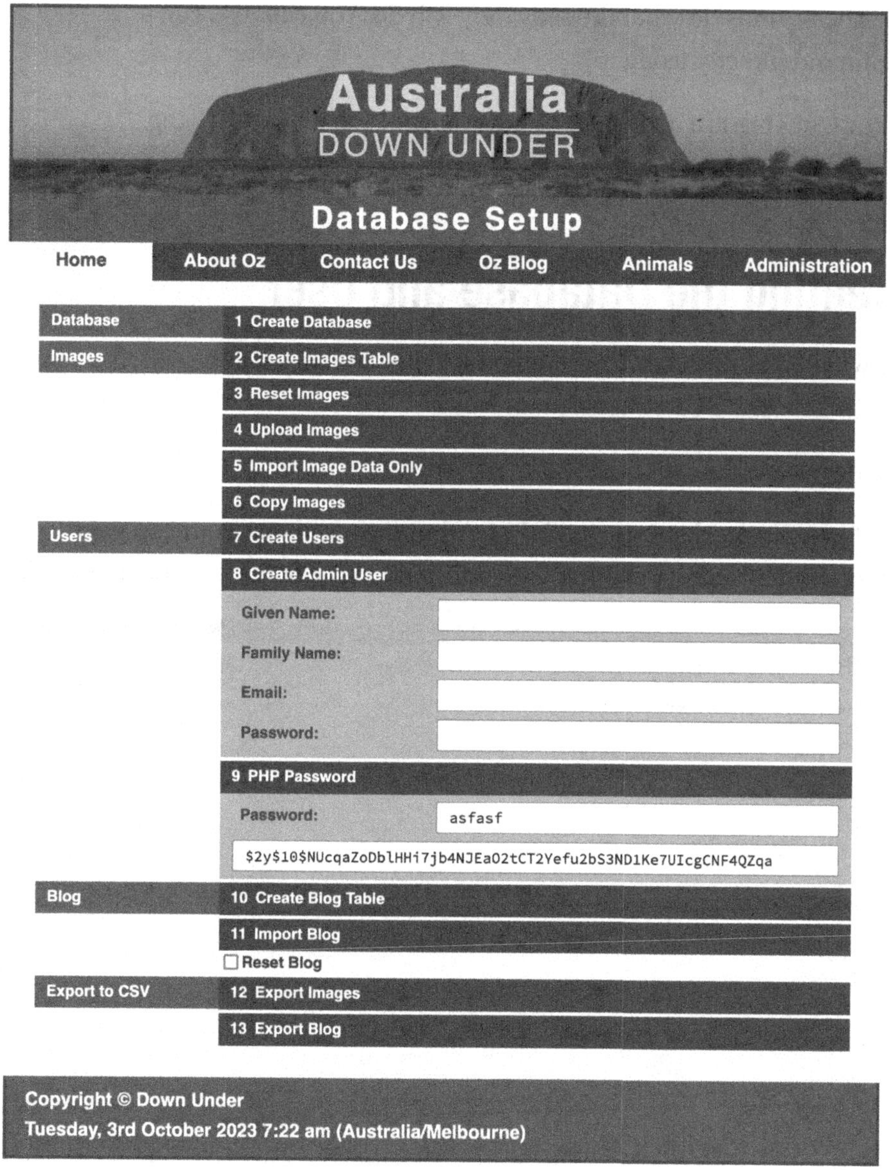

Figure 5-2. *The Setup Page*

The buttons do what they say they will do. You can also run a command directly using

```
http://australia.example.com/setup?action=do-something
```

These links will be given as alternatives in the following sections.

Creating the Database and User

We will begin by creating our database. The database will be called australia. The SQL statement for this is

```
CREATE DATABASE australia;
```

To create the database in PHPMyAdmin, you can use some on page buttons, but it's easier to enter the command in the SQL tab as in Figure 5-3.

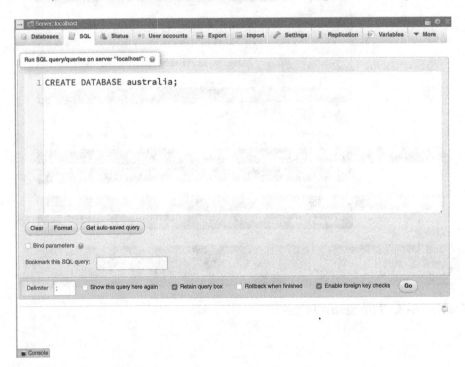

Figure 5-3. *PHPMyAdmin Create Database*

Locate and click the **Go** button.

Using the setup page instead, you can simply click

```
1 Create Database
```

The shortcut for this step is

```
http://australia.example.com/setup?action=australia
```

We now need to create a database user.

Although we could use the default **root** user, the root user has too much power. This creates an opening for anybody trying to break into the database. It is best to create a user with privileges limited to managing the data in this particular database.

For our special database user, the details are as follows:

Detail	Property
Name	ozadmin
Server	localhost
Password	Test@321
Database	australia
Privileges	SELECT, INSERT, UPDATE, DELETE

For this user

- The ozadmin user will be restricted to a specific database on a specific server. Here, the database is australia, of course, and the server is localhost. Even though the web server is remote to the user, the database is local to the web server.

149

- The database server can have many users, and the users can access multiple databases. The name ozadmin implies that this user will be the administrator for the australia database.

- You can use any password you like, of course, but the dummy one suggested gets through the standard password tests, even if it's not very strong. *Needless to say, don't use this password in real life!*

  If you feel the need to use a different password, of course you can. However, don't forget it—otherwise, you'll need to go through the process of setting a new one.

- The special user is restricted to the four data operations on this specific database. The user can't change the structure of the database and can't access any other database.

The SQL statement to create the user is

```
USE australia;

CREATE USER 'ozadmin'@'localhost' IDENTIFIED BY 'Test@321';
GRANT SELECT,INSERT,UPDATE,DELETE,DROP ON australia.*
    TO ozadmin@localhost;
```

- The USE australia; statement makes sure that the following SQL applies to the australia database, and not another.

The script is available in the file /setup/mysql/australia.sql in your project folder.

The preceding setup step which created the database also creates the user.

MySQL may have some issues with creating users, especially if you've tried to create the user before. The SQL script in the australia.sql file includes statements to drop and recreate the ozadmin user.

Preparing the Images Table

The next thing to do is to create our tables.

The basic command to create a table is

```
CREATE TABLE ... (
    ...
);
```

The parentheses will contain a collection of column definitions.

Although it is possible to store images in a database, it is generally not recommended as it makes the database harder to manage and requires extra work in your PHP script. Rather, we will store the image file name in the database. Because we will use the same name for the original image as well as its thumbnails, we need only store one image name, without the path. This makes it easier to adapt to moving your images around if you need to.

The structure of the images table is as follows:

Column	Type
id	INT UNSIGNED AUTO_INCREMENT PRIMARY KEY
title	VARCHAR(60) NOT NULL
name	VARCHAR(48) NOT NULL
src	VARCHAR(60) NOT NULL
description	TEXT
gallery	BOOLEAN DEFAULT false

As regards the columns

- Every row in a database table should have a unique identifier; the technical term for this is a **primary key**. In this case, the primary key is called id, and it's an auto-incremented integer (whole number)—we don't need to assign it ourselves.

- The title and description columns will store the title and description when we upload an image. The title is a string limited to 60 characters. The description is also a string, but without a limit.

- The name column will be the original file name of the column as uploaded, slightly modified. The src column will contain a uniquely modified version which will be used when displaying the image later. They are both limited length strings.

- Not all images will be used in the gallery. Those that will have the gallery value set to true. By default, it isn't.

The MySQL statement to create the preceding table is

```
USE australia;

DROP TABLE IF EXISTS images;

CREATE TABLE images (
    id INT UNSIGNED AUTO_INCREMENT PRIMARY KEY,
    title VARCHAR(60) NOT NULL,     -- descriptive name
    name VARCHAR(48) NOT NULL,      -- original file name
    src VARCHAR(60) NOT NULL,       -- current file name
    description TEXT,
    gallery BOOLEAN DEFAULT false
) CHARACTER SET utf8mb4 COLLATE utf8mb4_unicode_520_ci
    ENGINE = INNODB;
```

The DROP TABLE IF EXISTS statement will remove the table and any data if the table already exists. It's used here to restart the database project.

The syntax for other SQL flavors is similar. However, the auto_ increment keyword and more especially the instruction at the end are specific to MySQL. Roughly translated the additional instructions define how the table is to be organized internally.

The script is available in the file setup/mysql/imagescreate.sql, and you can run it in the PHPMyAdmin SQL tab. Don't forget to click the **Go** button.

You can also use the setup screen shortcut:

2 Create Images Table

Or use the following link:

http://australia.example.com/setup?action=imagescreate

That will do for now. There are other tables to be created, but we can do that later.

The next step will be to see how we connect to the database.

Using the Database with PHP

The database runs independently of PHP, but is also accessible from PHP, which is good for what we're trying to do. This isn't handled by PHP itself, but through one of a number of libraries which are loaded with PHP.

There are many functions built in to PHP to work with databases. Many of them are specific to the different databases (such as PostgreSQL, MySQL, and SQLite). A better alternative is to use PDO, which is also part of PHP. This is a more generic package which allows a single set of functions to access all the different databases.

In this book, we will be using PDO (PHP Data Objects) as our means of communication.

Connection

Before you can communicate with the database, you will have to establish a connection.

To make our code manageable, we'll put the connection data into a separate file. We can call it `pdo.php` and put it in the `includes` folder.

Included files can optionally have a `return` statement. This gives an opportunity to generate a result to be used by the main program:

```
$variable = require_once ...;
```

If there's no return statement, the returned value will be 1 to indicate that the include was successful; we haven't bothered with that in the other included files.

Add the following to the `pdo.php` file:

```php
<?php
    // connection code

    return $pdo;
```

Note that again we don't close the block.

The $pdo variable will be generated during the rest of the script. (If you try to load the page at this point, you'll get an error, since the $pdo variable hasn't yet been set.)

Connection String

Before we establish a connection, we will need to describe it. This is done in a DSN (Data Source Name), which is a database-specific string which describes the database and possible settings.

For MySQL, the string is

```
$dsn = 'mysql:host=localhost;dbname=australia;charset=utf8mb4';
```

- The mysql: part tells PDO to use the MySQL driver. (This also applies to MariaDB.) You can change this to the driver for a different DBMS if you have it set up, such as pgsql for PostgreSQL.

- host is the name or IP address of the database server. Presumably, it's on the same machine as the web server.

- dbname is the name of the database.

- charset defines which character encoding we'll use. Here, we'll use UTF8, which is a compact form of Unicode.

We can add it to our code:

```
<?php
    $dsn='mysql: host=localhost; dbname=australia;
    charset=utf8mb4';

    return $pdo;
```

We'll now make the connection to the database.

Creating a Connection

To create a PDO object, you will require the DSN, username, and password.

For easy maintenance, you can set the username and password in separate variables:

```php
<?php
    $dsn = 'mysql: host=localhost; dbname=australia;
    charset=utf8mb4';

    $user = 'ozadmin';
    $password = 'Test@321';
```

We can now create the PDO object with the new keyword, supplying the necessary data:

```php
<?php
    $dsn = 'mysql: host=localhost; dbname=australia;
    charset=utf8mb4';

    $user = 'ozadmin';
    $password = 'Test@321';

    $pdo = new PDO($dsn, $user, $password);
```

The new keyword creates a PDO object from the PDO class.

A Crash Course in Classes and Objects

The PDO object gives you a taste of **Object-Oriented Programming**, or **OOP** for short. OOP is a methodology which works with **objects**.

From a programming point of view, an object is a package. The package may contain data, or it may contain functions; typically, it contains both.

Object data are referred to as **properties** and would presumably be data directly related to the particular object. Object functions are referred to as **methods** and are presumably functions that work on the particular object. It's also possible that an object's properties and methods are not directly related to a particular object and that the object is simply a convenient way of bundling data and functions.

In this case, the PDO object will definitely have properties and methods related to the individual object.

The standard method for working with objects is first to design it. This design is called a **class**, and it outlines the properties and methods which will comprise the object. You can design your own classes, but you may find that a class design has already been provided, such as the **PDO** class.

To create an object from a class, you use the new keyword:

```
$pdo = new PDO(...);
```

This invokes the class's **constructor** method to create and initialize the object. A constructor is an initialization method which is automatically called and uses the parameter values to set up the object.

The return value is the object you have just created.

In some cases, you only need a single object, but in some cases you'll create multiple objects of the same class. Each object has its own property data.

If you want to reference an object's property or class, you use a **thin arrow** (->). For example:

```
$pdo -> prepare();
```

In this case, we're referencing the prepare() method of the $pdo object. The thin arrow is, of course, made up of two characters, but is totally unrelated to either "minus" or "greater than"; it's meant to be a pointer to the property or method.

The important part of methods such as this is that whatever happens in that method can use or change other properties in the object. That is, they have access to the rest of the object, so the object is self-contained.

When working with PDO, we'll be working largely with a single PDO object, called $pdo for convenience. However, many of the object methods will generate a complementary object of the PDOStatement class. This additional object may contain data from the database or some additional code to be used when working with the database.

More on that later.

Handling Connection Errors

When PHP tries to make contact with an external process, there is always a chance of failure. In this case, you might have got the username or password wrong, or there may be an issue with the database, such as someone forgetting to start it up.

PHP will, of course, report on the error, but it will dump the sort of information you may not wish to share with the outside world, such as the $user and $password values. For example, if MySQL is not running, you'll get an extensive error message which includes this handy detail:

```
PDO->__construct('mysql:host=localhost','ozadmin','Test@321')
```

You probably don't want that information to get out. You'll want to trap the error and handle it yourself.

PHP has the ability to trap certain runtime errors, called exceptions, including those generated by a failed PDO creation:

```
try {
    $pdo = new PDO($dsn, $user, $passwd);
}
catch (PDOException $e) {

}
```

The try ... catch block will first attempt the code inside the try block. If a problem occurs, PDO will generate an exception (i.e., an error) object of type **PDOException** and run the code inside the catch block. You don't have to use this exception object, but you do have to receive it.

We can pass on the error message generated in the PDOException object, using the throw command:

```
try {
    $pdo = new PDO($dsn, $user, $passwd);
}
```

```
catch (PDOException $e) {
    throw new PDOException($e->getMessage(), $e->getCode());
}
```

This is slightly better, but still too much information. For our purposes, it is sufficient to display a simple message and give up. In practice, you might, for example, redirect to a different page first.

exit or die

PHP has a statement with two names: exit and die. Both do exactly the same job, which is to terminate the PHP script at that point and go no further. Both also allow the option of including a message:

```
exit;
exit('Bye Bye');
```

```
die;
die('Goodbye Cruel World');
```

Note that, even though exit and die are not technically functions, the message must be inside parentheses.

The difference between the two is entirely up to you. We'll be using exit when the exit is orderly and planned, while die will be used when the exit is the result of a disaster.

Here, we'll exit with a message:

```
try {
    $pdo = new PDO($dsn, $user, $passwd);
}
catch (PDOException $e) {
    die('Problem connecting to the Database');
}
```

Add the following code to your pdo.php file:

```php
<?php
    $dsn = 'mysql: host=localhost; dbname=australia;
    charset=utf8mb4';
    $user = 'ozadmin';
    $password = 'Test@321';

    try {
        $pdo = new PDO($dsn, $user, $passwd);
    }
    catch (PDOException $e) {
        die('Problem connecting to the Database');
    }

    return $pdo;
```

Adding Options

PDO allows you to pass certain options to modify its behavior. You can
pass them in one of two ways.

We can set up an array of options as a fourth parameter:

```php
$options = [ ... ];

try {
    $pdo = new PDO($dsn, $user, $password, $options);
}
catch (PDOException $e) {

    ...
}
```

We can also set an option after the event:

```
$pdo->setAttribute(..., ...);
```

We'll describe them individually, but we'll add them in an array.

Error Reporting

By default, if PDO errors occur, PDO fails quietly, presumably so as not to give away too much detail to the casual observer. This is fine for a live server, but very frustrating during development. One of the first things we can do with our newly created PDO object is to set error reporting to something more verbose:

```
$pdo->setAttribute(PDO::ATTR_ERRMODE, PDO::ERRMODE_EXCEPTION);
```

This instructs PDO to treat all errors seriously enough to halt the code and report. You should not be so verbose in a production server.

Prepared Statements

We will discuss prepared statements later. They're a way of protecting your database from problematic code.

Prepared statements are available for most modern databases, but PHP is prepared to emulate them if necessary. Unfortunately, it may also emulate them if unnecessary. The following will instruct PDO not to emulate them:

```
$pdo->setAttribute(PDO::ATTR_EMULATE_PREPARES, false);
```

It's generally better to let the DBMS do its own prepared statements.

Setting the PDO Options

We can combine these two statements using the $options parameter:

```php
<?php
    $dsn = 'mysql: host=localhost; dbname=australia;
charset=utf8mb4';
    $dsn = 'mysql: host=localhost; dbname=australia;
charset=utf8mb4';

    $user = 'ozadmin';
    $password = 'Test@321';

    $options = [
        PDO::ATTR_ERRMODE => PDO::ERRMODE_EXCEPTION,
        PDO::ATTR_EMULATE_PREPARES => false,
    ];

    try {
        $pdo = new PDO($dsn, $user, $password, $options);
    }
    catch (PDOException $e) {
        die('Problem connecting to the Database');
    }

    return $pdo;
```

For the most part, this is the pattern you would use to connect to a database, and you would include this file whenever a page needs access to the database.

Using the Alternative Script

The script we've developed will certainly do the job, but the `includes` folder contains a more elaborate script to connect to the database. This is in `db.php`.

The script includes additional options for MySQL, as well as some code to extend the functionality of the PDO object.

The additional features are

- Switching MySQL from "traditional" mode to "ANSI" mode. This is to do with how the SQL language is written and would be recommended if you want your database to be more compatible with SQL standards. In the code for this book, there won't be any differences, so adding this feature is simply a matter of form—it's not necessary here.

- Adding an `interpolate()` method. This will be useful later when we need to troubleshoot prepared statements.

This added functionality is not really required, but it's useful to have it there just in case. So, instead of your beautifully crafted `pdo.php` file, we're going to use the `db.php` file.

Summary

A database will be an important part of our work with PHP, and this chapter explores what a database is and how we work with it in PHP.

The database is usually managed by a separate process in the form of a Database Management System, or DBMS. The DBMS we'll be using with PHP is probably MySQL or MariaDB.

A database comprises tables, which, in turn, comprise rows of instances and columns of details. In this chapter, we set up

- A database to store the tables

- A user who has access to the database

- A table to store image details

There are graphical tools, such as PHPMyAdmin, but we'll be using SQL statements for our database management.

Having set up the database, we need to connect to the database in PHP. The preferred method is to use PDO—we create an object which is connected to the database and use various methods to send to and read from the database.

Part of the process of connecting to the database will be to set up authorization, anticipating connection errors, and modifying the connection to suit how we intend to use the database.

This ended in a connection script saved in a separate file to be included whenever we need database access.

Coming Up

Having made a connection to the database, we can now finish the job started in Chapter 4. There, we uploaded files and processed text data without yet saving it to the database. In Chapter 6, we'll do just that and add the data.

This will involve learning how to write to the database and how to make changes to existing data.

We'll also look at protecting ourselves from SQL injection attacks and fixing text data for inclusion.

Once we have that in place, we'll look at implementing bulk uploads using a ZIP file, CSV data, and refactored code.

CHAPTER 6

Adding Data to the Database

We are now ready to complete the uploading task begun in Chapter 4. The ultimate goal is to be able to retrieve the images and to display them, together with information about the images. However, there isn't much information you can keep with the image file itself, so we use a database to store the information.

When working with the database, we'll need to first make a connection to the database, which we started on in Chapter 5. In PHP, this connection is represented as a PHP object, which we use to manipulate the data.

One problem we need to prepare for is the risk of attack from outside. In this case, it's the risk of an SQL injection attack, which is when an outsider attempts to crack into our database using additional SQL code. We'll have a look at how that works and how we go about protecting against that.

Once we've added the data to the database, we can also finish the job of renaming the image files. Each row in a database table has a unique ID, which we'll use to modify the original name of the file. This modified name will be stored in the database and used when saving and retrieving the image file.

That should do the job, but we're also going to plan for the future. In the next chapter, we'll look at doing a bulk upload. To prepare for that, we'll rework the current code, adapt it, and make it work from another source, rather than just this upload form.

© Mark Simon 2024
M. Simon, *An Introduction to PHP*, https://doi.org/10.1007/979-8-8688-0177-8_6

In the process, we'll learn a little more about writing functions and using variables to pass data between sections of our code.

Connecting to the Database

In Chapter 5, we developed a script to connect to the database. The script was saved as includes/pdo.php. However, there's a more comprehensive script already saved as includes/db.php. It's included with the files you set up at the beginning of the project.

You can use either script, but the latter script does include some additional modifications useful for future projects. It also includes some code which may help in troubleshooting.

At the beginning of the manage-images.code.php file, add the following:

```php
<?php
    require_once 'includes/db.php';
```

You'll note that the path is a relative path, which is always risky. In this case, it might also be confusing.

You might think that since the included file db.php (or pdo.php) is in the same directory as the including file (manage-images.code.php), you shouldn't reference the includes directory again. However, *both* files are bing included in the original file (uploadimages.php), and the includes directory is relative to there.

It would be much simpler if we could use absolute path names. Remember, PHP doesn't have a simple way of doing that, so we calculated a variable $root to assist us. We can rewrite the include as follows:

```php
<?php
    $root = str_replace($_SERVER['SCRIPT_NAME'], '',
        $_SERVER['SCRIPT_FILENAME']);
```

```
require_once "$root/includes/db.php";
require_once "$root/includes/default-library.php";

// Configuration
    $CONFIG['images']['directory'] = 'images';
    ...
```

At the same time, we've moved the assignment statement to the beginning and rewritten the default-library.php include statement.

We should now be ready to write the code to add the data to the database. However, first, we'll need to learn about something called **SQL injection**.

SQL Injection

For the most part, getting data into the database is a matter of writing a few SQL statements and combining them with the supplied data. However, this can lead to serious weaknesses in your code.

For example, suppose you have the following SELECT statement, which will be used as a simple login test:

```
SELECT count(*) FROM users
WHERE username='...' AND password='...';
```

This would count the number of users whose name and password match some input. If you're using this to log in, you would assume that the result is either 1 when they match (the username would need to be unique) or 0 if they don't match, because either the username or password was wrong.

You might plan to interpolate the data in a PHP string:

```
$user = 'fred';            //  from the login form
$password = 'Test@321';    //  from the login form
```

167

```
$sql = "SELECT count(*) FROM users
    WHERE username='$user' AND password='$password'";
```

```
print $sql;
```

You would get the output:

```
SELECT count(*) FROM users
    WHERE username='fred' AND password='Test@321';
```

which should be fine.

Note the line break in the string. PHP is one of the few programming languages which let you include a line break this way. In SQL, the extra line break is ignored, so both languages are happy. You could, of course, have written the string on a single line, but it's too wide for this page.

However, suppose your attacker supplies the following username and password:

- Username: `fred' or 1=1; -`

- Password: `whocares`

While admittedly an odd username, there is no accounting for taste, so you might insert the data directly into the SQL statement as follows:

```
SELECT count(*) FROM users
    WHERE username = 'fred' or 1=1; -- ' AND
    password='whocares';
```

You have now hijacked the statement:

- The username is a dummy. The or 1 = 1 will always evaluate to true.

- The semicolon terminates the SQL statement.

- The -- marks the beginning of an SQL comment and thus causes the rest of the statement to be ignored.

The result is that user has faked a successful login.

It could have been worse. It is also possible to include more destructive SQL statements such as drop table, which will have unfortunate consequences.

You'll see later that storing and handling the password this way is also disastrous. There's a much safer way to manage logging in, so you should never use this sort of code in real life. However, the point is that it's possible for evil visitors to inject SQL this way. And they certainly will try ...

The problem arises because the database gets the completed SQL statement *after* the fake data has been included. This makes it impossible to distinguish it from genuine SQL code, and so it will be interpreted along with the rest of the statement.

PHP has a number of solutions to this. Earlier PHP tended to automatically escape embedded quotes which might trigger the misinterpretation, using the magic quote behavior. However, this is itself problematic and should no longer be used.

There are also functions available to escape strings. However, the best solution is to use **prepared statements** which avoid the problem altogether.

Prepared Statements

Prepared statements help to reduce the risk of SQL injection by separating the interpretation of the statement from the data.

Without prepared statements, the sequence of including user data is as follows:

Using Interpolation

Original SQL   The SQL statement is written with gaps

Data is added   Using interpolation or other methods, the data is inserted to the SQL statement

Interpretation   The database interprets the SQL statement complete with injected data

Execution   The database then executes the interpreted statement

A prepared statement is a statement which has *already* been interpreted, with placeholders where the data will be inserted later. The data is then given to the prepared statement, and the statement will then be executed.

This will ensure that no data, no matter how well constructed, will be interpreted as part of the SQL and so will be incapable of causing this type of attack. This basically switches the processing order:

Using a Prepared Statement

Original SQL   The SQL statement is written with **placeholders**

Interpretation   The database interprets the SQL statement, but only with placeholders

Data is added   The data is now added separately

Execution   The database then executes the interpreted statement with data

Preparing an SQL statement means that the SQL is interpreted *before* any data has been added, so the data won't be misinterpreted as part of the instruction later.

Prepared statements can also be used if you need to execute the statement many times, such as adding multiple rows. Since the statement has already been interpreted and optimized, executing the statement with new data is much simpler for the database.

When to Worry About SQL Injection

When writing the code in PHP, you'll find that using prepared statements does require an extra step. It is also less possible to simplify code when using prepared statements. For this reason, it may be more convenient to use unprepared (direct) statements if you can be sure that it is safe.

- Numbers are safe.

  Note that this type of problem only occurs when the data is a string. Pure numbers can never create this problem, since they can never be interpreted as SQL statements.

  This doesn't mean that user input which is *supposed* to be a number is necessarily safe. However, if your code has processed the data in such a way that the result is a genuine number, then the data will be safe.

- Your own statements are safe.

  If the SQL statement is generated entirely without outside data, then it is safe to use direct statements. This doesn't mean that you can't make a mess of your database. It just means that using prepared statements is an unnecessary precaution.

- All other statements with user-generated data are unsafe.

  Trust no one. Even if the user is benign, some data may accidentally include what appears to be SQL and may yet cause damage to your database.

As a rule, we'll use prepared statements whenever we're including data from forms. The exception will be when we've reprocessed the incoming data to be a pure number, which won't be very often.

Adding the Image Data to the Table

Having established a connection to the database, we will add the data collected from the form.

To add an image row to the table, we will need the following SQL statement:

```
INSERT INTO images(title, description, name, src, gallery)
VALUES ('...', '...', '...', '...', ...);
```

- This is called an **INSERT** statement, for reasons which should be obvious. It comprises two clauses: the **INSERT** clause and the **VALUES** clause.

- The INSERT clause names the table, as well as a list of columns to be populated, one row at a time.

- The VALUES clause lists the values to fill the columns. SQL doesn't care whether the values are correct or even make sense. What it does care about, however, is that the values are compatible.

  In this case, the first four must be strings, no longer than allowed in the table definition. The last value must be either true or false or, in MySQL, 1 or 0.

Note that the id is not included here: it's generated automatically by the database. When the time comes, we'll need to get the newly inserted id, so that we can make any necessary changes to the newly created row.

For the moment, the name and the src values will be the same: both refer to the file name of the image. However, to avoid conflicts, we'll need to set a new value for the src which is unique.

Ultimately, the src will rely on the id, which won't be available until *after* the row has been inserted. For this reason

- The src will be supplied with a temporary value (the same as name).

- Afterward, the src will be updated to a new value.

The SQL statement to update (modify) a row later is

```
UPDATE images SET src='...' WHERE id=...;
```

- The **UPDATE** statement has two or three clauses. The UPDATE clause names the table to be updated.

- The **SET** clause has one or more column/value pairs for columns whose value is to be changed.

- The optional **WHERE** clause limits the update only to matching rows; otherwise, all rows would be updated with the same value. In this case, we're going to limit the update to a single row, since the id must be unique.

The UPDATE statement is particularly risky, as you can use it to change every row in the table, whether you mean to or not. Here, we limit the damage to a single row by specifying its id in the WHERE clause.

Line Breaks

The description is a mass of text which may include line breaks. Line breaks *can* be stored directly in the database, but they may make management of the data a little more awkward. For this reason, we'll encode the line breaks using a special character.

We can use any character we like, of course, but to make it more obvious, we will use the **pilcrow** character ¶. Most people don't know the name of the character, but it's immediately recognizable.[1]

To enter the pilcrow:

Environment	Enter	Comments
HTML	&pilcrow;	Necessary in the days before UTF was standard
Macintosh	opt-7	
Windows	alt-0182	Hold down the alt key, press 0182 on the *numeric keypad*, then release alt

We won't need the HTML version, since we can type the pilcrow character directly, once we know how. In fact, we won't need to type it very much either; for the most part, we'll use custom functions to convert to and from the pilcrow when needed.

The only other issue is what we mean by a line break. Different operating systems have different opinions on combinations of the carriage return (CR) and line feed (LF). The three standard versions are

- MacOS, Linux, and other Unix type OS: LF ⇒ \n

- Windows (and DOS): CRLF ⇒ \r\n

- Ancient Macintosh: CR ⇒ \r

---

[1] If you use your imagination, you can see that the pilcrow character is really a stylized reverse P, which was used in ancient texts to mark a paragraph break. That's no weirder than using <p></p> in HTML.

We can use the PHP `str_replace()` function to do the fixing:

```
$description = str_replace(["\r\n","\r","\n"], '¶',
$description);
```

The first value in the `str_replace()` function can be a single string or, as you see here, an array of strings. Note again that we're using double quotes for the line break characters since they're not interpreted in single quote strings.

Creating Line Break Functions

The preceding task isn't difficult, but we may need to do it again in the future. In any case, we may wish to make some changes in the future. For this reason, we can create a function and add it to a library file.

Three functions, actually. There will be three line break conversions to work with, so we'll write three conversion functions:

- Text coming from a text field will need the line breaks converted to pilcrows for the database. For that, we'll write a function called `nl2pilcrow()` ("new line to pilcrow").

- Text from the database to populate a text field, such as when editing the text later, will need to be converted back to line breaks. We'll call that function `pilcrow2nl()`.

- Text from the database to be displayed on a page will need pilcrows converted to HTML paragraphs. This will be `pilcrow2p()`.

To begin with, we can create a new file called `library.php` and save it in our `includes` folder. This will be for any new functions we want to create and reuse.

We can then start it off with a PHP block and a comment:

```php
<?php
/*  Pilcrow Functions
    ==================================================
    ================================================== */
```

Remember not to close the PHP block.

To create a function, you use the following pattern:

```php
function something(...) {
    ...
    return ...;
}
```

- The function has a unique name. You can't have two functions with the same name; any attempt to do this will result in a fatal error.

- The parentheses *may* contain input variables. These variables are properly called **parameter** variables. Some functions don't require input and so don't have parameter variables; however, the function definition must still include parentheses, even if they're empty.

- There *may* be a **return** statement which would return the output of the function. If there isn't a return statement, or the return statement has no value, then there's an implied return value of `null`.

- The parameter variables may have an optional data type, which limits the type of data you can input to the function. The function may also have an optional return type.

Input and return data types have been available in various forms since PHP 5, but have always been optional. You'll very often see functions defined without data types.

It's generally a good idea to include data types if practical, since it will help in limiting invalid values.

For the first function, we can write

```php
<?php
/*  Pilcrow Functions
    ================================================
    ================================================ */

    function nl2pilcrow(string $text): string {
        return str_replace(["\r\n","\r","\n"], '¶', $text);
    }
```

The function expects a string input and will return a string result.

The variable $text will contain the text to be converted. The function simply replaces the line break characters using str_replace() as before. The result is immediately returned as the output.

We can do something similar with the pilcrow2nl() function, but there's a complication. We'll want to convert the pilcrow to the correct line break for the operating system, but we have no way of knowing what the user is using. Fortunately, PHP has that information from the form submission and has a built-in constant called PHP_EOL which is the correct line break for that operating system.

The `pilcrow2nl()` can be written as

```php
<?php
...

function pilcrow2nl(string $text): string {
    return str_replace('¶', PHP_EOL, $text);
}
```

Now for the tricky one. Although the pilcrow comes *between* paragraphs, HTML puts tags *around* paragraphs. This means that you'll need to convert something like this:

```
text ¶ text ¶ text
```

to something like this:

```
<p> text </p><p> text </p><p> text </p>
```

It's not so very tricky:

- Replace the pilcrow with the closing and opening tags:
  ¶ → `</p><p>`

- Wrap the whole text between opening and closing tags:
  `<p> ... </p>`.

To do that, we'll use a `str_replace()` to replace the pilcrows and `sprintf()` to wrap the string:

```php
<?php
...

function pilcrow2p(string $text): string {
    return sprintf('<p>%s</p>', str_replace('¶', '</p><p>',
        $text));
}
```

We now have three functions we can use to manage the line breaks later on. For now, we'll just need one to prepare the description from the uploaded data for the database.

If you reopen the manage-images.code.php file, you can begin with adding a reference to the library:

```php
<?php
    $root = str_replace($_SERVER['SCRIPT_NAME'], '',
        $_SERVER['SCRIPT_FILENAME']);

    require_once "$root/includes/db.php";
    require_once "$root/includes/default-library.php";
    require_once "$root/includes/library.php";
```

We can then apply the nl2pilcrow() function to the description. We'll do that as part of the section to add to the database:

```php
if(!$errors) {  //  proceed
    // Get Name

        ...

    //  Add to the Database
        $description = nl2pilcrow($description);
    ...

}
```

The Prepared SQL Statement

The title and description are strings that clearly come from the outside, so we'll definitely need to use prepared statements. This involves the following steps:

1. Define the SQL statement.

2. Generate a prepared statement from the SQL.

3. Define the data.

4. Execute the prepared statement with the data.

Steps 2 and 3 can be in either order. The preceding order is probably what you'd expect. You can also combine some of the steps, though for now we'll keep them separate.

We'll start by defining the SQL statement:

```
// Add to the Database
   $description = nl2pilcrow($description);

   $sql = 'INSERT INTO images(title, description, name, src,
   gallery)
       VALUES(?, ?, ?, ?, true)';
```

The four actual values are replaced by question mark placeholders, to be replaced when the prepared statement is executed.

The last value is set to true for all of the images uploaded here. We don't need an additional data value for that, so we can hard-code it.

Note that, even though the values are strings, *you don't put the placeholders in quotes*. Remember, you only use quotes when you are defining a string literal; here, the strings will have already been defined.

The next step will be to use the SQL string to prepare the statement:

```
// Add to the Database
   $description = nl2pilcrow($description);

   $sql = 'INSERT INTO images(title, description, name, src,
   gallery)
       VALUES(?, ?, ?, ?, true)';
   $pdoStatement = $pdo -> prepare($sql);
```

The prepare() method of a PDO object takes a string as its input. Presuming that it's valid SQL, it will return a complementary **PDOStatement** object, which we can think of as a proxy.

Note that we could have inserted the SQL statement as a string literal in the prepare() method:

```
//  Add to the Database
    $description = nl2pilcrow($description);

    $pdoStatement = $pdo -> prepare('INSERT ... VALUES (...)');
```

This might be slightly more efficient, since the $sql variable's value is not reused anywhere else. However, the code will be easier to read and maintain if you separate the two. On the other hand, we will occasionally reduce the code to one statement if it makes our code easier to work with.

Executing with Data

The next step is to gather the data. For PDO, the data is always in an array, even if it's a single value.

We already have the values in various variables, so we can gather them together:

```
//  Add to the Database
    $description = nl2pilcrow($description);

    $sql = 'INSERT INTO images(title, description, name, src,
    gallery)
        VALUES(?, ?, ?, ?, true)';
    $pdoStatement = $pdo -> prepare($sql);
    $data = [$title, $description, $name, $name];
```

For now, we'll use the $name variable for both the name and src columns. We don't yet have enough detail to finish the src, so we just need something to fill in.

Finally, we'll execute the statement. To do this, we call the execute()
method with the array of data:

```
// Add to the Database
$description = nl2pilcrow($description);

$sql = 'INSERT INTO images(title, description, name, src,
gallery)
    VALUES(?, ?, ?, ?, true)';
$pdoStatement = $pdo -> prepare($sql);
$data = [$title, $description, $name, $name];
$pdoStatement -> execute($data);
```

Notice how we've used the two different objects:

- The PDO object ($pdo) was used to generate a
  PDOStatement object ($pdoStatement).

- The PDOStatement object was used to add the data.

Again, we might have combined the data and execute statements:

```
$pdoStatement -> execute([$title, $description, $name, $name]);
```

For now, however, it's easier to follow and easier to maintain in these
four separate steps.

PHP allows you to bind the data separately, using a series of **bind**
statements. This is especially useful if you're repeatedly using the same
prepared statement with different data. However, it is usually simpler and
more convenient to include the data in an array with the execute statement.

Retrieving the New ID

To generate the src value, we're going to use the image's id value, which
will be unique. The problem is that we don't yet know what it is, since it
was auto-generated by the database. Only the database knows, so we'll
need to ask it.

The tricky part with an auto-incremented ID is that we won't know until after the row is created what its value will be. To retrieve the new value, we can call the lastInsertId() method after we've added the data:

```
// Add to the Database
...
$pdoStatement->execute($data);

$id = $pdo->lastInsertId();
```

You'll notice that this method is called on the original PDO object. This method is pretty indiscriminate, fetching the last auto-incremented value regardless of which table you are using. The good news is that it's valid for a particular database session—if another process had added a row to the same table, its lastInsertId() will be distinct from this one. However, we need to fetch this one as soon as we can or lose it forever.

Modifying the Name

Previously, we changed the name from the uploaded file by changing it to lower case and replacing all the spaces. It is this name which has been saved twice.

This was risky because if we upload a new file with the same (adjusted) name, then it will overwrite the older file.

We will now modify the name to make it unique and use it as the src of the file. We will use this new src value as follows:

- When keeping the file, we will use this instead of the original name.

- When making the various resized copies, we will use this new name.

We will construct the src value by taking the original name and combining it with the id of the inserted image.

Constructing the New Name

To guarantee a unique name, we will include the id in the new name. For consistency, we will zero-pad the id to a set number of digits, say 6, which should be enough.

In principle, the id alone should be enough, but for management, we also include the original name, so that we know what we are looking at.

The adjusted name will be something like

000042-koala.jpg

By zero-padding the number, the renamed images will always appear in numerical order in a directory listing.

Zero-Padding a Number

Most of the time, when we use the sprintf() function, we use the %s parameter which will insert a string. Even if the value is a number, it will be treated as a string at this point.

We can add additional padding of certain characters by inserting the padding character and a width. In this case, we use %06s to specify padding with zeroes up to six digits in total. That should be enough, but if you think you'll want more than a million images, feel free to increase that.[2]

The sprintf() function call is

sprintf('%06s-%s', $id, $name);

The $id value will have come from the lastInsertId() function and will be padded to six digits. The $name value is the original name.

---

[2] All right, that's not strictly correct. The auto-incremented id isn't normally reused, even if the data has been deleted. It's quite conceivable that your auto-incremented id has reached a very high value, but you don't have quite so many actual images in your collection.

Add the following to your code:

```
// Add to the Database
  ...
  $id = $pdo->lastInsertId();
  $src = sprintf('%06s-%s', $id, $name);
```

Now that the new src value has been generated, we will

- Update the database with the new value.

- Modify the keep image code to use the new value.

- Modify the resize code to use the new value.

Updating the Database

To update the table, we will use the same steps as to insert the data. This time, we'll use the following prepared SQL statement:

```
UPDATE images SET src=? WHERE id=?
```

For the data, we'll use the newly calculated $src variable and the $id variable. In the code, we can add

```
// Add to the Database
  ...
  $id = $pdo->lastInsertId();
  $src = sprintf('%06s-%s', $id, $name);

  $sql = 'UPDATE images SET src=? WHERE id=?';
  $pdoStatement = $pdo -> prepare($sql);
  $data = [$src, $id];
  $pdoStatement -> execute($data);
```

If you try this now, you'll see your next database row with the new src value, but the images won't have their new names yet.

Keeping the File and Creating the Resized Copies

Now that we have the new name, we can modify the code which keeps the file and creates the thumbnail by changing the $name references to $src.

Modify the move_uploaded_file statement to include the new $src variable:

```
// Keep Original
move_uploaded_file($_FILES['image']['tmp_name'],
    "$root/{$CONFIG['images']['directory']}/originals/$src");
```

Now, modify the resizing code to include the new $src variable:

```
// Make Thumbnails
resizeImage(
    "$root/{$CONFIG['images']['directory']}/originals/$src",
    "$root/{$CONFIG['images']['directory']}/display/$src",
    $CONFIG['images']['display-size']
);
resizeImage(
    "$root/{$CONFIG['images']['directory']}/originals/$src",
    "$root/{$CONFIG['images']['directory']}/thumbnails/$src",
    $CONFIG['images']['thumbnail-size']
);
resizeImage(
    "$root/{$CONFIG['images']['directory']}/originals/$src",
    "$root/{$CONFIG['images']['directory']}/icons/$src",
    $CONFIG['images']['icon-size']
);
resizeImage(
    "$root/{$CONFIG['images']['directory']}/originals/$src",
    "$root/{$CONFIG['images']['directory']}/scaled/$src",
    $CONFIG['images']['scaled'], ['method'=>'scale']
);
```

Now, if you try it, the copied image names should include the id from the database. It's also a good way of checking that the database work is correct, since you won't have a new id unless it is.

Refactoring the Code

In the next chapter, we will be importing image details from an uploaded text file. This means calling our code multiple times.

While what we've written will do for a single upload, it needs to be rewritten to make it more suitable. This is called **refactoring**.

In our case, we'll move the code to two functions, so that we can call them to do all the hard work. The functions will be called from our current code, but will also be called from the code which imports the data.

The Function Outline

We're going to create two functions which do the following:

- One function will save the data to the database. It will return the new id and the src values to be used by the next function.

- The other function will save the image and copy the resized versions. This will need the data returned from the first function.

The reason we're doing this in two functions is partly to make the two jobs easier to appreciate, but also partly for a later development. We're going to write code to edit existing data. That will include the ability to upload a different image without adding anything new to the database.

PHP functions can be defined anywhere in the code. PHP is actually processed in more than one stage, and function definitions are processed at an earlier stage than running the actual code.

Deciding whether to define your functions before or after you need them is a matter of taste and, to some extent, a subject of some bitter disputes. In our code, we'll define them beforehand to make the process a little more obvious.

Exactly where is, of course, another matter. Here, we'll define them between the configuration and initialization sections:

```php
<?php
    ...
    // Configuration
        ...
    // Functions

    // Initialise
        ...
```

We can declare the two functions as follows:

```php
// Functions
    function addImageData(string $name, string $title,
        string $description) {

    }

    function addImageFile(string $file, string $src) {

    }
```

The functions will need to be given the details which were collected from the form. The same details will be in the import file. To add the details, we will put them in parameters.

Most of the code will be cut and pasted into the functions, but first we have to deal with another problem.

Scope

Variables are contained in an environment called their scope. This defines where the variable is available.

The rules of scope in PHP are a little different than in most other languages, so your experience with another language may mislead you.

Suppose we have the following code:

```
$a = 3;
function test() {
    $a = 4;
}
test();
print $a; // 3
```

In most languages, the variable $a will have been set to the new value, since functions inherit the variables defined outside—not in PHP, however.

In PHP, the function creates a *new* variable $a, which it then assigns. The original variable is untouched.

The outer variable is referred to as a **global** variable. The inner variable is a **local** variable. In PHP, variables inside a function are *always* assumed to be new local variables.

If we really want to use the global variable inside the function, we will need to say so using the global keyword:

```
$a = 3;
function test() {
    global $a;
    $a = 4;
}
test();
print $a; // 4
```

189

Our `addImageData()` function will need access to the global `$pdo` variable to work with the database. For this function, we'll need to have an additional `global` statement:

```
// Functions
    function addImageData(string $name, string $title,
        string $description) {
        global $pdo;

    }
```

You'll see a lot of discussion over the use of global variables. The general consensus is that you should rely on them as little as possible. For example, you might have decided to pass the `$pdo` variable as an additional parameter, and you'd be in good company. Here, we justify using the global variable by noting that it's already defined that way.

Writing the addImageData() Function

For the most part, the main purpose of this function is to add data to the database. In the process, however, we'll have fetched the `id` of the new data and used it to generate a `src` value to be used when coping the image and its clones.

We may not need the `id` for now, but it doesn't hurt to have it. We'll certainly want the `src` for the next function call to copy the image. To do that, we'll begin at the end: we'll have a `return` statement with the two values:

```
// Functions
    function addImageData(string $name, string $title,
        string $description) {
        global $pdo;

        return [$id, $src];
    }
```

Technically, a function can only have a single return value, but the loophole is that the return value may be an array or some other collection. Here, we're returning an array with the two values.

From the original code, cut the code which prepares the name and adds the data to the database. Paste this code into the function:

```
// Functions
   function addImageData(string $name, string $title,
       string $description) {
       global $pdo;

       $name = strtolower($name);
       $name = str_replace(' ', '-', $name);

   // Add to the Database
       $description = nl2pilcrow($description);

       $sql = 'INSERT INTO images(title, description, name,
       src) VALUES(?, ?, ?, ?)';
       $pdoStatement = $pdo -> prepare($sql);
       $data = [$title, $description, $name, $name];
       $pdoStatement->execute($data);

       $id = $pdo -> lastInsertId();
       $src = sprintf('%06s-%s', $id, $name);

       $sql = 'UPDATE images SET src=? WHERE id=?';
       $pdoStatement = $pdo->prepare($sql);
       $data = [$src, $id];
       $pdoStatement->execute($data);

       return [$id, $src];
   }
```

Don't include the line with $name = $_FILES['image']['name'];. In the original code, you should be left with

```
if(!$errors) {  //  proceed
    //  Get Name
      $name = $_FILES['image']['name'];

    //  Keep Original
      ...
}
```

You also can dispense with the comment // Get Name, as there's not much more going on here:

```
if(!$errors) {  //  proceed
    $name = $_FILES['image']['name'];

    //  Keep Original
      ...
}
```

Of course, now it won't work, since the original code no longer does the database work. For that, we'll need to call our function:

```
if(!$errors) {  //  proceed
    $name = $_FILES['image']['name'];
    [$id, $src] = addImageData($name, $title, $description);

    //  Keep Original
      ...
}
```

Remember the addImageData() function returns two values in an array. The left-hand side of the statement receives those two values into the $id and $src variables. The $id won't be used, but the $src variable is used for the code which copies the image.

The array notation on the left-hand side is called **array destructuring**—you're taking an array and destructuring it into a number of variables. Prior to PHP 7.1, and even since 7.1 if you insist, you would use the list() statement list($id, $src) = instead.

You can try this out. If it's working correctly, you'll get exactly the same result as before, but now the database work is done in a separate function.

Writing the addImageFile() Function

To begin with, the process will be similar to that for the previous function. We'll need to make a few more changes, however, because the file isn't always uploaded individually.

First, cut the code out of the main section, and paste it to the addImageFile() function:

```
function addImageFile(string $file, string $src) {
    move_uploaded_file($_FILES['image']['tmp_name'],
        "$root/{$CONFIG['images']['directory']}/
        originals/$src");

    resizeImage(
        ...
    );
    resizeImage(
        ...
    );
    resizeImage(
        ...
    );
    resizeImage(
        ...
    );
}
```

We won't need the comments in here.

You'll notice a reference to the $root variable and the $CONFIG array, which are global variables. This will require another global statement:

```
function addImageFile(string $file, string $src) {
    global $root, $CONFIG;

    ...
}
```

A global statement, as you can see, can reference more than one variable.

There is a problem with the move_uploaded_file() function. One of its jobs is to check that the file is a genuine upload. This won't work for the bulk upload we'll be doing later, so we need to make three changes:

- Change the reference to $_FILES['image']['tmp_ name'] to the $file parameter. Instead of referencing the uploaded file directly, we'll rely on the $file parameter.

- Change the move_uploaded_file() function to a different function to copy files.

- Check for the uploaded file differently.

For the first two changes, we can use the copy() function:

```
function addImageFile(string $file, string $src) {
    global $CONFIG;

    copy($file,
        "$root/{$CONFIG['images']['directory']}/
        originals/$src");

    ...
}
```

We'll add a separate check for the uploaded file in a moment. First, we'll test our changes. Having removed the code from its original location, we can replace it with a call to the function:

```
if(!$errors) {  //  proceed
    $name = $_FILES['image']['name'];
    [$id, $src] = addImageData($name, $title, $description);
    addImageFile($_FILES['image']['tmp_name'], $src);

    ...
}
```

This should work now.

To be 100% safe, we'll need to check that the file is indeed a properly uploaded one. We can do that while we're checking for other errors—specifically, while we're checking the uploaded file.

We can add the following test:

```
if(!isset($_FILES['image'])) $errors[] = 'Missing File';
else switch($_FILES['image']['error']) {
    case UPLOAD_ERR_OK:
        //  if($_FILES['image']['size'] > 0x100000)
        $errors[] = ... ;
        if(!in_array($_FILES['image']['type'], $imagetypes))
            $errors[] = 'Not a suitable image file';
        if(!is_uploaded_file($_FILES['image']['tmp_name']))
            $errors[] = 'Not an uploaded file';
        break;
    ...
}
```

The is_uploaded_file() file does the same check as move_uploaded_file(), obviously without moving it. We don't normally need it if we're using the latter function.

195

Using the Code in the Future

We've put in some effort to modify the code to do the same thing it was doing before the changes. However, by moving sections of the code into separate functions, we'll be able to reuse it in later code:

- When we implement a bulk upload, we'll be able to add the details to the database and copy the images without having to individually upload single images.

- When we implement editing existing image details, we'll be able to replace the image without affecting the database otherwise.

It's often the case that developing code goes through multiple stages, starting with just trying to make it work. You then go through a refining process to make the code more maintainable and more reusable, as we have done here.

Summary

In this chapter, we worked on adding data to the database and refactoring the code to be able to use it in scripts later in the project.

Working with the database involves establishing a connection using the sort of script we developed in Chapter 5. The script generates an object variable, which we called $pdo through which we call the database functions.

Before dealing with the database, however, we need to look out for SQL injection. This is where some additional SQL has been added to the user-generated data in an attempt to break into the database. It can also occur when certain text and characters are included in the text which may be misinterpreted as SQL.

To deal with possible SQL injection, we use prepared statements. These are SQL statements which are first interpreted without data and then executed with the data afterward, when it's too late to misinterpret the data.

Databases are easiest to handle with simple text and numbers; line breaks can be awkward to work with. To allow for richer descriptions, we can convert line breaks to a special character, such as a pilcrow, and convert it back when the time comes.

It's possible for multiple image files to be uploaded with the same original name. We can adapt this name using the ID of the database row we've just added. This involves retrieving the ID, modifying the name, and saving the changed name back into the database. We can then use the modified name for our permanent copies of the image files.

When everything is working, we can then refactor it to make it more reusable. In this case, we can package sections of the code into functions which can be called when needed. We supply the data to be used as parameter variables.

Sometimes, the function needs additional data from outside the function. By default, PHP variables are local in scope, but we can add a reference to global variables using a `global` statement.

We are now ready to use the code in the next chapter.

Coming Up

If you like, you can go ahead and add images and text data one at a time, but it would be convenient if we could upload a folder full of images together with the text to be added.

You can't upload a folder, but you can easily upload a ZIP file with the folder contents. In the next chapter, we'll look at how to unzip a file and put the contents in a convenient location. We'll also look at how to read a CSV file with data and use the CSV file in place of the upload file.

CHAPTER 7

File Handling

PHP includes built-in functions to work with the filing system. This includes functions to read directories and to read and write files. Although typically these files are text files, PHP can work with any binary file. Some binary files, such as image files, can be manipulated by other PHP functions, while others will need additional coding or libraries of code.

Processing text files can be very useful if you have configuration data which you want to use, but need to keep in a simple format for maintenance. Text files can also be useful as a means of importing existing data into your site. And, of course, you may be working on a project which manages text documents.

In this chapter, we'll look at reading text files only. Writing text files isn't something that you would do much, especially if you're keeping data in a database. Text files, on the other hand, are the sorts of files you might use to import data into a database.

In Chapter 12, we will look at exporting from a database out to a text file.

Although we are designing the site to allow adding image files one at a time, we may already have existing data which we want to load. This would include the image files, which will need to be copied with thumbnails made, and text data, which will need to be added to the database.

Our upload page includes a form to allow the mass import of image data. We'll do this as a ZIP file. In the process, we'll develop skills in

© Mark Simon 2024
M. Simon, *An Introduction to PHP*, https://doi.org/10.1007/979-8-8688-0177-8_7

- Checking and uploading a ZIP file

- Reading and interpreting a CSV file

- Working with numbered and associative arrays as collections of data

- Checking the MIME type of existing files

- Redirecting to another page

- Clearing database tables and directories

First, however, we'll need to learn a little more about the import form.

Preparation

In the uploadimage.php file, there is a section to upload an import file. It includes an upload button. Using CSS, the submit button is hidden until a List file has been added.

Here is the relevant part of the form:

```
<form id="editimage-import" method="post"
    enctype="multipart/form-data">
    <label for="import-file">Import File</label>
    <input type="file" name="import-file" id="import-file"
        accept="application/zip,.zip" required>
    <button type="submit" name="import">Import</button>
</form>
```

- The form, of course, has method="post" and enctype="multipart/form-data" because it's going to upload a file.

- The input is called import-file and the submit button is called import. We'll use this information when processing the submitted form.

- The `input` also includes an `accept` attribute which limits the type of file which the browser will allow, either by MIME type or by file extension.

- The `input` has a `required` attribute. You'd think that for this form it should be obvious, but we're going to use this to show or hide the submit button. In the CSS, if the form isn't valid (as when a required field is missing), the submit button will be hidden.

Both the `accept` and `required` properties could form part of the form validation. However, as always, we won't trust the browser, and the PHP will do its own checking. Browser-side validation is purely for the convenience of the user. Server-side validation is always essential to protect the server.

Technically, you don't need a separate form—the form contents could have been part of the previous form, as long as the form elements all have different names. If they have the same names, however, you'll need to keep them separate.

Here, we've kept the form separate purely for logistic reasons. We can keep them in separate parts of the page and style them differently.

The ZIP File

The ZIP file will be a compressed version of a folder of images and a CSV file with the image details. For convenience, we'll expect the CSV file to be called `@index.csv`. There's nothing special with the @ sign—it's there so that the file will appear at the top of the list when the folder is unzipped.

The structure will be something like this:

```
folder/
    @index.csv
    image.jpg
    another.jpg
    yetanother.jpg
    etc.jpg
```

Of course, they aren't necessarily JPEG files—just whatever image types we're prepared to accept.

The complicating factor is that, depending on how the ZIP file was generated, the files may or may not appear in a folder as you've seen earlier. That's going to make unzipping the file trickier.

The CSV File

The CSV file will be expected to have a header row:

```
name, title, description
```

When the time comes, we will remove the header row.

The rest of the data will follow, one line per image. This is one reason why it was so important to translate between line breaks and pilcrows. CSV files can't really handle multiple line values, so we'll encode them with the pilcrow.

We will allow a small variation from standard CSV files. CSV files shouldn't have empty lines, but it's easy to ignore them, so we'll allow them if you want to make the file a little more readable.

The other standard features of CSV files are that the comma is used to separate values (the C in CSV), and double quotes are used to enclose value strings which might be misread, such as when they include commas.

Processing the Uploaded Zip File

Before we go ahead, we'll need to make a change to the settings file. The sample project includes a sample ZIP file with images and text to be imported. It's much larger than the 2 or 8Mb limits we have allowed in the standard configuration.

Note although zipping files does compress, you won't get much compression of image files, as standard image formats are already compressed. The main benefit of zipping is that a folder full of multiple files has been transformed into a single file to be uploaded.

In order to allow the upload, we'll need to increase the limits. We should do this in both the .htaccess and .user.ini files, in case the deployment server uses either of them.

For the .htaccess file, change the settings to the following:

```
#   Uploads
    php_value    post_max_size 40M
    php_value    upload_max_filesize 20M
```

That should be more than enough for the sample file, but if you have your own file to test on, you'll want to check that again.

For the .user.ini file, we'll set the same values:

```
#   Uploads
    post_max_size=40M
    upload_max_filesize=20M
```

We'll put the processing code in the manage-images.code.php file. Naturally, we're going to use the addImageData() and addImageFile() functions we developed earlier, which is why we made sure to lift them out of the original code.

It doesn't matter where we put the code for the import, but it makes some sense to put this code after the earlier upload image code, reasoning that it's the next stage in development.

At the very end of the PHP block, add the following:

```php
<?php

    ...

    //  Import Zip File
    if(isset($_POST['import'])) {

    }
```

Much of the testing will be similar to when we uploaded a single image file.

Checking the Zip File

Since there's only one field in this field, there's not much that can go wrong. In this case, it may be missing, or it may be the wrong type.

The web form uses some CSS to hide the button if a file hasn't been selected, so you'd think that a missing file is unlikely. Besides, who would submit the form when there's nothing else on the form?

The point is we *always* need to check submitted data. The CSS only works on modern browsers, so the submit button may be visible anyway. A user may have clicked on the wrong button. It's always possible to bypass browser validation. Browser validation is purely for user convenience, and server validation is for real protection.

You can copy and paste and adapt the code from the upload section to make it easy.

To begin with, we won't need an $errors array, since there'll only be one error message. We can leave it as an empty string.

We can go straight into testing the uploaded file:

```
//  Import Zip File
    if(isset($_POST['import'])) {
        if(!isset($_FILES['import-file'])) $errors =
        'Missing File';
        else switch($_FILES['import-file']['error']) {
                case UPLOAD_ERR_OK:
                    if(
                        $_FILES['import-file']['type']
                        != 'application/zip'
                    ) $errors = 'Not a suitable ZIP file';
                    break;
                case UPLOAD_ERR_INI_SIZE:
                case UPLOAD_ERR_FORM_SIZE:
                    $errors = 'File too big';
                    break;
                case UPLOAD_ERR_NO_FILE:
                    $errors = 'Missing File';
                    break;
                default:
                    $errors = 'Problem with file upload';
        }
    }
```

The code is very similar to the code we used for an individual image file. However

- The file uploaded is in $_FILES['import-file']; the reference has changed.

- There's only one error message, so we don't bother with an array. Here, we assign the error message directly to the variable. We're still calling it $errors (plural) to be consistent with the rest of the application.

205

- There's only one MIME type to test (application/zip), so we don't need an array test. Here, we test for not equal to (!=).

There'll be a little more testing later after we've unzipped the file. For now, we can go ahead and unzip the file if there's no error so far:

```
//  Import Zip File
   if(isset($_POST['import'])) {
       if(!isset($_FILES['import-file'])) $errors =
       'Missing File';
       else switch($_FILES['import-file']['error']) {
            ...
       }

       if(!$errors) {
           // unzip file
       }
   }
```

We won't yet output the error message in case we discover other errors after unzipping the file.

Unzipping the File

There's a folder into which we can unzip the file contents. It's called uploads. As regards doing the unzip, there's some good news and some bad news.

The good news is that PHP has a built-in method to unzip a file. It involves creating an object of the ZipArchive class:

```
$zip = new ZipArchive;
```

Using this object, we can open the source file, extract the contents, and close it:

```
$zip = new ZipArchive;
$zip -> open($source);
$zip -> extractTo($destination);
$zip -> close();
```

That should do the job. Now for the bad news. It won't quite.

You'll remember from the description of the folder structure that all of the images and the CSV file are in a folder. The problem is that the folder, whatever it's called, may be part of the ZIP file contents, and the images and CSV file may be nested inside this folder—or maybe not. It depends on how the folder was zipped.

We don't want to get caught out on how the folder was zipped, so we're going to take a different, more complex approach. Instead of using the extractTo() method, we'll read the contents of the ZIP file one by one and copy the file directly, one by one.

The default-library.php file includes a function called unzip(). Appendix D discusses the function in detail, but here are the main points of interest.

We open and close the ZIP file as before:

```
$zip = new ZipArchive;
$zip -> open($source);

//  extract files

$zip -> close();
```

However, instead of using the extractTo() method, we need to iterate through the contents of the ZIP file to get at the individual files. To do this, we need two things:

207

- The numFiles property has the number of files or directories in the archive. Note that a directory is treated as a file.

- The getNameIndex() method extracts the *name* of one of the files, by index number.

To iterate through the archive, we use a for() statement:

```
$zip = new ZipArchive;
$zip -> open($source);

for($i = 0; $i < $zip -> numFiles; $i++) {
    //  extract the file
}

$zip -> close();
```

The for() statement is an ancient and counterintuitive statement which is basically used for counting through something. It has three parts, separated by semicolons:

```
for(start ; while ; next)
```

- In this case, the start is to set a counter variable to 0: $i = 0. Calling it $i is simply a very old tradition.

- The statement will *repeat* while the while condition is true. Here, the statement will repeat while the counter is less than the number of files.

- After each iteration, increment the counter variable. The expression $i++ basically means add 1 to $i.

Within each iteration, get the name of the file. The name will be the full path name including the enclosing directory, if any, so we'll need to deal with that in a moment. For now, we'll test whether it's the name of a directory by testing its last character:

```
for($i = 0; $i < $zip -> numFiles; $i++) {
    $file = $zip -> getNameIndex($i);
    if($file[-1] == '/') continue;
}
```

- We use the counter number to reference each file
  name, using getNameIndex().

- To get a single character from a string, we can use
  a notation which treats the string as an array of
  characters. The negative index counts from the end.
  Using $file[-1] means the first character from
  the end.

- If the last character is the forward slash (/), it's a
  directory name. Note that this is true even on Windows
  which prefers the backslash (\).

- If it's a directory, skip the rest and move on to the next
  one. The continue statement basically moves to the
  end of the block.

We'll now want to copy the file out of the archive into the real
destination. For our particular case, we want to dispense with the internal
path and just use the file name. We do that with the basename() function:

```
for($i = 0; $i < $zip -> numFiles; $i++) {
    $file = $zip -> getNameIndex($i);
    if($file[-1] == '/') continue;
    $name = basename($file);
}
```

Having got the base name, we'll do the copy:

```
for($i = 0; $i < $zip -> numFiles; $i++) {
    $file = $zip -> getNameIndex($i);
    if($file[-1] == '/') continue;
    $name = basename($file);
    copy("zip:// ... #$file", " ... /$name");
}
```

The copy(from, to) function, as the name suggests, copies the file. The special odd-looking notation zip:// ... #$file copies from what was a virtual file in the ZIP archive. Here, we use the $file and $name values from the previous lines. The from part of the function references the original ZIP file; the to part of the function references where it's going.

That's how the code works. There's a function we prepared earlier in the default library called unzip() which does all of this:

```
$result = unzip($_FILES['import-file']['tmp_name'],
"$root/uploads");
```

This will unzip and copy the files; there's also a result, if you want it. The result is an array of arrays. The library unzip function also builds arrays of original file names and base names, just in case you're interested, and returns them in an array. We won't need the $files array, but we'll want the $names array for further testing.

The return array is an associative array: it has string keys. The array would look like this:

```
['files' => [ ... ], 'names' => [ ... ]]
```

Recall in Chapter 6 that you can copy a numbered array into multiple variables using an array notation on the left-hand side:

```
[$a, $b] = ... ;
```

That's called destructuring an array. That won't quite work with associative arrays. Since PHP 7.1, we can use a similar notation to destructure associative arrays:

```
['files' => $files, 'names' => $names] = ... ;
```

Here, we associate the array key with a variable name:

```
//  Import ZIP File
    if(isset($_POST['import'])) {
        if(!isset($_FILES['import-file'])) $errors =
        'Missing File';
        else switch($_FILES['import-file']['error']) {
            ...
        }

        if(!$errors) {
            ['files' => $files, 'names' => $names]
                = unzip($_FILES['import-file']['tmp_name'],
                    "$root/uploads");
        }

    }
```

The next step will be to read the CSV file and use it to copy the images to the images directory.

Reading Text Files

The file that will control what's being added and copied is a CSV file. A CSV file is really just a text file with a special format.

PHP has many functions to handle files, particularly text files. Many of these functions allow you to write files, modify files, or update files. However, if all you want to do is to read their content, then there are two simple functions which do the rest of the hard work.

The `file()` function is the simplest to use. It reads the file into an array of strings, one string per line. What we mean by a line here is whenever we encounter a line break.

In this case, we expect to find a file called `@index.csv` in the `uploads` directory. We can read this way:

```
$file = "$root/uploads/@index.csv";
$data = file($file);    // array of lines
```

Of course, we could have done that in one line without the variable, but we're going to pre-check the file in a moment.

The other simple way to read a text file is using `file_get_contents()`. This will read the entire file into a single string:

```
$file = "$root/uploads/@index.csv";
$contents = file_get_contents($file);    // string of contents
```

You can split the string up into an array yourself using `explode()`, but you might have other plans for the file contents.

For our CSV file, we'll stick to the `file()` function because we'll want the lines individually.

There's one quirk with the `file()` function. When splitting the file into an array of lines, each line also includes the line break at the end. It's mostly useless, so it would be better if we can leave it out. We can do that by adding an optional flag:

```
$file = "$root/uploads/@index.csv";
$data = file($file, FILE_IGNORE_NEW_LINES);
```

The constant `FILE_IGNORE_NEW_LINES` is really just a number. In fact it's the number 2, but presumably using the name makes it a little more readable.

While we're at it, we can also instruct the `file()` functions to skip empty lines:

```
$file = "$root/uploads/@index.csv";
$data = file($file, FILE_IGNORE_NEW_LINES | FILE_SKIP_
EMPTY_LINES);
```

The constant `FILE_SKIP_EMPTY_LINES` is also a number: 4. The `|` operator between them is a binary "or" operator. This is just a way of combining two binary numbers. The result will actually have the value of 6, but we're not supposed to care about that—what's important is that it's the combination of the two flags.

Wherever possible, you should use PHP constant names instead of the numbers they represent, no matter how cumbersome they are. Using the numbers makes your code a little harder to follow.

The other reason is that technically, the values of the constants aren't necessarily guaranteed. If in a future version of PHP they decide to change the values for some sort of logistic reason, the constant names will stay the same and would still work.

We can now add the `file()` function to our code:

```
// Import ZIP File
   if(isset($_POST['import'])) {
       ...

       if(!$errors) {
           ...
       }

       $file = "$root/uploads/@index.csv";
       $data = file($file, FILE_IGNORE_NEW_LINES |
           FILE_SKIP_EMPTY_LINES);
   }
```

Note that we've added the extra code *after* the test for no errors. Really, we should only do this if there are no errors. Later, we'll add more error checking code, so, for now, we'll just have to trust it.

Once we have the file in an array, we can process it line by line. First, however, we need to do something about the header row.

Removing the Header Row

The CSV file includes a header line as the first line. We'll want to remove that, so that we can process the rest of the lines as real data. We can do that with the array_shift() function:

```
//  Import ZIP File
    if(isset($_POST['import'])) {
        ...

        $file = "$root/uploads/@index.csv";
        $data = file($file, FILE_IGNORE_NEW_LINES |
            FILE_SKIP_EMPTY_LINES);
        $header = array_shift($data);
    }
```

The array_shift() function removes the first item of an array and renumbers the rest of the array down.

The return value of array_shift() is the item we've just removed; in this case, it's the first line, the header line. Sometimes, that's exactly what you want as you're fetching one item at a time from the beginning. If you are, then you're treating the array as a **queue**—a data structure where new items are added to the end and old ones removed from the beginning. A queue is also known as a **FIFO** structure—First In, First Out.

In this case, we don't really need the header, so we can just ignore the variable. In fact, we can call the function without bothering with its return value:

```
array_shift($data);
```

Now we have an array with real data. We now need to split it.

Splitting CSV Data

Each line has three items separated by commas. At the moment, each line is still just a string. We'll want to split these strings using the commas.

The str_getcsv() function will split a string into its comma-separated parts. For example:

```
$test = 'apple,banana,cherry';
$test = str_getcsv($test);
print_r($test);
```

The print_r() function will output a complex structure. In this case, we would see

```
Array
(
    [0] => apple
    [1] => banana
    [2] => cherry
)
```

The reason why we use str_getcsv() and not explode(), which would also split a string, is that str_getcsv() is more intelligent. If there's a field in double quotes with a comma inside, it knows not to split at that comma. It's also more flexible if you check its options—you can decide whether to use commas or some other separator character and whether to use double quotes or otherwise for strings.

We want to run the `str_getcsv()` function over all the lines in the
$data array. You can do this one line at a time:

```
foreach ($data as &$line) {
    $line = str_getcsv($line);
}
```

You've seen the `foreach()` before: it iterates through the array one
item at a time. The ampersand (&) character before the $line variable is
special.

Normally, the variable after the `as` has a *copy* of the data. By putting the
ampersand before it, the variable will be a *reference* to the original data.
This way, assigning a new value will be changing the content of the original
array. In this case, we're replacing each string in the original array with an
array of split values.

If all you're doing with each item of an array is running it through a
function, PHP has a simpler way to do this. The `array_map()` function is
used to run every item of an array through a function:

```
$data = array_map('str_getcsv', $data);
```

This is the equivalent of the `foreach` earlier. We can add this to
the code:

```
//  Import ZIP File
    if(isset($_POST['import'])) {
        ...
        $file = "$root/uploads/@index.csv";
        $data = file($file, FILE_IGNORE_NEW_LINES |
            FILE_SKIP_EMPTY_LINES);
        $header = array_shift($data);
        $data = array_map('str_getcsv', $data);
    }
```

- The array_map() function takes the name of the function we want to apply as a string in the first parameter.

- The return value of array_map() is a new array with the modified contents. Here, we're assigning it to the original $data variable.

We're now ready to add the data to our collection.

Importing the Data

When we uploaded images and data individually, we read the data from the form and copied the image file from its temporary location. To prepare for this part of the project, we moved that part of the code to separate functions. We'll now use these functions to finish the import.

This time, we'll use foreach() to iterate through the array of CSV data:

```
// Import ZIP File
  if(isset($_POST['import'])) {

      ...

      $file = "$root/uploads/@index.csv";
      $data = file($file, FILE_IGNORE_NEW_LINES |
          FILE_SKIP_EMPTY_LINES);
      $header = array_shift($data);
      $data = array_map('str_getcsv', $data);

      foreach($data as $item) {
          // import item
      }
  }
```

217

Remember each item in the array is another array of three values, the name of the file, the title, and the description, in that order. We can start by adding the data to the database:

```
foreach($data as $item) {
    [$id, $src] = addImageData($item[0], $item[1], $item[2]);
}
```

The addImageData() function returns the id and the modified src of the newly added image. Again, we don't really need the id, so we could have written

```
foreach($data as $item) {
    [, $src] = addImageData($item[0], $item[1], $item[2]);
}
```

The current location of the file is in the uploads directory. The full path of this file is

```
"$root/uploads/$item[0]"
```

We can use that and the src value to process the images:

```
foreach($data as $item) {
    [, $src] = addImageData($item[0], $item[1], $item[2]);
    addImageFile("$root/uploads/$item[0]", $src);
}
```

We can now test it by uploading the ZIP file again. This time, the database should be populated with the new data, and the image folders should fill up with the new images.

Checking the MIME Types

We've checked the MIME type of the uploaded file, but we've assumed its contents are OK. With an uploaded file, you can check the MIME type from the $_FILES array, but you can't use the same method after the ZIP file has been expanded into our directory.

PHP has a method of getting various pieces of information about existing files, such as the MIME type. Unlike relying on the information in the $_FILES array, this method looks at the file itself.

The PHP method involves creating and using a finfo object. It's somewhat indirect, so the default library includes a convenience function which wraps the method:

```
function MimeType($filename) {
    $finfo = new finfo(FILEINFO_MIME_TYPE);
    return $finfo->file($filename);
}
```

We should now check whether the @index.csv file actually exists and whether it's actually a CSV file.

Remember that we've unzipped the file in a test for no errors:

```
if(!$errors) {
    ['files'=>$files, 'names'=>$names]
        = unzip($_FILES['import-file']['tmp_name'], "$root/
        uploads");
}
```

We can now test whether the @index.csv exists and is the right MIME type:

```
if(!$errors) {
    ['files'=>$files, 'names'=>$names]
        = unzip($_FILES['import-file']['tmp_name'], "$root/
        uploads");
```

219

```
if(
    !file_exists("$root/uploads/@index.csv")
    || MimeType("$root/uploads/@index.csv") != 'text/csv'
) $errors = 'No valid @index.csv file';
}
```

- The file_exists() function does what it says: it tests whether there is a file at that location.

- Putting ! before something means "not." Here, !file_exists() tests whether a file doesn't exist.

- The || operator means "or." The file may exist, but it may not be the right type.

- The correct MIME type for a CSV file is text/csv. If the MIME type isn't text/csv, then we have an error.

If you follow the logic closely, there is a possible point of failure. If the file doesn't exist, how can we test its MIME type? If we tried, we'd end up with a fatal error. Fortunately, the || is **short-circuited**.

In logic, the **OR** operation requires one or more values to be true. More precisely, it only requires one value to be true, and it doesn't matter about the rest. Languages such as PHP (as well as JavaScript but *not* SQL) take advantage of this fact by short-circuiting the operation.

If the first value is true, PHP won't evaluate the second part at all. Not only is it (slightly) more efficient, it's safer.

In this expression, if the file *doesn't* exist, that satisfies the OR operation, so PHP won't attempt to check its MIME type.

We can now wrap the rest of the code inside another error test:

```
if(!$errors) {
    ['files'=>$files, 'names'=>$names]
        = unzip($_FILES['import-file']['tmp_name'], "$root/
        uploads");
```

```
    if(
        !file_exists("$root/uploads/@index.csv")
        || MimeType("$root/uploads/@index.csv") != 'text/csv'
    ) $errors = 'No valid @index.csv file';
}

if(!$errors) {
    $file = "$root/uploads/@index.csv";
    $data = file($file, FILE_IGNORE_NEW_LINES |
        FILE_SKIP_EMPTY_LINES);
    $header = array_shift($data);
    $data = array_map('str_getcsv', $data);

    foreach($data as $item) {
        [, $src] = addImageData($item[0], $item[1], $item[2]);
        addImageFile("$root/uploads/$item[0]", $src);
    }
}
```

We're now only copying the image files if we can't detect any other errors.

Checking the Images

The other additional check we need is for the images we're supposed to be uploading. Here, two things might go wrong:

- The image referenced in the CSV file might not have been included.

- The image referenced in the CSV file might not actually be an image.

We can check them as we iterate through the $data array. We'll use a similar test as for the CSV file, but, if we find an error, we'll just skip the iteration instead of creating an error message.

We'll first need to set up an array of MIME types as we did when uploading a single image file:

```
if(!$errors) {
    ...

    $imagetypes = ['image/gif', 'image/jpeg', 'image/png',
        'image/webp'];

    foreach($data as $item) {
        [, $src] = addImageData($item[0], $item[1], $item[2]);
        addImageFile("$root/uploads/$item[0]", $src);
    }
}
```

We can now add the test inside the foreach:

```
if(!$errors) {
    ...

    $imagetypes = ['image/gif', 'image/jpeg', 'image/png',
        'image/webp'];

    foreach($data as $item) {
        if(
            !file_exists("$root/uploads/$item[0]")
            || !in_array(MimeType("$root/uploads/$item[0]"),
                $imagetypes)
        ) continue;

        [, $src] = addImageData($item[0], $item[1], $item[2]);
        addImageFile("$root/uploads/$item[0]", $src);
    }
}
```

- Remember that $item[0], the first item, is the name of the file. We're checking whether a file of that name is in the uploads directory.

- We're using the in_array() function to check the MIME type against an array of MIME types.

- The continue statement skips the rest of the iteration.

It's not perfect, of course, but we've improved the safety of our import process by checking for missing or wrong files.

So far, however, we've ignored the error. We'll do that when we're finishing up.

Finishing Up

For testing purposes, it makes sense to keep on the page until we've got everything working. In reality, once you've uploaded the file, you should move on to the next task.

At the end of our code block, we can prepare to either move on or display the error message:

```
// Import ZIP File
    if(isset($_POST['import'])) {
        ...

        if(!$errors) {
            ...
            foreach($data as $item) {
                ...
            }

            // Move On

        }
```

```
    else {
        // Display Error Message
    }
}
```

Here, we've added a comment at the end of the upload and an `else` block for errors.

Displaying the errors is simple enough. It's not even an array so we don't need to implode it. We can just write

```
if(!$errors) {
    ...

}
else {
    $errors = sprintf('<p class="errors">%s</p>', $errors);
}
```

This puts the `$errors` string inside an error paragraph. This paragraph will be displayed in the form in the `<?= $errors ?>` block.

As for moving on, that means redirecting to another page.

There is a page called `imagelist.php`. In Chapter 9, it will be part of a bigger scheme to maintain our image collection. For now, we'll just use it as a landing page.

PHP can't go on to the next page directly, but it can request the browser to do so. To do this, we need to send a special instruction to the browser.

A Crash Course in HTTP(S)

All communication between the browser and the server uses the **HTTP** protocol, which defines how the communication is structured. When you see **HTTPS**, it's the same thing, but it's been encrypted to make the communication more secure; it works the same way.

HTTP communication has three important parts:

- From the browser, the **URL** itself has information about which site we're dealing with as well as possible data on the query string.

- There is a **header** section which has information about the communication. From the browser, it may include **cookies** used to save some data; from the server, it may also include cookies. We'll see more about cookies later.

  The header also includes messages from the server. This may be informational, such as whether the resource is missing (the dreaded 404) or whether it's been moved to a new location. It may also include an instruction for the next page.

- The **body** section from the server is what we've been working with all this time. All of the HTML output is sent in the body section.

Coming from the browser, data sent using the POST method is included in the body.

From PHP's point of view, there are two types of output:

- *Most* output is to the body. This includes any HTML not in a PHP block as well as whatever is output from `print` or `echo`.

- You can also output to the header. This is sometimes done implicitly, such as when you set a cookie, which we'll do a little later. This can also be done explicitly using the `header()` function.

Headers Already Sent

PHP is very strict about writing to the HTTP header. It must be done *before* anything is written to the body. If you attempt to write to the header *after* writing to the body, you'll get

> Headers Already Sent

which breaks everything.

New PHP developers aren't always aware that they're doing this until they get the error message. Here are some subtle ways this might have happened:

- If you have any blank lines or comments before the first PHP block, you've already started writing to the body, so it's too late to write to the header.

  If you include a file, there may be additional (blank) lines after the PHP block. This is why we don't close the PHP block; we let PHP do it automatically at the end of the PHP file.

- Saving a cookie or using sessions (which we'll do later) also write to the header. If you do any of this after any other output, there'll be an error.

The safest way to handle this is to write your code carefully.

If you look in the `.htaccess` and `.user.ini` settings files, you'll find that there's a setting for output buffering. This would cause PHP to hold on to its body output until at the end, after the headers have been written. You'll also notice that it's turned off, which it is by default anyway. It can be handy if you can't work out what's going wrong, but it's better to try to write your code not to need it.

If you follow the principle of separating PHP processing from the output, which is what we've been doing, it will be easier to organize your code so that headers won't be sent after the body has been written.

Redirecting to the Next Page

To redirect to the next page, we can use the following PHP:

```php
if(!$errors) {
    ...

    // Move On
    header("Location: URL");
    exit;
}
else {
    $errors = sprintf('<p class="errors">%s</p>', $errors);
}
```

The header() function is used to simply write into the HTTP header. You're expected to know enough HTTP to know what to write. In this case, the Location: command is the URL of the next location for the browser.

Once we've written the new location, there's no point in filling the body with the rest of the page, since the user won't see it. For that reason, we've followed the header() function with exit, which stops PHP processing at this point.

This won't work yet since you need to supply a real URL for the Location: command.

You can probably get away with just using the short name of the page:

```php
// Move On
header("Location: imagelist.php");
exit;
```

227

Technically, however, it should be a full URL, complete with a protocol and host—something like this:

```
header("Location: https://www.example.com/imagelist.php");
exit;
```

This poses some difficulty when you are testing on one server (such as www.example.com) but deploying on another. You will need to programmatically determine your host. You'll also have a problem with the protocol: it may be http on the development server, but https (hopefully) on the live server.

PHP has this sort of information in its $_SERVER array, which contains information about the server environment. In particular, the item $_SERVER['HTTP_HOST'] has the URL of the current host, and $_SERVER['HTTPS'] will indicate that the current protocol is https.

To properly direct the user to another page, we should first extract the data in a more useful form. We can do this at the beginning of the script as we're setting up:

```
<?php
    $root = str_replace($_SERVER['SCRIPT_NAME'], '',
        $_SERVER['SCRIPT_FILENAME']);

    $host = $_SERVER['HTTP_HOST'];
    $protocol = isset($_SERVER['HTTPS']) && $_
    SERVER['HTTPS'] == 'on'
        ? 'https'
        : 'http';
```

The $host variable is simply a copy of the data from the $_SERVER array, to make it easy to interpolate it later.

The $_SERVER['HTTPS'] value is a little complex: it may not be set, in which case you must be using http. Even if it is set, it may not be on. Using the conditional operator

- isset($_SERVER['HTTPS']) tests whether this
  value exists.

- $_SERVER['HTTPS'] == 'on' tests whether this value is
  set to on.

- The && operator means "and." It requires *both* values to
  be true.

Like the || operator, the && operator is also short-circuited. In this case,
if the first test *fails*, there's no point in going on. The second test will only
be applied if the first value is true.

Using the conditional operator, the $protocol variable is set to either
https or http.

Using these variables, we can complete the redirect:

```
// Move On
header("Location: $protocol://$host/imagelist.php");
exit;
```

When you test this now, you'll see that it's taken you to the imagelist.
php page.

You'll also find that it's taken some time to get there. Copying and
transforming the images is very resource intensive, and so you'll have to
wait a little.

If you have a large collection to upload, you may find that PHP gives up
after a while. That's because it has a default timeout of 30 seconds.

If you really need more time, you can increase the timeout. For the
.htaccess file, change the settings to the following:

```
php_value    max_execution_time 30
```

For the .user.ini file, we'll set the same value:

```
max_execution_time=30
```

You probably won't want to keep a higher value. This would allow some incorrect PHP scripts to keep running too long and possibly hang the system.

On the `imagelist.php` page, there's a link to add a new image. It won't work yet, as we'll need to rename the page first. We'll worry about that in Chapter 9.

Starting Over

By now, there will be a great deal of test data, as well as the old uploaded images. We will need to clean up both the images folders and the images table.

There is a setup link which will clean everything up:

`http://australia.example.net/setup?reset-images`

For testing purposes, however, you can incorporate the code directly.

To clean up the table, SQL has a `TRUNCATE` command. It clears the old data and resets the auto-increment counter to start again.

We can add that to the beginning of the import code:

```
// Import Zip File
    if(isset($_POST['import'])) {
        $pdo -> exec('TRUNCATE TABLE images');

        ...

    }
```

- The exec() method runs an SQL statement directly and doesn't expect a result other than whether it worked. We don't need to prepare this statement, since there's no user-supplied data.

Clearing the directories is more involved, since there are multiple images in multiple directories.

To delete a file, we use a function called unlink(). That may sound like a strange thing to call it, but it reflects the fact that files are not actually deleted—the file system removes the reference to the file and is free to reuse the space later.

For example, to delete the @index.csv file, we can use

```
unlink('uploads/@index.csv');
```

To delete a whole directory, you would use the wildcard *. When using this in an operating system, the * is always expended to the names of the files, an operation called **globbing**. To do the same thing in PHP, you need the glob() function:

```
$files = glob('uploads/*');
```

The glob() function returns an array of file names, so we would have to unlink all of the array items. We can do this with the array_map() function:

```
$files = glob('uploads/*');
array_map('unlink', $files);
```

We don't really need to keep the $files array, so we can do this in one line:

```
array_map('unlink', glob('uploads/*'));
```

There's more than one directory to clear out, so we can start with an array of directory names:

```
$directories = ['uploads', 'images/originals', 'images/display',
    'images/thumbnails', 'images/icons', 'images/scaled'];
```

Using this array, we can use foreach to clear the directories:

```
$directories = ['uploads', 'images/originals', 'images/display',
    'images/thumbnails', 'images/icons', 'images/scaled'];
foreach($directories as $dir)
    array_map('unlink', glob("$root/$dir/*"));
```

We've changed the string in the glob() function to double quotes, so that we can interpolate the $root and $dir variables. The $dir variable is a reference to each directory in the $directories array.

The code at the beginning now reads

```
// Import ZIP File
    if(isset($_POST['import'])) {
        $pdo -> exec('TRUNCATE TABLE images');
        $directories = ['uploads', 'images/originals',
            'images/display', 'images/thumbnails',
            'images/icons', 'images/scaled'];
        foreach($directories as $dir)
            array_map('unlink', glob("$root/$dir/*"));

        ...
    }
```

There's one more task in cleaning up. Just as we've cleared out the images directories in preparation, we'll want to clean out the uploads directory when we've finished with the import.

We can add one more unlink statement at the end of the upload:

```
if(!$errors) {
    ...

    foreach($data as $item) {
        ...
    }
```

```
array_map('unlink', glob("$root/uploads/*"));
```

```
//  Move On
    header("Location: $protocol://$host/imagelist.php");
    exit;
}
else {
    ...
}
```

We can now test the import button again, but it won't be until the next chapter that we can fully appreciate the results.

After you've finished your testing, you should comment out the code at the beginning to clear out the old data or possibly even remove it:

```
//  Import ZIP File
    if(isset($_POST['import'])) {
        $pdo -> exec('TRUNCATE TABLE images');
    /*
        $directories = ['uploads', 'images/originals',
            'images/display', 'images/thumbnails',
            'images/icons', 'images/scaled'];
        foreach($directories as $dir)
            array_map('unlink', glob("$root/$dir/*"));
    */
        ...
    }
```

When using this for real, we probably want to add imported data to existing data, rather than replace it.

Summary

PHP includes the ability to work with files on the server. This includes creating and deleting files, as well as reading and writing them.

In this chapter, we uploaded a ZIP file and expanded it with a view to importing multiple images. This process involved reusing code written in the previous chapter to add individual images.

Since the ZIP files are likely to be quite large, you probably need to increase the upload limits in the `.htaccess` or `.user.ini` file. We also need to agree on the content format of the zipped file. In this case, it's supposed to be a collection of images and a CSV file which describes them.

Having first checked that a ZIP file has been properly uploaded, PHP has the ability to expand a zipped file, but the fact that it may contain nested folders complicates things, so it's more reliable to extract the files one at a time.

There are multiple functions to read text files, including CSV files. The simplest involves reading the file into an array of lines using the `file()` function. From there, we can remove the header line and process the rest of the lines individually as CSV strings. We can use this to get the file name, the title, and description for each image.

Using this information, we can add the data to the database and copy the image files to the various image folders.

When working with extracted files, we don't get the benefit of the information otherwise available in the `$_FILES` array, particularly in checking the MIME type of the files. However, we can use PHP's ability to get information on existing files to test for this.

When we've finished, we would want to move on to another page. We can do this by adding an instruction in the HTTP header to redirect, using the `header()` function. Writing to the header can be tricky if we're also writing to the body, which is what most PHP output is doing. We need to make sure that all of the header is completed before we start writing to the body.

The `Location:` header command is used to redirect the browser. Because this should include a properly formed URL, we also need to fetch the protocol and the current URL from the `$_SERVER` array.

Testing involves uploading and copying files many times and adding a lot of data to the database. When we're convinced that everything's working, we need to clean out the database table with the `TRUNCATE` command and to empty out the images directories.

We also want to clean up the `uploads` directory after completing the import, which we can do using the same method as clearing the other directories previously.

Coming Up

We now have a collection of images. In the next chapter, we're going to turn that collection into an image gallery.

In the process, we'll learn more about extracting data from the database, generating HTML from the data, and controlling what we want with query strings.

We'll also learn about fetching random images and saving results in cookies.

The image gallery code we'll be developing is also going to be the basis for developing pages to manage the database.

CHAPTER 8

The Image Gallery

One of the features of the sample project is an image gallery. We've put in a lot of effort to upload the images and populate the database with image data, and now we're going to put it all together and display the images.

When we have finished, it will look something like Figure 8-1.

Figure 8-1. *The Image Gallery*

© Mark Simon 2024

M. Simon, *An Introduction to PHP*, https://doi.org/10.1007/979-8-8688-0177-8_8

Because of the size of the gallery, we will display a catalogue of a few thumbnail images per page and allow the user to page through the catalogue. The catalogue page will also display one larger image.

When the visitor clicks a thumbnail image, the catalogue page will update with the chosen image for display.

The catalogue and display image will be handled on the page `gallery.php`, using code developed in a separate file `gallery.code.php`.

There will be three main sections on the page:

- A gallery of some of the images

- A paging bar to select the next page of images

- A larger image, selected by the user

Although we're focusing on the image gallery, what we're really learning about is fetching data from a database and responding to requests from the visitor.

In the process, we'll learn how to fetch one or more rows with the SQL select statement and how to get that data into PHP variables. These variables will then be used to construct HTML elements for display on the page.

Visitors will request a page or image using a query string, and we'll learn how query strings work in PHP. We'll also learn how to generate query strings in code.

For convenience, we'll store some of this in browser cookies, and we'll see how cookies are managed.

We'll also look at how to fetch random data from the database, and we'll use this to display a random image in other pages.

Preparation

Not surprisingly, the page for the gallery is `gallery.php`. It's mostly ready to go, but we'll need to add an include for the code we're developing.

If you load the page now, it will fall apart, since it references a number of variables which don't exist. We'll fix that in a moment.

First, create a new file called gallery.code.php and save it in the includes directory. Next, add an include for this file in the gallery.php file, at the very beginning:

```
<?php require_once 'includes/gallery.code.php'; ?>
```

In the gallery.code.php page, add a PHP block (without closing it), and start with the following variables:

```
<?php

    $images = $paging = $displaying = '';
    $title = $image = $description = '';
```

The first three variables—$images, $paging, and $displaying—relate to the gallery section. The other three variables—$title, $image, and $description—relate to the larger image.

If you reload the page, it now looks terribly blank, but at least it's not full of error messages.

The gallery will need access to the database and possibly some library functions:

```
<?php
    $root = str_replace($_SERVER['SCRIPT_NAME'], '',
        $_SERVER['SCRIPT_FILENAME']);

    $pdo = require_once "$root/includes/db.php";
    require_once "$root/includes/default-library.php";
    require_once "$root/includes/library.php";

    $images = $paging = $displaying = '';
    $title = $image = $description = '';
```

Again, we've calculated the $root variable, so we can have absolute references to the included files.

Fetching the Thumbnails

If you look at the live site, you'll see

- A collection of thumbnail images

- A navigation block

- A gallery page number

The information comes from two main sources:

- A visitor selects a gallery page.

- The database supplies the rest of the information.

For now, we'll hard-code the page number and focus on the database side of things.

Fetching from the Database

We've put a lot of effort into populating the database. Now it's time to retrieve the data.

If you want, you can play along using PHPMyAdmin and the SQL tab. If you do, you should start by first selecting the australia database.

Don't forget to press GO after every example.

To get data from a database table, we use a SELECT statement:

```
SELECT * FROM images;
```

This is called the SELECT statement and has two clauses: the FROM clause indicates which table to fetch from, and the SELECT clause indicates which columns. Using SELECT * means fetch all of the columns—the column order is whatever was set up when the table was created.

It's usually not a good idea to use SELECT * as you have no control over which columns or which order they come in. It's better to specify the columns directly:

```
SELECT id, title, src, gallery FROM images;
```

For the gallery thumbnails, we won't need the other columns.

You'll see that we still have all of the rows. We won't want all of them for a single page of images. There are three things we can do to improve our fetch:

- Select only those images which have the gallery property set to true. For now, that's all of them, but, in principle, there might be others not to be included.

  We do that by adding the filter clause: WHERE gallery=true.

- Limit the number of rows to, say, three at a time.

  To limit the number of rows, we use the LIMIT ... OFFSET clause: LIMIT 3 OFFSET 0. The OFFSET is the number of rows to skip first.

- Show the newest images first.

  The table is sorted with the ORDER BY clause. Here, we sort by the id column and reverse the direction with the DESC (descending) keyword: ORDER BY id DESC. This comes *before* the LIMIT ... OFFSET clause.

Putting this together, we get

```
SELECT id, title, src
FROM images
WHERE gallery=true
ORDER BY id DESC LIMIT 3 OFFSET 0;
```

- SQL can, and should, be written on multiple lines when the statement gets a little complex. You can still write it on one line if it's more convenient.

- We've elected not to select the `gallery` column, since we're only selecting where it's `true`. You can still select it if you like.

- Technically, MySQL doesn't use `true` and `false` values. They're synonyms for 1 and 0. However, the boolean names make the intent a little clearer.

Using the `LIMIT ... OFFSET` clause allows us to page through a large set of results. There are two parts, both of which are a matter of choice:

- The `LIMIT` value is arbitrary—you can have any number you like, of course. Effectively, we use that as a page size. We'll set that in the configuration section of the script.

- The `OFFSET` will depend on the page number. The first page will have an `OFFSET` of 0. The subsequent pages will be offset by the page number and the page size.

We can now start writing this in PHP.

Fetching a Gallery Page

To begin with, we'll set up the page size in a configuration section at the beginning:

```php
<?php
    $root = str_replace($_SERVER['SCRIPT_NAME'], '',
        $_SERVER['SCRIPT_FILENAME']);

    $pdo = require_once "$root/includes/db.db";
    require_once "$root/includes/default-library.php";
    require_once "$root/includes/library.php";
```

```php
$CONFIG['gallery']['page-size'] = 3;
$CONFIG['images']['display-size'] = '480 x 360';
$CONFIG['images']['thumbnail-size'] = '240 x 180';

...
```

We've also included the dimensions for the images we'll be displaying. We'll use them later when it comes to generating the img elements for display. They're the same values that we used when uploading and resizing the images. In a later chapter, we'll consolidate all of these configuration values.

After setting the main variables, we can add the variable for the gallery section:

```php
<?php
    ...

    $CONFIG['gallery']['page-size'] = 3;
    $CONFIG['images']['display-size'] = '480 x 360';
    $CONFIG['images']['thumbnail-size'] = '240 x 180';

    $images = $paging = $displaying = '';
    $title = $image = $description = '';

    $page = 1;

    $limit = $CONFIG['gallery']['page-size'];
```

Currently, the $page variable is hard-coded to page 1, which we'll change later to the visitor's selection. The $limit variable is just a copy of the configuration value.

We're going to set up the preceding SELECT statement, but we'll need to calculate the offset. That will depend on the page number and the page size.

For example, suppose the visitor wants page 4. To calculate the offset:

1. Skip past the first *three* pages: 4 - 1.

2. Multiply those three pages by the page size:
    (4 - 1) * 3.

Of course, the page number may change, and the page size may change, so we'll use the variables instead:

```php
<?php

    ...

    $limit = $CONFIG['gallery']['page-size'];
    $offset = ($page - 1) * $limit;
```

We can now create the SQL string:

```php
<?php

    ...

    $limit = $CONFIG['gallery']['page-size'];
    $offset = ($page - 1) * $limit;

    $sql = "SELECT id, title, src
        FROM images
        WHERE gallery=true
        ORDER BY id DESC LIMIT $limit OFFSET $offset";
```

Remember PHP will happily accept line breaks in strings, and SQL will ignore them. This makes it reasonable to write the SQL statement on multiple lines.

In Chapter 5, we made a big deal of *not* directly using user input in the SQL, for fear of SQL injection. The page number will indeed come from the user, but it's different.

By the time we've finished processing the page number, all that will be left will be an integer. Remember that numbers can't be misinterpreted as SQL—only strings can. At this point, the number is hard-coded, but when we do accept it as user input, we'll definitely make sure that it's a harmless number.

Having got the SQL string, we now need to use it.

The PDO method has two functions to use SQL statements without going through the prepare ... execute process. The exec() method is used to change something in the database. Here, we'll use the query() method to fetch something:

```
$pdo -> query($sql);
```

The query() method doesn't directly give you the results. Instead, you get a PDOStatement object, from which you can then fetch the results. Yes, a PDOStatement is also used for prepared statements, but not in this case.

We can now get the PDOStatement:

```
<?php
    ...

    $sql = "SELECT id, title, src
        FROM images
        WHERE gallery=true
        ORDER BY id DESC LIMIT $limit OFFSET $offset";
    $results = $pdo -> query($sql);
```

You can call a variable anything you like, of course. Previously, we called the PDOStatement something like $prepared because that was how we planned to use it. Here, we plan to extract the results, so it makes sense to call it $results.

Fetching the Rows

In the trade, we say a PDOStatement is traversable. That means you can iterate through the PDOStatement if it's a simple collection. It isn't a simple collection, but we'll let PHP treat it that way.

It's possible to retrieve data from one row at a time:

- fetch() will fetch a single row of data. If you keep calling this method, it will fetch the next and so on till you get to the end.

- fetchColumn() will fetch a single column from a single row. Again, you can call this repeatedly, getting that column from the next row.

You can also retrieve the whole lot into an array:

- fetchArray() will copy all the rows into an array. An array *is* a simple collection.

In this case, we want to fetch one row at a time, but there's a simpler way to do that. You can also use foreach() on a PDOStatement:

```
foreach($results as $row) {
    ...
}
```

This looks like an array, but there are some differences. Importantly, the data isn't there yet. Each iteration will fetch the data from the PDOStatement. If you have a large set of data, this can be important, since you're not using up so much memory as you might if it was all there in an array.

Each row, however, *is* an array. You can see the contents of each row using print_r():

```php
<?php

...

$sql = "SELECT id, title, src
    FROM images
    WHERE gallery=true
    ORDER BY id DESC LIMIT $limit OFFSET $offset";
$results = $pdo -> query($sql);
foreach($results as $row) {
    print_r($row);
}
```

When you do, you'll see each row appear a little like this:

```
Array
(
    [id] => 17
    [0] => 17
    [title] => Saltwater Crocodile
    [1] => Saltwater Crocodile
    [src] => 000017-crocodile.jpg
    [2] => 000017-crocodile.jpg
)
```

For your convenience, and possible confusion, the selected data appears *twice* in the array, first with a string key and next with a numeric key. That's the default behavior. In a small set of data such as this, it doesn't matter, but if you like, you can change what you get in the query() call:

- `$pdo->query($sql, PDO::FETCH_NUM)` fetches only with numeric keys.

- `$pdo->query($sql, PDO::FETCH_ASSOC)` fetches only with associative (string) keys.

- `$pdo->query($sql, PDO::FETCH_BOTH)` fetches both; this is the default.

You don't generally need to make a choice. In this case, we're going to use the associative keys and ignore the rest, but we'll fetch both anyway.

Generating the Gallery Images

The gallery part will simply be a collection of images. In HTML, an image looks like this:

```
<img src="..." alt="..." title="..." width="..." height="...">
```

- The src is the URL of the image file; it's the whole point of the img element.

- The alt is a required text attribute. It's used when the image is not viewable, such as when the file is missing or delayed, or the visitor is visually impaired.

- The title is an optional short description of the image. You'll often see the title pop up when you hover over the image, but it may be used in other ways.

- The width and height are also optional and are used to help the browser plan for placing the image. It can also be used to scale the image.

Later, we'll use the images as links to a larger image. To do that, we need to wrap the image in an anchor:

```
<a href="..."><img src="..." alt="..." title="..." width="..."
height="..."></a>
```

- The href attribute is the URL of the link.

Most of these values will come from the database or the configuration values, so we'll need to fill them in as we iterate through the result set.

To generate the images, we can start by creating a template string to be used in an sprintf() function:

```php
<?php
    ...

    $a = '<a href="%s"><img src="%s" alt="%s" title="%s"
        width="%s" height="%s"></a>';
    foreach($results as $row) {
        print_r($row);
    }
```

Two of the values need adjusting. First, the src needs to refer to the directory where the images are located. In this case, it will be the thumbnails directory:

```
src="/images/thumbnails/%s"
```

Second, the href needs to be modified to a request. We'll go through the details later, but for now we'll add

```
href="?image=%s"
```

The template string is now

```php
<?php
    ...

    $a = '<a href="?image=%s"><img src="/images/thumbnails/%s"
        alt="%s" title="%s" width="%s" height="%s"></a>';
    foreach($results as $row) {
        print_r($row);
    }
```

Now that we have our template, we can build the collection of images. We can do that using an array and sprintf():

```php
<?php
    ...

    $a = '<a href="?image=%s"><img src="/images/thumbnails/%s"
        alt="%s" title="%s" width="%s" height="%s"></a>';

    $images = [];
    foreach($results as $row) {
        $images[] = sprintf($a, ...);
    }
    $images = implode($images);
```

This is the same technique we used to generate the navigation links for the menu in Chapter 2.

We'll need to get the values for the width and height attributes. We have them in the $CONFIG array, but only as a combined string.

In the default-library.php file, there's a simple function, splitSize(), which can be used to extract the width and height values from the string. They will come back in an array which we can destructure into two variables.

You can learn more about how this function works in Appendix D.

We can add that before the foreach:

```php
<?php
    ...

    $a = '<a href="?image=%s"><img src="/images/thumbnails/%s"
        alt="%s" title="%s" width="%s" height="%s"></a>';

    $images = [];
    [$width, $height]
        = splitSize($CONFIG['images']['thumbnail-size']);
```

```
foreach($results as $row) {
    $images[] = sprintf($a, ...);
}
$images = implode($images);
```

For the sprintf() function, we'll fill it in with each row:

```
<?php
    ...

$images = [];
[$width, $height]
    = splitSize($CONFIG['images']['thumbnail-size']);
foreach($results as $row) {
    $images[] = sprintf($a, $row['id'], $row['src'],
        $row['title'], $row['title'], $width, $height);
}
$images = implode($images);
```

Remember each row is an array of data. Here, we're using the associative keys to reference the relevant columns:

- The ?image= reference will get the id of the image we want to select.

- The src is a reference to the file name of the image. We've already hard-coded the folder.

- We're using the title from the database for both the alt and title attributes. In reality, they're not necessarily the same, but we're taking the easy way here.

- The width and height are from the split configuration size value.

251

If you load the page now, you'll see three images. You can change the page number ($page) to see another three. Don't go too far, of course. If you select the last page of images, you may get fewer than three.

You can also experiment with changing the page size value.

Selecting the Page

In the next section, we'll work on a navigation block. For now, we'll see how to manually select a particular page number.

You can send data to the server with a form, but that's a little too heavy-handed for a simple task like this. You can also send data via **query string**. A query string is additional information on the URL. There are two ways to generate a query string:

- A form using the GET method puts the data on a query string. This is often used for search forms, where you can bookmark the result page.

- You can simply write the query string directly on the URL after a question mark (?).

We'll use the second method for our page number.

You can write a query string on a complete URL this way:

```
http://australia.example.com/gallery.php?page=2
```

At the server end, the query string will be in the $_GET superglobal array:

```
$_GET['page']
```

We can start by adding this to our code, replacing the hard-coded 1:

```php
<?php
    ...

    $images = $paging = $displaying = '';
    $title = $image = $description = '';

    $page = $_GET['page'];

    $limit = $CONFIG['gallery']['page-size'];
    $offset = ($page - 1) * $limit;
```

Now, *many* things can go wrong at this point. First, the page number may be missing, as it will be when you first select the gallery page. You can handle this with the following expression:

```php
<?php
    ...
    $page = $_GET['page'] ?? 1;
```

The ?? operator is called a **null coalescing** operator, and it can be used to replace a null or missing value with an alternative.

The second problem is that the value may not be a number, but a string. We can fix that with the intval() function:

```php
<?php
    ...
    $page = intval($_GET['page'] ?? 1);
```

The intval() function will attempt to interpret the input as an integer. If it's already a number, there's not much to do, except that will truncate a decimal if it exists. If it's a string, it will start from the beginning and interpret digits as far as it can. If the string doesn't start with digits, the result will be 0.

The next problem is that we don't have a page zero. We'll have to change that to a one:

```php
<?php
    ...
    $page = intval($_GET['page'] ?? 1) ?: 1;
```

The `?:` operator is called a short ternary operator (a.k.a. "elvis" operator, if you twist your head to the side). We've already seen the full ternary or conditional operator before, where you choose between two values. The short ternary operator selects the second value if the first value is falsy, like a zero.

Note the subtle difference between the two operators. The `??` operator is an alternative for a `null` or missing value. The `?:` is an alternative for a falsy value. The `null` qualifies for both, but missing values don't work with the second operator, and zero values don't work with the first.

There are a few more problems, which we'll deal with in a moment, but you can now try this with various values for the page query string. You'll notice the following:

- Values with pure strings will give you page 1.

- Values which start with digits will give you a numbered page.

- Numbers which are too high will give you nothing.

- Negative numbers will give you an error.

At least we'll always get a number, even if it's out of range. We'll now look at squeezing the number between the first and last pages.

Negative numbers are easy enough to handle:

```php
$page = intval($_GET['page'] ?? 1) ?: 1;
if($page < 1) $page = 1;
```

A negative number is, of course, less than zero, but even page zero is no good for us. If the page is less than one, we'll set it to one.

As for the maximum page, well, that depends on the number of images and could easily change for next time. For that, we'll need to fetch the number of images first.

To get the number of rows in a table, you use a statement like

```
SELECT count(*) FROM images WHERE gallery=true;
```

The expression count(*) counts rows in a table. The result will be a virtual table with one row and one column:

count(*)
19

There's no user input for this one, so we can use the query() method and fetchColumn() to get the result:

```
$sql = 'SELECT count(*) FROM images WHERE gallery=true';
$result = $pdo -> query($sql);
$imageCount = $result -> fetchColumn();
```

The fetchColumn() would fetch the default first column (column 0) from the first row.

Of course, the query is so simple, we don't need the separate $sql variable:

```
$result = $pdo -> query('SELECT count(*) FROM images WHERE
gallery=true');
$imageCount = $result -> fetchColumn();
```

And, since we're reading the result immediately, we don't need
$result either:

```
$imageCount = $pdo -> query('SELECT count(*) FROM images
    WHERE gallery=true') -> fetchColumn();
```

We can now add this to the code:

```
<?php

    ...

    $limit = $CONFIG['gallery']['page-size'];
    $offset = ($page - 1) * $limit;

    $imageCount = $pdo -> query('SELECT count(*) FROM images
        WHERE gallery=true') -> fetchColumn();
```

You can, of course, use any variation of this statement that you prefer.

Having got the number of images, we now need the number of pages.
That will depend on the page size. You'll nearly get the right result if you
divide the two:

```
$pages = $imageCount / $limit;
```

The problem is when the number of images isn't exactly divisible—you
can't get part of a page. The simplest method is to round the result *up*:

```
$pages = ceil($imageCount / $limit);
```

The ceil() function rounds up a fractional result to the next integer.
PHP also has a floor() function which rounds down.

We now have the number of pages:

```
<?php

    ...

    $limit = $CONFIG['gallery']['page-size'];
    $offset = ($page - 1) * $limit;
```

```
$imageCount = $pdo -> query('SELECT count(*) FROM images
    WHERE gallery=true') -> fetchColumn();
$pages = ceil($imageCount / $limit);
```

Now we can use this information to squeeze the page number between the limits:

```
if($page < 1) $page = 1;
if($page > $pages) $page = $pages;
```

PHP also has two functions which do the same job as before:

```
$page = max(1, $page);          //  $page is at least 1
$page = min($page, $pages);     //  $page is up to $pages
```

The max() function returns the larger of the two, while the min() function returns the lesser.

If you're game enough, you can combine them:

```
$page = min(max(1, $page), $pages);
//  or
$page = max(1, min($page, $pages));
```

We can now finish the squeezing-in code:

```
<?php
    ...

    $imageCount = $pdo -> query('SELECT count(*) FROM images
        WHERE gallery=true') -> fetchColumn();
    $pages = ceil($imageCount / $limit);

    $page = max(1, $page);          //  $page is at least 1
    $page = min($page, $pages);     //  $page is up to $pages
```

Note that we no longer need the if($page < 1) $page = 1; statement we had earlier.

While we're here, there's a paragraph at the bottom of the page which tells us which page we're up to:

Page ... of ...

Well, not yet. There is a paragraph with a variable $displaying which will tell us that as soon as we set the value. That's easily done using a double-quoted string and string interpolation:

```php
<?php

    ...

    $page = max(1, $page);        //  $page is at least 1
    $page = min($page, $pages);   //  $page is up to $pages

    $displaying = "Page $page of $pages";
```

This will work, but it's hardly convenient for the visitor to have to type in the page number. We'll now work on a navigation block.

The Navigation Block

For our navigation block, we'll have four links:

First Page • Previous Page • Next Page • Last Page

When we've finished, each of these links will have a URL of ?page=something, where something is, of course, a page number.

Although you would expect a full URL, your web browser is going to help us out here. You probably realize that a partial URL is always completed by the browser. For example, if you have a link of the form

```html
<a href="something.php">
```

the browser will finish the job and fill in the URL with that of the current site:

```
<a href="http://australia.example.com/something.php">
```

The same goes for just a query string. If your link says something like

```
<a href="?page=4">
```

the browser will complete it with the current URL as

```
<a href="http://australia.example.com/gallery.php?page=4">
```

You won't see that in the HTML, but you will see that if you hover over such a link. We don't have any of these page links yet, but you'll see something similar if you hover over one of the images inside their links.

That means all we need to worry about is getting the correct page numbers.

There'll be an added complication. If we're on the first page, we really shouldn't have links to the first page (we're already there) or previous page (there isn't one). The same goes for the last page and the links to the last or next page.

Rather than leave out the links altogether, we'll replace these links with a span element, styled to look like a disabled link. This is similar to what we did for the site menu and the current page.

The code we're about to write will be useful in future parts of this project and possibly in other projects, so we'll write it as a function and add it to our library.

In the library.php file, add the following at the bottom:

```
/*  Paging Function
    =================================================
    ================================================= */

function paging(int $page, int $pages) {

}
```

The comment block at the beginning helps to organize the function. The two variables will be for the current page and the total number of pages. They're both expected to be integers.

For convenience, we'll build the four links in an array and implode the result to return it:

```
/*  Paging Function
    ================================================
    ================================================ */

    function paging(int $page, int $pages) {
        $paging = [];

        return implode($paging);
    }
```

For the first link, to Page 1, we already know its destination. The only thing we want worry about is whether we're already on Page 1, in which case the link will be a span. We can do that with a conditional (ternary) operator:

```
function paging(int $page, int $pages) {
    $paging = [];

    $paging[] = $page == 1
        ? '<span>«</span>'
        : '<a href="?page=1"  data-page="1">«</a>';

    return implode($paging);
}
```

The expression can be confusing, so we've spread it out to three lines. Also note that there's an additional attribute data-page with the same value. That's for a special trick which you'll see later.

Note the two different uses of =. A single = is an assignment, and we're assigning the result to the array item. A double == is a test, and we're testing whether $page is equal to 1.

You may be wondering where that « symbol came from. It's called a "left angle quote" and is commonly used for this purpose. To get these special symbols, you can enter the following:

Character	Name	HTML Entity	Macintosh[1]	Windows[2]
«	Left Single Angle Quote	&laquo;	opt-\	alt-0171
‹	Left Angle Quote	&lsaquo	shift-opt-3	alt-0139
›	Right Angle Quote	&rsaquo	shift-opt-4	alt-0155
»	Right Single Angle Quote	&raquo;	shift-opt-\	alt-0187

You don't normally need the HTML entities anymore, since modern web pages should be using UTF, but some developers prefer them. You may also need them on Windows.

The second link, for the previous page, will be similar, but the link can't be hard-coded. We'll need to calculate that and put it inside the string. We can do that with sprintf():

```
function paging(int $page, int $pages) {
    $paging = [];

    $paging[] = $page == 1
        ? '<span>«</span>'
        : '<a href="?page=1" data-page="1">«</a>';
```

---

[1] Macintosh: Hold down the option key or shift-option while pressing the other key.

[2] Windows: Hold down the alt key while typing the four digits *on the numeric keypad* and then release the alt key. If you don't have a numeric keypad, then you're out of luck and you'll either have to copy and paste the character from somewhere or use the HTML entity.

```
    $paging[] = $page == 1
        ? '<span>‹</span>'
        : sprintf('<a href="?page=%s" data-page="%s">‹</a>',
            $page - 1, $page - 1);

    return implode($paging);
}
```

Again, the link will be a span if we're on the first page. If we're not, the link should be to $page - 1, which we've dropped in to the %s placeholder.

Don't forget to change the text of the second span and link to ‹.

For the next two links, we need to test whether we're on the last page with $page == $pages:

```
function paging(int $page, int $pages) {
    $paging = [];

    $paging[] = $page == 1
        ? '<span>«</span>'
        : '<a href="?page=1" data-page="1">«</a>';
    $paging[] = $page == 1
        ? '<span>‹</span>'
        : sprintf('<a href="?page=%s" data-page="%s">‹</a>',
            $page - 1, $page - 1);

    $paging[] = $page == $pages
        ? '<span>›</span>'
        : sprintf('<a href="?page=%s" data-page="%s">›</a>'
            $page + 1, $page + 1);
    $paging[] = $page == $pages
        ? '<span>»</span>'
        : sprintf('<a href="?page=%s" data-page="%s">»</a>',
            $pages, $pages);
```

```
    return implode($paging);
}
```

Here, the next page is $page + 1 and the last page is $pages.

Again, don't forget to use the › and » characters.

Once we've saved the function, we can add the following to the end of our gallery.code.php file:

```
<?php

    ...

    $paging = paging($page, $pages);
```

The gallery page already has a place for the $paging variable:

```
<p id="paging"><?= $paging; ?></p>
```

If you reload the page, you should now see a navigation block at the bottom, making it much easier to move between pages.

If you hover over one of the links, you'll see the link appear as a page number. That's a bit of CSS magic, which uses the data-page attribute as the content of the link. You'll see how it's done in Appendix B.

Remembering the Page

If you've been flicking through the image gallery and have reason to leave it, it would be convenient to come back to the same page later. Since the page number appears on the URL, you can always bookmark it, but you don't need to take it so seriously. You can always save the current page as a cookie.

A cookie is a small item of data saved on the browser. It's normally generated on the server and sent back to the browser in the headers together with the current page content.

Writing a cookie is one of those cases where you'll be writing to the header indirectly, so you'll need to make sure that you haven't written anything to the body before. This is one reason why it's always a good idea to put all of your PHP processing at the beginning before you get to the HTML output.

To write a cookie, you use the setcookie() function:

```
setcookie(name, value, expiry)
```

At the very least, you'll need the cookie name and its value. The cookie name can be anything you like; we'll call it gallery-page. The value will be the currently selected page.

All cookies must be allowed to expire. If you don't set an expiry time, the cookie will expire when the page is closed. Here, we'll set the expiry to, say, one hour. Of course, one hour is much too short for this sort of thing, but you'll easily be able to test whether it's working. Later, you can set it to a much longer time.

The expiry time needs to be in a special format, but PHP handles that automatically. All you need to do is give the function the time in PHP format.

In PHP, the current time (and date) can be obtained with the time() function. In fact, it will be a so-called Unix time stamp, which is the number of seconds since the beginning of time, which, apparently, is January 1, 1970.

If you want to set the cookie for a future time, you can add a number of seconds. For example, to set the cookie for seven days, you can use

```
time() + 7 * 24 * 60 * 60
```

Of course, you could have added 86400 in this case, but using the multiplication makes it easier to see what's going on.

An alternative is to use PHP's strtotime() function. This very clever function will take a string and try its best to interpret it as a date and time. You can also use expressions like 'Next Wednesday'. You can even use expressions such as '+ 1 week'.

We'll use that to set the cookie for the page number:

```php
<?php

    ...

    $page = max(1, $page);        //  $page is at least 1
    $page = min($page, $pages);  //  $page is up to $pages
    setcookie('gallery-page', $page, strtotime('+ 1 hour'));

    $displaying = "Page $page of $pages";
```

This sets a use-by date of only one hour. That's too short in real life, but just fine for testing.

Note that once again, the time used is that on the server, which is all that PHP knows about. It's subject to the time zone of the server and may be different to that on the browser machine. A short expiry date will highlight the problem, and you might find yourself even setting the expiry time to the past on the browser.

For development purposes, your server and browser are on the same machine, so it won't be a problem right now.

Setting the cookie isn't enough. We need to read the cookie. In the end, the page number will be one of three possible values:

1. The page number from the query string

2. The cookie value

3. The default, which is 1

... *in that order.* You want the query string to take precedence over the cookie and the cookie to take precedence over the default.

We can do that with the following expression:

```php
intval($_GET['page'] ?? $_COOKIE['gallery-page'] ?? 1) ?: 1;
```

Here, we use the null coalescing operator twice: once for a missing page number and again for a missing cookie.

We can now add that to our code:

```php
<?php

    ...

    $images = $paging = $displaying = '';
    $title = $image = $description = '';

    $page = intval($_GET['page'] ?? $_COOKIE['gallery-page'] ?? 1)
        ?: 1;
```

It's important to get the order right; otherwise, we'll be stuck on a cookie value or page 1.

Cookies have had some bad publicity. It's not the cookie's fault—it's all those first- and third-party cookies which are intent on spying on you and tracking you.

The situation has got so bad that some jurisdictions, such as the EU, require some sort of consent on the part of the second party (the visitor) regarding cookies.

In this case, you'll find that this sort of cookie is OK, as it's simply remembering what the visitor has requested, without actually tracking the user.

If you open the developer tools in your browser, you should be able to see the cookie and its current value.

Displaying a Larger Image

On the right-hand side of the page is a space for a larger image. We're going to populate it with one of the following:

- An image the visitor has selected from the gallery on the left.

- If the visitor hasn't selected an image, then it will be one of the images in the gallery. Which one is something we'll look at.

There are three variables which comprise the larger image:

- $title is the stored title of the image. We'll use that as a heading.

- $image is the actual image element. We'll build that up from the database data.

- $description also comes from the database. We'll need to adapt it through the pilcrow2p() function to convert the pilcrows to HTML paragraphs.

First, however, we'll need to fetch an image.

Fetching a Miscellaneous Single Image

Even though we've fetched some image data for the gallery on the left, we have yet to fetch the data for the larger image.

We could, in principle, use data from the image data we've already fetched for the gallery. However, we'll make this a separate fetch to allow us to use an image not on the current page.

Remember, we already have a link to a larger image with the query string ?image=.... We'll process that in a similar way to processing the page number. First, however, we'll deal with no selection.

Unlike the gallery page number, we won't default to image number 1. Instead, we'll default to one of the other images. We basically have a number of choices:

- The first image in the gallery

- The last image in the gallery

- A random image in the gallery

- The first, last, or random image from the whole collection

To get one of the images in the gallery, we need to keep track of the image IDs for the current page. We can build a collection of IDs in an array as we're iterating through the rows.

We can modify the iteration to include an array for IDs:

```
$images = [];
$ids = [];
[$width, $height] = ... ;
foreach($results as $row) {
    $images[] = sprintf($a, $row['id'], $row['src'],
    $row['title'],
        $row['title'], 240, 180);
    $ids[] = $row['id'];
}
```

This creates an empty array for $ids and then adds each fetched ID to the array. There are three functions to choose one of these IDs:

- The array_shift() function will fetch the *first* item. It treats the array as a **queue**—a First In First Out (FIFO) data collection.

- The array_pop() function will fetch the *last* item. It treats the array as a **stack**: a Last In First Out (LIFO) data collection.

- The array_rand() function will fetch a random *key* from the array. Unfortunately, it's not a random *item*, so we'll need to use the random key to get a random item.

You can use one of the preceding functions to fetch a random ID:

```
$imageid = array_shift($ids);        // First id
$imageid = array_pop($ids);          // Last id
$imageid = $ids[array_rand($ids)];   // Random id
```

In the last case, you use array_rand() to fetch the random key and then use the result as an index into the $ids array.

At the end of your code, you can add the following:

```
...

$paging = paging($page, $pages);

// $imageid = array_shift($ids);        // First id
// $imageid = array_pop($ids);          // Last id
$imageid = $ids[array_rand($ids)];   // Random id
```

In this case, the first two statements are commented out, because you'll only need one of the statements. Of course, you can decide you don't want a random image and choose one of the others instead. You can also decide to delete the other statements.

So far, we've only got an id. What we really need is the image data. We can get this from the database directly:

```
<?php
    ...

    $imageid = ... ;
```

```
$sql = "SELECT title, src, description FROM images
    WHERE id=$imageid";
$row = $pdo -> query($sql) -> fetch();
```

The $imageid variable is purely an integer, so it's safe to interpolate it into the SQL string.

Remember, the result from the query() method is a PDOStatement, from which the fetch() method will give us the first (and only) row.

Remember also that the row is an array with everything twice. We used the associative keys before, but this time it's easier to use the numeric keys. That allows us to use simple array destructuring to read the results into variables:

```
[$title, $src, $description] = $row;
```

In fact, we can dispense with the $row variable altogether:

```
<?php
    ...

    $imageid = ... ;
    $sql = "SELECT title, src, description FROM images
        WHERE id=$imageid";
    [$title, $src, $description] = $pdo -> query($sql) ->
    fetch();
```

The ability to destructure the results this way is one reason why the row also has numeric keys. In this format, only numerically keyed values, starting with 0, are assigned. You can destructure with associative keys, but it's not so neat:

```
['title' => $title, 'src' => $src, 'description' =>
$description] = $row;
```

The data isn't ready to go yet. Well, the $title is, since it's going straight into an h3 element, but the $description variable needs a little fixing, and we need to generate an image variable.

For the $description, we just need to change the pilcrows to HTML paragraphs. We can do that with the pilcrow2p() function:

```php
<?php

    ...

    $imageid = ... ;
    $sql = "SELECT title, src, description FROM images
        WHERE id=$imageid";
    [$title, $src, $description] = $pdo -> query($sql) ->
    fetch();

    $description = pilcrow2p($description);
```

For the image, we can use a similar technique as for the gallery and use the sprintf() function to fill in a template string. We'll do it in two steps for readability.

First, we'll create the template string:

```php
<?php

    ...

    $imageid = ... ;
    $sql = "SELECT title, src, description FROM images
        WHERE id=$imageid";
    [$title, $src, $description] = $pdo -> query($sql) ->
    fetch();

    $description = pilcrow2p($description);
    $image = '<img src="/images/display/%s" alt="%s" title="%s"
        width="%s" height="%s">';
```

We've used the $image variable here because that's the variable which will be displayed on the page.

Next, we use sprintf() to fill in the values:

```php
<?php
    ...

    $imageid = ... ;
    $sql = "SELECT title, src, description FROM images
        WHERE id=$imageid";
    [$title, $src, $description] = $pdo -> query($sql) ->
    fetch();

    $description = pilcrow2p($description);
    [$width, $height]
        = splitSize($CONFIG['images']['display-size']);
    $image = '<img src="/images/display/%s" alt="%s" title="%s"
        width="%s" height="%s">';
    $image = sprintf($image, $src, $title, $title, $width,
    $height);
```

Again, we've derived the $width and $height variables from the configuration value, this time for the display version.

You can now reload the page and see a larger image. We haven't yet enabled selecting the particular image, but we'll do that in a moment.

Selecting a Random Row from the Database

If you choose to default to a random image from the database, rather than a random image on the page, we'll need to take a different approach. The simplest method is to let the database do the randomizing and fetch the ID of the first row of the result.

You can do this with

```
SELECT id FROM images WHERE gallery=true ORDER BY rand();
```

The rand() function in MySQL generates a random number. The table is thus sorted in random order. This will, of course, return the whole table, but we only want the first row of that.

In PHP, we can use fetchColumn() to get the only column from the first row. Remember, repeated calls to fetchColumn() would give us subsequent rows, but we won't do that.

We can now add the following:

```
<?php
    ...

    $imageid = $pdo -> query('SELECT id FROM images
        WHERE gallery=true ORDER BY rand()') -> fetchColumn();
    $sql = "SELECT title, src, description FROM images
        WHERE id=$imageid";
    [$title, $src, $description] = $pdo -> query($sql) ->
    fetch();

    $description = pilcrow2p($description);
    [$width, $height]
        = splitSize($CONFIG['images']['thumbnail-size']);
    $image = '<img src="/images/display/%s" alt="%s" title="%s"
        width="%s" height="%s">';
    $image = sprintf($image, $src, $title, $title, 480, 360);
```

We can test this now. Of course, what we really want is to allow the visitor to select an image from the gallery.

Fetching a Selected Image

To get the visitor's image selection, we'll use the same method as we did for the page number. However, instead of defaulting to 1 as we did for the page, we'll default to 0:

```php
<?php
    ...

    $paging = paging($page, $pages);

    $imageid = intval($_GET['image'] ?? $_COOKIE['gallery-
    image'] ?? 0)
        ?: 0;

    ...

    $imageid = ... ;        // one of the fallback methods

    $sql = "SELECT title, src, description FROM images
    WHERE id=$imageid";
    [$title, $src, $description] = $pdo -> query($sql) ->
    fetch();
```

Put the new statement before the code to fetch a default image.

The reason we'll default to 0 for this is that we'll use that as a test: if the value is 0, then it can't be a valid selection, since the id starts at 1.

There's one more test we need to make to be sure: there's no guarantee that the query string came from one of our links, since you can easily type it yourself. Having gone through the intval() function, it's guaranteed to be a number, so it's harmless enough, but we still need to check whether it's a valid image ID.

Suppose we try the following with a valid ID, such as 3:

```
SELECT id FROM images WHERE gallery=true AND id=3;
```

Of course, we'll get 3.

Note that we have two conditions here, gallery=true and id=3, combined with the AND operator, which means that both conditions must be satisfied. In theory, the ID might not be for one of the gallery images.

In PHP, you could use

```
$imageid = 3;
$sql = "SELECT id FROM images WHERE gallery=true AND id=$imageid";
$imageid = $pdo -> query($sql) -> fetchColumn();
```

You'd still get the same result. You wouldn't normally select for something you already know. However, if we try this with an invalid ID, such as a negative number:

```
$imageid = -3;
$sql = "SELECT id FROM images WHERE gallery=true AND
id=$imageid";
$imageid = $pdo -> query($sql) -> fetchColumn();
```

the result would be null. You can then test the result before deciding to fall back on a default:

```
$imageid = intval($_GET['image'] ?? $_COOKIE['gallery-
image'] ?? 0)
    ?: 0;
$sql = "SELECT id FROM images WHERE gallery=true AND
id=$imageid";
$imageid = $pdo -> query($sql) -> fetchColumn();

if(!$imageid) {
    $imageid = ... ;         // one of the fallback methods
}

$sql = "SELECT title, src, description FROM images
    WHERE id=$imageid";
[$title, $src, $description] = $pdo -> query($sql) -> fetch();
```

Remember the if() will test for true or something truthy; if(!) will test for false or something falsy. In this case, null or 0 are both falsy, so the fallback image ID will be used.

The only other thing you might want to do to complete the page involves the cookie. In the code to fetch the image ID, you'll notice that we examined the cookie gallery-image in the same way we checked the page number before.

You can set the cookie the same way. It would need to be set after you've worked out a valid image ID:

```
$imageid = intval($_GET['image'] ?? $_COOKIE['gallery-
image'] ?? 0)
    ?: 0;
$sql = "SELECT id FROM images WHERE gallery=true AND
id=$imageid";
$imageid = $pdo -> query($sql) -> fetchColumn();

if(!$imageid) {
    $imageid = ... ;        //  one of the fallback methods
}

//  setcookie('gallery-image', $imageid, strftime('+ 1
hour'));

$sql = "SELECT title, src, description FROM images
    WHERE id=$imageid";
[$title, $src, $description] = $pdo -> query($sql) ->
fetch();
```

Note, however, that this has been commented out. There's nothing wrong with the idea *per se*, but remember that the cookie takes precedence over a missing image ID; that is, it takes precedence over whatever we've decided on a fallback image. That means the first or last image won't ever be used once a cookie has been set. Of course, that's up to you.

Displaying a Random Image on Other Pages

If you go back to the home page, you'll notice that there's a space on the right for an image. The same appears on a few other pages, such as the contact page.

The space is in a separate section called an **aside**, which is what HTML5 calls a section that's meant to be additional to the main content.

When we've finished, we'll see a random image similar to Figure 8-2.

Figure 8-2. *The Aside with a Random Image*

We've already got the aside itself in a separate included file. This was cut from the original index.php file and still has the placeholders for the data:

```
<aside id="photo">
    [image]
    <h2>[title]</h2>
    <div>
        [description]
    </div>
</aside>
```

Now would be a good time to change those placeholders to PHP output blocks:

```
<aside id="photo">
    <?= $image ?>
    <h2><?= $title ?></h2>
    <div>
        <?= $description ?>
    </div>
</aside>
```

We'll now write the code to populate the aside with a random image.

First, create a new file in the includes directory called aside.code.php and include it in the index.php file:

```
<?php require_once 'includes/aside.code.php'; ?>
<?php
    //  Page Title and Heading
        $pagetitle = 'Home';
        $pageheading = 'Australia Down Under';

    require_once 'includes/head.inc.php';
?>
```

You'll have to do that with the contact page as well. That can go before the code for the contact form:

```php
<?php require_once 'includes/aside.code.php'; ?>
<?php require_once 'includes/contact.code.php'; ?>
<?php
    // Page Title and Heading

        ...
?>
```

There will be one or two other pages to fix, but this will do for now.

In the aside.code.php script, create the PHP block (without closing it) and include the database and library files, as well as a configuration setting for the image we'll be displaying:

```php
<?php
    $root = str_replace($_SERVER['SCRIPT_NAME'], '',
        $_SERVER['SCRIPT_FILENAME']);

    $pdo = require_once "$root/includes/db.php";
    require_once "$root/includes/default-library.php";
    require_once "$root/includes/library.php";

    $CONFIG['images']['thumbnail-size'] = '240 x 180';
```

We have already written the code to fetch a random ID from the database. We'll adapt that to fetch a random row:

```php
<?php
    ...

    $CONFIG['images']['thumbnail-size'] = '240 x 180';

    $sql = 'SELECT title, src, description FROM images
        WHERE gallery=true ORDER BY rand()';
```

We've put the SQL into a separate variable since it's a little longer than before. We've also changed it to select the title, src, and description rather than just the id.

We can now use the fetch() method to fetch the entire row instead of just one column. As before, this gives us an array of results, and we can destructure the numerically keyed values into the separate variables:

```php
<?php
    ...

    $sql = 'SELECT title, src, description FROM images
        WHERE gallery=true ORDER BY rand()';
    [$title, $src, $description] = $pdo -> query($sql) ->
    fetch();
```

We can now finish fixing the $description variable and setting the $image variable:

```php
<?php
    ...

    $sql = 'SELECT title, src, description FROM images
        WHERE gallery=true ORDER BY rand()';
    [$title, $src, $description] = $pdo -> query($sql) ->
    fetch();

    $description = pilcrow2p($description);
    $image = '<img src="/images/thumbnails/%s" alt="%s"
    title="%s"
        width="%s" height="%s">';
    [$width, $height]
        = splitSize($CONFIG['images']['thumbnail-size']);
    $image = sprintf($image, $src, $title, $title, $width,
    $height);
```

You'll notice that the image is coming from the thumbnails directory. We've also set the width and height values.

You can now reload index.php as many times as you like and see the random image, the same with the contact page. Remember that a random image may appear twice in a row.

Summary

In this chapter, we learned more about accessing the database with PHP. This was in the process of fetching data to generate a gallery of images.

Fetching data from a database table involves the SQL SELECT statement:

```
SELECT ...
FROM ...
WHERE ...
ORDER BY ... LIMIT ... OFFSET ...;
```

This statement defines the table (FROM ...) and the columns (SELECT ...). We can qualify which rows we want (WHERE ...), sort the results (ORDER BY ...), and limit the number of rows (LIMIT ... OFFSET ...).

We use the query() method in the PDO object to run the query and get a PDOStatement as the result. From there, we can use the fetch() method to fetch one row at a time as a mixed array of numeric and associative keys. We can also iterate through the PDOStatement result using foreach().

For each row, we can generate HTML elements by embedding the data into HTML strings. This is readily done using the sprintf() function.

The LIMIT and OFFSET values determine which section of the table we're extracting. Using the incoming page value, we can adjust these values to page through the collection.

A query string is additional data appended to the query and can be used to request something at the server. The query string can be added by the visitor, embedded in a URL, or generated from a GET form.

Query strings can be read in PHP from the $_GET array. Because this data comes from the outside, you would need to preprocess it before using it in your SQL. The intval() function forces the value into an integer, which is harmless in SQL.

The incoming query may be missing or invalid. We can use the null coalescing operator (??) to substitute for a missing value and the short ternary operator ?: to substitute for a zero or falsy value.

For the visitor's convenience, we can create a navigation block consisting of a number of links to other pages. These links are in the form of query strings and can be generated from the current page number. We can also modify the block if the current page happens to be the first or last of the catalogue.

We can use cookies to save a current (valid) page number using the setcookie() function and fetch from existing cookies using the $_COOKIE array.

The images in the gallery section are wrapped in anchors with query strings; these have an image ID to view a larger version of the image, complete with description.

Using similar logic to getting a page number, we can retrieve the selected image ID, if any. If there isn't an image ID, we can substitute one from the other images on the page or a random image from the database. From there, we can generate the HTML to display the larger image and description.

Using the same ideas, we can also display a random image in the aside section on other pages.

Coming Up

In the following chapters, we're going to use code similar to the gallery code to generate lists of database data to be edited. Once we select one of the images, we'll be able to implement a data management system. This includes

- Reading existing data

- Deleting data

- Editing existing data

And, of course, we've already seen how to add new data, which we'll incorporate in the above.

In the next chapter, we'll work on two pages: one to list the images and another to maintain them.

CHAPTER 9

Managing Data

When it comes to working with data, there are four main operations. In SQL, these operations are

- INSERT: Add data to a database table.
- SELECT: Read data from one or more tables.
- UPDATE: Change existing data.
- DELETE: Delete one or more rows from a table.

When we added the image data, we used the INSERT statement. When we created the image gallery, it was the SELECT statement.

In this chapter, we will look at maintaining the image data. This will involve all of the major SQL statements, including UPDATE and DELETE.

As with inserting and selecting the data, the process will be to use PHP to generate and populate the SQL statements. When we have finished, we will have the means to fully maintain a database table.

We'll see that maintaining the data will consist of two parts: a table of existing data and a form to manipulate individual data. We'll see how to generate the table and how to adapt the form to the particular task.

There will be a lot of activity between the tasks, and we'll learn more about processing form submission. This will include changing the content of pages, such as adding or removing page elements and changing their behavior.

© Mark Simon 2024
M. Simon, *An Introduction to PHP*, https://doi.org/10.1007/979-8-8688-0177-8_9

We'll learn about the UPDATE and DELETE statements in particular and how they manipulate existing data. We'll also learn more about using PDO to work with the database, working with individual rows, and reading and changing database table rows.

Maintaining the database is only a part of managing the image collection, and we'll learn more about uploading and deleting files.

We'll know something about submitted text and file data, but we'll also learn a little about using checkboxes in PHP. We will add a checkbox and modify the code to work with the new element.

There is a lot going on here, but we'll find that much of the hard work has already been done. In fact, you'll find that copy and paste is definitely your friend. In this chapter, we'll be able to integrate much of what we have already learned so far.

The Image Pages

We're going to do the maintenance work in two stages:

1. Select one of the images to edit.

2. Make changes to the image data.

That's the general idea. To do this, we'll need two pages.

The first page will be a list of existing images, such as in Figure 9-1.

Figure 9-1. *The List of Images*

Some of the elements will be familiar, such as the navigation block at the bottom. In fact, this is essentially a modified version of the gallery page, and the code for this page will be similar.

Those buttons on the right side of the table will be used to select one of the images for editing or deleting. In fact, those buttons will all take us to the second page.

There's also a button Add New Image to add a new image. It will also take us to the second page.

The second page is basically a form and looks something like Figure 9-2.

Figure 9-2. *Editing an Image*

The second page will actually appear differently and do different jobs, depending on which button you used in the first page:

- If you select Add New Image, the second page will be empty. In fact, it will be essentially the page you've already used to upload a new image in Chapter 4.

- If you select one of the Edit or Remove buttons, the second page will be populated with existing data. You can then finish the job by selecting the submit button or cancelling this particular edit.

The second page will be the same page as the page to upload images, but we'll modify it to do the different jobs.

All of the activity will be triggered by forms and submit buttons:

- The Image List page will have a from with submit buttons to add a new image, edit an exiting image, or delete an image.

  These buttons won't do anything to the database yet. Instead, they will prepare the form in the Edit Image page.

- The Edit Image page will have a submit button to insert, update, or delete an image and its data.

There's also a cancel button. It's not really a button—it's a link back to the Image List page, styled to look like a button. If you suddenly go off to another page, the changes will be lost, which is what you want when you cancel.

The relationship between the two pages is something like Figure 9-3.

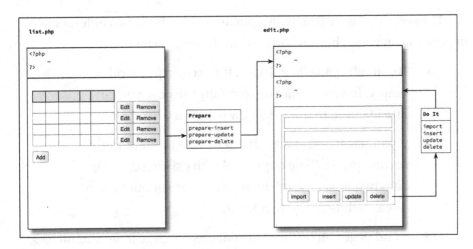

Figure 9-3. *The List and Edit Pages*

We'll refer to the particular activity as an **event**—that's not meant to be a technical term, but just a convenient way of describing what we're doing. The name of the event will simply be the name of the submit button.

The Image List page will trigger one of three events:

- **prepare-insert**: Prepare the form to insert a new image.

- **prepare-update**: Prepare the form to update an existing image.

- **prepare-delete**: Prepare the form to delete an existing image.

You'll see that all three events prepare the form. On the Edit Image page, we'll have the form with the following events:

- **insert**: Insert the new data into the database.

- **update**: Update the existing data in the database.

- **delete**: Delete the current data from the database.

We've already written the code for the **insert** event. There's also an **import** event which we've also already written.

Note that the names of the submit buttons, and their events, can be anything we like. The names of the last three, from the form, are the same as the SQL statement we'll be running. That's just to make our plan more obvious.

The names of the first three have the `prepare` prepended, again, to make the intention obvious.

To get ready for the code, we'll make one small but significant change: change the name of the `uploadimage.php` page to `editimage.php`.

The Image List Page

We'll begin by working on the list page, `imagelist.php`. Much of this will be similar to the work we did for the gallery page.

First, create a new file in the `includes` directory called `imagelist.code.php`.

In the body of the `imagelist.php` page are two variables which will need to be initialized in the code:

```php
<?php
    $tbody = $paging = '';
```

The $tbody will be used for our list of images, and the $paging will be for a navigation block, similar to the gallery page.

In the `imagelist.php` page, include a reference to the code at the beginning:

```php
<?php require_once 'includes/imagelist.code.php'; ?>
<?php
    ...
?>
```

Preparatory Code for the Image List

We've done most of this before for the gallery page. You can copy and paste much of the code, but you'll need to make sure to adjust the names and values.

The image list will comprise a table with details and buttons:

- There will be a small copy of the image.

- The details will include the id and the title of the image.

- There will be an Edit and Remove button for each image.

The following code will generate the data for the table.

First, we'll need some configuration values. This will be for the page size and the size of the image:

```php
<?php
    $CONFIG['imagelist']['page-size'] = 6;
    $CONFIG['images']['icon-size'] = '40 x 30';

    $tbody = $paging = '';
```

We've got a larger page size of six images per page. The smaller images will come from the icons directory.

We'll also need to include the database connection and the two library files. For this, we'll also need the $root variable:

```php
<?php
    $root = str_replace($_SERVER['SCRIPT_NAME'], '',
        $_SERVER['SCRIPT_FILENAME']);

    $pdo = require_once "$root/includes/db.php";
    require_once "$root/includes/default-library.php";
    require_once "$root/includes/library.php";
```

```
$CONFIG['imagelist']['page-size'] = 3;
$CONFIG['images']['icon-size'] = '40 x 30';

$tbody = $paging = '';
```

The page number will work as with the gallery, using the query string, cookie, or default first page. We'll also calculate the limit and offset the same way:

```
<?php
    ...

    $tbody = $paging = '';

    $page = intval($_GET['page'] ?? $_COOKIE['imagelist-
    page'] ?? 1)
        ?: 1;

    $limit = $CONFIG['imagelist']['page-size'];
    $offset = ($page - 1) * $limit;
```

The cookie for the page number will be called imagelist-page to distinguish it from the gallery page number. The query string name will still be page, as there's no risk of confusion.

To get the number of pages, we'll use a similar query to the one for the gallery, but not exactly the same:

```
<?php
    ...

    $limit = $CONFIG['gallery']['page-size'];
    $offset = ($page - 1) * $limit;

    $imageCount = $pdo -> query('SELECT count(*) FROM images')
        -> fetchColumn();
    $pages = ceil($imageCount / $limit);
```

This version doesn't filter WHERE gallery=true. In principle, the images might include non-gallery images.

We'll adjust and store the page number:

```php
<?php
    ...
    $imageCount = $pdo -> query('SELECT count(*) FROM images')
        -> fetchColumn();
    $pages = ceil($imageCount / $limit);

    $page = max(1, $page);            //  $page is at least 1
    $page = min($page, $pages);       //  $page is up to $pages
    setcookie('imagelist-page', $page, strtotime('+ 1 hour'));
```

Don't forget to change the cookie name to imagelist-page.

Finally, you can add the paging block:

```php
<?php
    ...
    $page = max(1, $page);            //  $page is at least 1
    $page = min($page, $pages);       //  $page is up to $pages
    setcookie('imagelist-page', $page, strtotime('+ 1 hour'));

    $paging = paging($page, pages);
```

The next task is to generate the data for the image list itself.

Unlike the image gallery, the image list will be presented in a table. In turn, the table will be inside a form. We'll need the form because the table will have a number of buttons to edit the data.

Something About HTML Tables

The list itself will be in the form of a table.

Tables are a two-dimensional structure comprising rows and columns. You can create tables in HTML, of course, but they're very cumbersome. There are many options, and the whole structure is crowded and confusing.

The table begins as an HTML container element:

```
<table>

</table>
```

You might think that tables have rows and columns, but you'd only be half right. In HTML, tables only have rows. These rows are tr ("table row") elements:

```
<table>
    <tr> ... </tr>
    <tr> ... </tr>
    <tr> ... </tr>
    <tr> ... </tr>
</table>
```

The rows, on the other hand, do have columns. Actually, they don't. What they do have are table cells, which *look like* columns. These cells are either td ("table data") or th ("table heading") elements:

```
<table>
    <tr><th>...</th><th>...</th><th>...</th></tr>
    <tr><td>...</td><td>...</td><td>...</td></tr>
    <tr><td>...</td><td>...</td><td>...</td></tr>
    <tr><td>...</td><td>...</td><td>...</td></tr>
</table>
```

A normal cell would be a td element, while a heading cell would be a th element. The th elements don't have to be in the first row or anywhere at all. It's up to the designer to decide where they belong.

The browser takes this data and gives you the *illusion* of a table by adjusting the widths of the table cells so that they all line up. There are no columns in HTML tables, only cells which line up. That explains why you can't select a column of data in a web table simply by dragging over it.

Tables can include another level of structure: the rows can be organized into sections. The sections would be a thead ("table header") section, a tbody ("table body"), and a tfoot section ("table footer"):

```
<table>
    <thead>
        <tr><th>...</th><th>...</th><th>...</th></tr>
    </thead>
    <tbody>
        <tr><td>...</td><td>...</td><td>...</td></tr>
        <tr><td>...</td><td>...</td><td>...</td></tr>
        <tr><td>...</td><td>...</td><td>...</td></tr>
    <tbody>
</table>
```

Such a table would look like Figure 9-4.

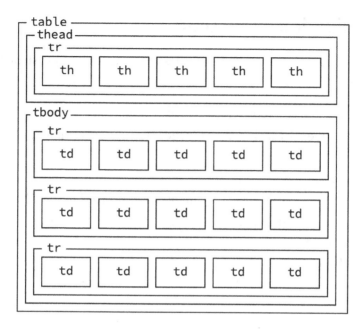

Figure 9-4. *An HTML Table Outline*

You can see we haven't bothered with a tfoot in this example. In fact, the sections are optional, but they do help to organize a table. This is helpful with assistive technology which has to work out what's happening in the table and with CSS which has the arduous task of making the table look presentable.

The default appearance of a table is astoundingly ugly, as you see in Figure 9-5.

Aye	**Bee**	**Sea**
Apple	Banana	Cherry
Accordion	Banjo	Cor Anglais
Another attempt at alliteration	Basically banal	Carefully crafted creations

Figure 9-5. *An Astoundingly Ugly Table*

Thankfully, CSS can do a much better job.

Generating the Table Data

If you look at the imagelist.php page, you'll see the following structure, simplified:

```
<form method="post" action="editimage.php" id="editblog">
    <input type="hidden" name="page" value="<?= $page; ?>">
    <table class="manage">
        <thead>
            <tr><th>ID</th><th> </th><th>Title</th>
                <th> </th><th> </th></tr>
        </thead>
        <tbody>
            <?= $tbody; ?>
        </tbody>
    </table>
</form>

<p id="paging"><?= $paging; ?></p>

<form method="post" action="editimage.php">
    <p><button type="submit" name="prepare-insert">
        Add New Image</button></p>
</form>
```

At the bottom is a separate form with just the one button to add a new image. The button could have gone into the same form as the other, but this way we can separate it visually.

In the main form is the table. The thead section is hard-coded and has the headings. The tbody will be output of the $tbody variable, and it is this data we'll be working on.

The form uses the POST method and sends the data on to the editimage.php page.

In the table, there will be five columns:

id	icon	title	edit button	remove button
…	…	…	…	…

To fetch the data from the form, we'll use something similar to the gallery:

```php
<?php
    ...

$sql = "SELECT id, title, src
    FROM images
    ORDER BY id LIMIT $limit OFFSET $offset";
$results = $pdo -> query($sql);
```

The difference is that we don't filter for gallery only images. Note that we haven't reversed the order either.

As with the gallery, we'll iterate through the results and put the data into an array, which will be imploded afterward:

```php
<?php
    ...

$sql = "SELECT id, title, src
    FROM images
    ORDER BY id DESC LIMIT $limit OFFSET $offset";
$results = $pdo -> query($sql);

$tbody = [];

foreach($results as $row) {

}

$tbody = implode($tbody);
```

This time, the variable is $tbody to reflect how it's going to be used. We'll also use a template string:

```php
<?php
    ...

    $tr = '<tr><td>%s</td><td>%s</td><td>%s</td><td>%s</td>
        <td>%s</td></tr>';

    $tbody = [];

    foreach($results as $row) {

    }

    $tbody = implode($tbody);
```

The template is called $tr because it's for a table row. Inside, there are five td elements, as there are five columns.

As usual, the string doesn't have to wrap around to the next line—it just fits better on this page.

Now things will get a little complicated. We'll use sprintf(), of course, to fill in the placeholders, but the values won't all be simple values. In fact, three of them will also be HTML elements. Just for now, we'll ignore that and fill in with simple values:

```php
<?php
    ...

    $tr = '<tr><td>%s</td><td>%s</td><td>%s</td><td>%s</td>
        <td>%s</td></tr>';

    $tbody = [];

    foreach($results as $row) {
        $tbody[] = sprintf(
            $tr,
```

```php
        $row['id'],          //  id
        $row['src'],         //  img element
        $row['title'],       //  title
        $row['id'],          //  edit button
        $row['id']           //  remove button
    );
}

$tbody = implode($tbody);
```

You can actually test this now, but you won't see the image or the actual buttons—just the raw data.

For the image, we'll need to construct an `img` element. We'll create the image template string:

```php
<?php

    ...

    $tr = '<tr><td>%s</td><td>%s</td><td>%s</td><td>%s</td>
        <td>%s</td></tr>';
    $img = '<a href="/images/display/%s"><img src="/images/
icons/%s"
        alt="%s" title="%s" width="%s" height="%s"></a>';

    $tbody = [];

    ...
```

This is the same as for the gallery, but with two significant changes:

- The surrounding anchor isn't a query string but a reference to another image. We'll discuss that later. For now, we can ignore that.

- The `src` attribute for the image is for the `icons` directory.

We'll also need to extract the width and the height from the
configuration value, using the splitSize() function in the default library:

```php
<?php

    ...

    $tr = '<tr><td>%s</td><td>%s</td><td>%s</td><td>%s</td>
        <td>%s</td></tr>';
    $img = '<a href="/images/display/%s"><img src="/images/
    icons/%s"
        alt="%s" title="%s" width="%s" height="%s"></a>';
    [$width, $height]
        = splitSize($CONFIG['images']['icon-size']);

    $tbody = [];

    ...
```

We can now use this for the image element in the row:

```php
<?php

    ...

    foreach($results as $row) {
        $tbody[] = sprintf(
            $tr,
            $row['id'],          // id
            sprintf(             // img element
                $img,
                $row['src'], $row['src'],
                $row['title'], $row['title'],
                $width, $height
            ),
```

```
        $row['title'],      //  title
        $row['id'],         //  edit button
        $row['id']          //  remove button
    );
}

$tbody = implode($tbody);
```

Note that we've used $row['src'] for both the anchor and the image and $row['title'] for both the alt and title attributes.

You can test this now, and you should see the icon images.

As for the buttons, they'll take the following form:

```
<button name="..." value="..."> ... </button>
```

We haven't worried about the value attribute for the other buttons before, but here we'll use it to identify which image we're editing. As for the name attribute, it will be either prepare-update or prepare-delete. It's OK to have multiple buttons with the same name—it's the value which will make the difference.

We can set up the template strings:

```php
<?php
    ...

    $tr = '<tr><td>%s</td><td>%s</td><td>%s</td><td>%s</td>
        <td>%s</td></tr>';
    $img = '<a href="/images/display/%s"><img src="/images/
    icons/%s"
        alt="%s" title="%s" width="%s" height="%s"></a>';
    [$width, $height]
        = splitSize($CONFIG['images']['icon-size']);
    $editButton = '<button name="prepare-update"
        value="%s">Edit</button>';
```

```
$removeButton = '<button name="prepare-delete"
    value="%s">Remove</button>';

$tbody = [];
...
```

There's only one value to replace, so the sprintf() will be simple. We can fill in the data as follows:

```
<?php

...

foreach($results as $row) {
    $tbody[] = sprintf(
        $tr,
        $row['id'],              // id
        sprintf(                 // img element
            $img,
            $row['src'], $row['src'],
            $row['title'], $row['title'],
            $width, $height
        ),
        $row['title'],       // title
        sprintf($editButton, $row['id']),   // edit button
        sprintf($removeButton, $row['id'])
        // remove button
    );
}
```

You can test the page now. Both the prepare-update and prepare-delete buttons will take you to the form's destination, which is editimage.php. Remember this is the old uploadimage.php page renamed. If you haven't renamed it yet, this would be a good time to do it.

However, when you do select an edit or remove button, you won't see anything new yet. We'll now work on the image editing page.

The Image Editing Page

When you select an edit or remove button, you will be landed on the editimage.php page, but you'll only see an empty form. There are a few changes we'll need to make first before we get started.

First, on the form itself, there is a hidden form field:

```
<form ... id="editimage-form">
    <input type="hidden" name="id" value="<?= $id ?>">
</form>
```

A hidden field won't appear on the page, but it's not meant to be secret. Anybody can view the page source and see the code. The real purpose is to hold a fixed value to be submitted with the rest of the data.

This one has the id, which is currently set to 0. To test the form, we'll make a small change to this field:

```
<form ... id="editimage-form">
    <input type="text" name="id" value="<?= $id ?>">
</form>
```

The field will now be displayed. This makes no difference to how it will behave, except that you will now be able to see it. You might be tempted to change it, but you should really leave it alone. Later, we'll change it back to hidden.

The code for the image editing page is in the `manage-images.code.php` file. So far, we've used it to process the `insert` and `import` buttons. Now, we'll use it to process a total of seven different buttons:

Button	Page	Process
prepare-insert	imagelist.php	Prepare form for adding a new image
prepare-update	imagelist.php	Prepare form for editing an existing image
prepare-delete	imagelist.php	Prepare form for deleting an existing image
insert	editimage.php	Insert a new image
import	editimage.php	Bulk upload images
update	editimage.php	Change existing image data
delete	editimage.php	Delete an image

There's one more change we'll make. Currently, the $pagetitle and $pageheading variables are both set to Upload Image. That was all right when that's all we did, but we'll now have to make adjustments for the different events.

To begin with, we'll process the three prepare buttons.

The Prepare Events

All of the processing code will be added to the `manage-images.code. php` file.

Three of the buttons we're going to process are to get the `editimage. php` page ready. For adding a new image, we'll need to set the id to 0 and clear the form. For editing or deleting an image, we'll need to set the id to whatever was submitted and populate the form with existing data.

We can add the following to process the three buttons in the manage-images.code.php file:

```
// Initialise
   ...

// Prepare Page
   if(isset($_POST['prepare-insert'])) {

   }
   if(isset($_POST['prepare-update'])) {

   }
   if(isset($_POST['prepare-delete'])) {

   }

// Upload Image
   ...
```

There's no requirement to put this code in this particular location, as it's independent from the rest. It just makes sense to put the prepare code before the event code.

Before we do anything else, we can adjust the page title and heading:

```
// Initialise
   ...

// Prepare Page
   if(isset($_POST['prepare-insert'])) {
       $pagetitle = 'Upload Image';
       $pageheading = 'Upload Image';
```

```
        }
        if(isset($_POST['prepare-update'])) {
            $pagetitle = 'Edit Image';
            $pageheading = 'Edit Image';

        }
        if(isset($_POST['prepare-delete'])) {
            $pagetitle = 'Delete Image';
            $pageheading = 'Delete Image';

        }

    // Upload Image
        ...
```

We should also remove these variables from the include block at the beginning of the editimage.php page to prevent them from overriding the values:

```
<?php require_once 'includes/manage-images.code.php'; ?>
<?php require_once 'includes/head.inc.php'; ?>
```

If you test the image list and edit image pages, you should see the new titles.

We'll also need to get the id of the image to be edited. For the prepare-insert event, there's nothing to do—it has already been set to 0 in the preceding code; we won't need it anyway.

For the prepare-update and prepare-delete events, we'll need to get it from the submitted data.

Remember that this time the submit button has specific value assigned, which is the id of the image we're editing. We can get it from the $_POST array:

```
// Prepare Page
    if(isset($_POST['prepare-insert'])) {
```

```
    $pagetitle = 'Upload Image';
    $pageheading = 'Upload Image';

}
if(isset($_POST['prepare-update'])) {
    $pagetitle = 'Edit Image';
    $pageheading = 'Edit Image';

    $id = intval($_POST['prepare-update'] ?? 0);
}
if(isset($_POST['prepare-delete'])) {
    $pagetitle = 'Delete Image';
    $pageheading = 'Delete Image';

    $id = intval($_POST['prepare-delete'] ?? 0);
}
```

In theory, the value might be missing, so we've used the null coalescing operator. We've also run it through the `intval()` function to make sure that we've got a genuine number.

If you test it now, you'll see the ID in the unhidden field.

Fetching the Data to be Edited

For the **prepare-insert** event, again, there's nothing to do. When you're adding a new image, there won't be any existing data, and the $title and $description variables have already been initialized to empty strings.

For the **prepare-update** and **prepare-delete** events, we'll need to populate the form with existing data. We can do that the same way we fetched a larger image for the gallery. At this point, the code to prepare for edit and remove will be identical:

```
// Prepare Page
   ...
   if(isset($_POST['prepare-update'])) {
       $pagetitle = 'Edit Image';
       $pageheading = 'Edit Image';

       $id = intval($_POST['prepare-update'] ?? 0);

       $sql = "SELECT title, src, description FROM images
           WHERE id=$id";
       [$title, $src, $description] = $pdo -> query($sql) ->
       fetch();
       $description = pilcrow2nl($description);
   }
   if(isset($_POST['prepare-delete'])) {
       $pagetitle = 'Delete Image';
       $pageheading = 'Delete Image';

       $id = intval($_POST['prepare-delete'] ?? 0);

       $sql = "SELECT title, src, description FROM images
           WHERE id=$id";
       [$title, $src, $description] = $pdo -> query($sql) ->
       fetch();
       $description = pilcrow2nl($description);
   }
```

Since the variable $id comes out of the intval() function, it's safe to interpolate that into SQL.

Note that we've adjusted the description through the pilcrow2nl() function which takes the saved pilcrows and replaces them with true line breaks for the text area.

Adjusting the Image Blocks

You'll see that we've also fetched the `src` value. That's so we can display a copy of the current image.

On the page, you'll see an upload button for a new image, but no old image. In the HTML, however, there is a commented block for this image:

```
<!-- if($id) get image:
    <p id="old-image">Current Image<br>
        <img id="preview" ... src="/images/thumbnails/
        <?= $src; ?>">
    </p>
endif; -->
```

The image block includes the `$src` variable which has been fetched for the **prepare-update** and **prepare-delete** events. Of course, it should only show if there is an existing image, that is, when the `$id` is something. We can replace the comment lines with PHP conditional blocks:

```
<?php if($id): ?>
    <p id="old-image">Current Image<br>
        <img id="preview" ... src="/images/thumbnails/
        <?= $src; ?>">
    </p>
<?php endif; ?>
```

There's also the upload button for a new image:

```
<p id="new-image" class="preview-image">
    <label>New Image (Shift-Click to Clear)<br>
        <input name="image" type="file"
            data-preview="preview-new-image">
    </label>
    <img id="preview-new-image">
</p>
```

Of course, you'll need it when adding a new image, but we'll also use it when editing an existing image in case you want to replace the photo itself. It's OK to leave it there when deleting an image, but it's pointless, so it's better to hide it then.

We've already tested for the **prepare-delete** event, and we'll use the same test to hide the new image block. However, this time it's the reverse: if the event is *not* **prepare-delete**, then show the block. Remember in PHP the not operator is the exclamation mark (!):

```php
<?php if(!isset($_POST['prepare-delete'])): ?>
    <p id="new-image" class="preview-image">
      ...
    </p>
<?php endif; ?>
```

If you test this, you should see the old image only for the **prepare-update** and **prepare-delete** events, and you should see the new image button only for the **prepare-insert** and **prepare-update** events.

Adjusting the Buttons

Currently, there's a submit button which we used to add a new image. Specifically, its name is insert which we tested for the **insert** operation.

There are additional buttons, commented out, which will trigger the **update** and **delete** events:

```
<!--[if edit]
    <button type="submit" name="update">Submit Changes</button>
[elseif remove]
    <button type="submit" name="delete">Delete Image</button>
[else]-->
    <button type="submit" name="insert">Add Image</button>
<!--[endif]-->
```

We'll need to test the current event to decide which button to show. Again, we can use the isset() test:

```php
<?php if(isset($_POST['prepare-update'])): ?>
    <button type="submit" name="update">Submit Changes</button>
<?php elseif(isset($_POST['prepare-delete'])): ?>
    <button type="submit" name="delete">Delete Image</button>
<?php else: ?>
    <button type="submit" name="insert">Add Image</button>
<?php endif; ?>
```

This conditional block is a little more complex in that there is more than one test. Additional tests start with elseif(...), which, in PHP, is one word.

You should now see the appropriate submit button for the different events.

Adjusting the Upload Form

There is also the separate form to bulk import images:

```
<form id="editimage-import" ... action="">
    <label for="import-file">Import File</label>
    <input type="file" name="import-file" id="import-file"
    required>
    <button type="submit" name="import">Import</button>
</form>
```

We could make that a separate event altogether, but we'll keep it as part of the **prepare-insert** event. However, we don't want it there for the **prepare-update** and **prepare-delete** events.

313

We can test for the id. Remember that it's zero for the **prepare-insert** event and nonzero for the other events. We'll test for nonzero:

```
<?php if(!$id): ?>
    <form id="editimage-import" ... action="">
        <label for="import-file">Import File</label>
        <input type="file" name="import-file" id="import-file"
            required>
        <button type="submit" name="import">Import</button>
    </form>
<?php endif; ?>
```

This is the *opposite* test for showing the old image.

Disabling Fields for Remove

There's one more thing. If you want to delete something, there's no point in changing its contents. Currently, if you select **prepare-delete**, you can still edit the title and description. That won't cause any damage, since all the changes will be lost, but the form should be smarter than that.

There is an HTML attribute called disabled which will disable parts of the form. You can use it on individual form elements or on whole sections. The fieldset element is a way of sectioning the form, and we'll disable the fieldset which has the title and description.

To begin with, the fieldset will be something like this:

```
<fieldset>
    <!-- images -->
    <p><label>Title<br>
        <input type="text" name="title"></label></p>
    <p><label>Description<br>
        <textarea name="description"></textarea></label></p>
</fieldset>
```

To disable the `fieldset`, we need only add the attribute:

```
<fieldset disabled>
    ...
</fieldset>
```

In the actual code, you'll see a PHP variable:

```
<fieldset <?= $disabled ?>>
    ...
</fieldset>
```

(Don't be confused by the two closing brackets >>: one closes the PHP block, while the other closes the `fieldset` tag.)

The default value for the `$disabled` variable is an empty string (`$disabled = ''`), which is why the `fieldset` and its contents are fully enabled. In the **prepare-delete** event, we'll set it to `' disabled'`:

```
if(isset($_POST['prepare-delete'])) {
    ...

    $disabled = ' disabled';
}
```

We've added a space at the beginning of the string in case it's not there in the `fieldset` tag; it doesn't hurt to have a few extra spaces to spare.

If you test it now, you'll find that the title and description can no longer be edited.

Implementing Update and Delete

All we've done so far is to prepare the form for updating and deleting. That includes having the right buttons appear. It also includes setting the ID of the image we're updating or deleting.

We'll now add two more blocks of code to update and delete. We can add them at the end of the PHP. At the same time, we can extract the ID from the $_POST array:

```php
<?php
    ...

    if(isset($_POST['update'])) {
        $id = intval($_POST['id'] ?? 0);

    }

    if(isset($_POST['delete'])) {
        $id = intval($_POST['id'] ?? 0);

    }
```

Deleting data is easy enough, so we'll handle that first. Updating will be nearly as complicated as adding a new one, not because of the SQL, but because of the error checking and options.

Once we've finished experimenting, we'll probably need to do a bulk import again.

Deleting Data

To delete a row from a database table, we use a DELETE statement:

```
DELETE FROM images WHERE id=...;
```

The WHERE clause isn't technically required if you really want to delete *all* rows. Here, we'll limit it to one row.

Note that if the id is zero, negative, or out of range, the DELETE statement will still run, but won't actually delete anything. That's because the id value is still a number, even if it doesn't match.

In PHP, we can write

```php
<?php
    ...

    if(isset($_POST['delete'])) {
        $id = intval($_POST['id'] ?? 0);

        $pdo -> exec("DELETE FROM images WHERE id=$id");
    }
```

However, don't run this yet.

Previously, we've used the query() method to run an SQL SELECT statement directly. Here, we're not expecting any data, so we use the exec() method. You can also use exec() for the UPDATE statement, but it will get more complicated, so we'll use a prepared statement when we get there.

Note that even though the value of $id comes from user input, we've run it through the intval() function, so it's reduced to a harmless number, which makes it safe to use with the exec() function. If the data were left in its original form, it would be safer to use a prepared statement.

The exec() method does have a return value, which we're ignoring here; it's the number of rows affected, which, in this case, is the number of rows deleted, which, in this case, should be 1.

The complication is that we will also want to delete the images for that row. For that, we'll need the src value, so we'll extract that *before* we delete the image:

```php
<?php
if(isset($_POST['delete'])) {
    $id = intval($_POST['id'] ?? 0);
```

```php
$src = $pdo -> query("SELECT src FROM images WHERE id=$id")
    -> fetchColumn();

$pdo -> exec("DELETE FROM images WHERE id=$id");
}
```

However, don't run this yet.

Once you've got the src value, you can use this to delete the images from the various directories. We've written similar code when doing the bulk import. We'll adapt it for a single image:

```php
<?php
if(isset($_POST['delete'])) {
    $id = intval($_POST['id'] ?? 0);

    $src = $pdo -> query("SELECT src FROM images WHERE id=$id")
        -> fetchColumn();

    $directories = ['images/originals', 'images/display',
        'images/thumbnails', 'images/icons', 'images/scaled'];
    foreach($directories as $dir) unlink("$root/$dir/$src");

    $pdo -> exec("DELETE FROM images WHERE id=$id");
}
```

Here, we don't have the uploads directory, and we're unlinking a single image from each directory, so the code is simpler.

However, don't run this yet.

When we've finished deleting the image, there's nothing more to look at. We should finish the job as we did for the import, which is to move on to the imagelist.php page:

```php
if(isset($_POST['delete'])) {

    ...

    $pdo -> exec("DELETE FROM images WHERE id=$id");
```

```
//  Move On
    header("Location: $protocol://$host/imagelist.php");
    exit;
}
```

Now you can run this.

Updating the Image Data

You can update data with an UPDATE statement:

```
UPDATE images SET title='...', description='...' WHERE id=...;
```

Again, you don't need the WHERE clause if you want to update the whole table to the same value, which would probably be a mistake.

Implementing the update code itself isn't too difficult, but there will be two complications:

- Because the incoming data presents the same risks as for adding a new image, we'll need to handle it the same way by testing for errors and using a prepared statement.

- We'll also allow a replacement image, but only if one's been included.

The code for updating the data can be largely adapted from the code for adding the data.

Updating the Text Data

We can begin extracting and testing the text data as we did for the **insert** event:

```
if(isset($_POST['update'])) {
    $id = intval($_POST['id'] ?? 0);
```

```
$title = trim($_POST['title']);
$description=trim($_POST['description']);

$errors = [];

//   Check Text
     if(!$title) $errors[] = 'Missing Title';
     if(!$description) $errors[] = 'Missing Description';

//   Process
     if(!$errors) {  //  proceed

     }
     else {              //  handle error
         $errors = sprintf('<p class="errors">%s</p>',
             implode('<br>',$errors));
     }
}
```

This is, of course, mostly copied from the previous code:

- Copy the data from the $_POST array.

- Check for no errors.

- Prepare error paragraph.

If there are no errors, we can proceed with the update.

Because of the risks associated with text data, we'll prepare the SQL statement:

```
if(isset($_POST['update'])) {

    ...

//   Process
     if(!$errors) { //  proceed
         $sql = 'UPDATE images SET title=?, description=?
             WHERE id=?';
```

```
        $prepared = $pdo -> prepare($sql);
    }
    else {            // handle error
        ...
    }

}
```

We'll need to fix the description for the database, using the nl2pilcrow() function. We can do that in the array for the execute() method:

```
if(isset($_POST['update'])) {

    ...

    // Process
        if(!$errors) {  // proceed
            $sql = 'UPDATE images SET title=?, description=?
                WHERE id=?';
            $prepared = $pdo -> prepare($sql);
            $prepared -> execute([$title,
            nl2pilcrow($description),
                $id]);
        }
        else {            // handle error
            ...
        }
}
```

At the end, we can move back to the imagelist.php page:

```
if(isset($_POST['update'])) {

    ...

    //  Process
        if(!$errors) {  //  proceed

            ...

        }
        else {              //  handle error

            ...

        }

    // Move On
        header("Location: $protocol://$host/imagelist.php");
        exit;
}
```

You can now test this by selecting an image and making a few changes to the text.

Replacing the Image

Unlike when we add a new image, we haven't tested whether an image has been uploaded, because we're just changing the text. However, we can also replace the image.

First, we need to see whether we want to. We're going to make a new image optional. With the edit form, we include a file upload for a new image. We'll need to check whether a file has been attached. This will be similar to testing for a new image:

```
if(isset($_POST['update'])) {

    ...

    $errors = [];
```

```
//  Check Text
    ...
```

```
//  Replace Image?
    if(isset($_FILES['image']) && $_FILES['error']
        != UPLOAD_ERR_NO_FILE) {

    }
```

```
//  Process
    ...

  ...
}
```

We put this text before the processing block in case we end up with an error.

Remember the && operator is short-circuited: the second test will only be applied if the first is successful. Here, we're first testing whether there is a file.

If there is an image, we'll test it as we did for a new image:

```
//  Replace Image?
    if(isset($_FILES['image']) && $_FILES['image']['error']
        != UPLOAD_ERR_NO_FILE) {
        $imagetypes = ['image/gif', 'image/jpeg', 'image/png',
            'image/webp'];

        switch($_FILES['image']['error']) {
            case UPLOAD_ERR_OK:
                if(!in_array($_FILES['image']['type'],
                $imagetypes))
                    $errors[] = 'Not a suitable image file';
                if(!is_uploaded_file($_FILES['image']['tmp_
                name']))
```

```
                $errors[] = 'Not an uploaded file';
            break;
        case UPLOAD_ERR_INI_SIZE:
        case UPLOAD_ERR_FORM_SIZE:
            $errors[] = 'File too big';
            break;
        default:
            $errors[] = 'Problem with file upload';
    }
}
```

This is basically copied from the insert image block, except that it's only used if there's an uploaded file, and we don't test for a missing file.

If we're satisfied that there's no error at this point, we can proceed to replace the old image with the new one:

```
// Replace Image?
    if(isset($_FILES['image']) && $_FILES['image']['error']
        != UPLOAD_ERR_NO_FILE) {

        ...

        if(!$errors {

        }
    }
```

First, we'll need to get the src value of the current image. We'll do that the same way as we did for deleting:

```
// Replace Image?
    if(isset($_FILES['image']) && $_FILES['image']['error']
        != UPLOAD_ERR_NO_FILE) {

        ...
```

```
    if(!$errors {
        $src = $pdo -> query("SELECT src FROM images
            WHERE id=$id") -> fetchColumn();
    }
}
```

Then we'll call the addImage() function:

```
//  Replace Image?
   if(isset($_FILES['image']) && $_FILES['image']['error']
       != UPLOAD_ERR_NO_FILE) {
       ...

       if(!$errors {
           $src = $pdo -> query("SELECT src FROM images
               WHERE id=$id") -> fetchColumn();
           addImageFile($_FILES['image']['tmp_name'], $src);
       }
   }
```

We're using the name of a preexisting image this time. The code in the addImage() function will readily create new images, but it will also replace images with the same name without asking.

You can now test the code by uploading a new image.

Checking a Checkbox

We've mentioned earlier that not all images are necessarily to be included in the gallery. There's a gallery column which was set to true when we uploaded the original image, but we don't appear to have the option to say otherwise.

We're going to add a checkbox to give us the choice. We'll default the checkbox to checked for a new image; otherwise, we'll set it to whatever's stored in the database when we prepare for edit or remove.

In HTML, a checkbox is a type of input element:

```
<input type="checkbox" name="...">
<input type="checkbox" name="..." checked>
```

If the checked attribute is present, then the checkbox will be preselected; otherwise, it's not. This doesn't stop you from changing it at any time.

When it comes to the submitted data, it's a little more complicated. In a typical form

- *All text fields* are submitted, even if they're empty.

- *Only selected buttons* are submitted. This includes checkboxes and radio buttons and, of course, any submit button, of which you can only submit one.

It was easy enough to test an empty text field; testing a missing button takes a slightly different approach.

Adding the Checkbox

We'll add a checkbox in a moment. First, we'll need another PHP variable, since we're going to use that in the checkbox.

With the other variables, add the following:

```php
<?php
    ...
    //  Initialise
        $id = 0;
        $title = $description = '';
```

```
$errors = '';
$disabled = '';
$gallery = ' checked';
```

Don't forget to include a leading space, just in case. We'll use this the same way we used the $disabled variable in the fieldset.

In the editimage.php file, add the following checkbox code:

```
<fieldset ...>
    ...
    <p><label>Title<br>
        <input type="text" name="title"
            value="<?= $title ?>"></label></p>
    <p><label>Description<br>
        <textarea name="description">
            <?= $description ?></textarea></label></p>
    <p><label><input type="checkbox" name="gallery"
    <?= $gallery ?>>
        Gallery</label></p>
</fieldset>
```

When you load the form now, you'll see the new checkbox at the bottom, but it tells us nothing yet. For the **prepare-update** and **prepare-delete** events, we'll need to get the current value from the database.

We can make a slight change to the SQL we used to fetch the current data and the code we used to set the variables:

```
if(isset($_POST['prepare-update'])) {
    ...

    $sql = "SELECT title, src, description, gallery FROM images
        WHERE id=$id";
    [$title, $src, $description, $gallery] = $pdo ->
    query($sql)
```

```
        -> fetch();
    $description = pilcrow2nl($description);
}
if(isset($_POST['prepare-delete'])) {
    ...

    $sql = "SELECT title, src, description, gallery FROM images
        WHERE id=$id";
    [$title, $src, $description, $gallery] = $pdo ->
    query($sql)
        -> fetch();
    $description = pilcrow2nl($description);
}
```

The value for $gallery will be 1 or 0 for true or false. We can use this to set the value of $gallery to either the string checked or an empty string:

```
if(isset($_POST['prepare-update'])) {
    ...

    $sql = "SELECT title, src, description, gallery FROM images
        WHERE id=$id";
    [$title, $src, $description, $gallery] = $pdo ->
    query($sql)
        -> fetch();
    $description = pilcrow2nl($description);
    $gallery = $gallery ? ' checked' : '';
}
if(isset($_POST['prepare-delete'])) {
    ...
```

```
$sql = "SELECT title, src, description, gallery FROM images
    WHERE id=$id";
[$title, $src, $description, $gallery] = $pdo ->
query($sql)
    -> fetch();
$description = pilcrow2nl($description);
$gallery = $gallery ? ' checked' : '';
}
```

Don't forget to include a leading space, just in case.

When you test this, you won't see anything different, since they're all gallery images so far.

Testing the Checkbox

The second half of the job is to use the checkbox value when adding or editing the image. This is slightly complicated by the fact that the checkbox may not be present in the $_POST array, but that's not hard to work with.

In the update code, add the following:

```
if(isset($_POST['update'])) {
    $id = intval($_POST['id'] ?? 0);
    $title = trim($_POST['title']);
    $description=trim($_POST['description']);
    $gallery = intval(isset($_POST['gallery']));

    ...
}
```

The isset() function will tell us whether the checkbox is set; wrapping it inside the intval() function will turn that into a 1 for true and a 0 for false.

You'll want to do the same thing for the insert code:

```
if(isset($_POST['insert'])) {
    $title = trim($_POST['title']);
    $description=trim($_POST['description']);
    $gallery = intval(isset($_POST['gallery']));

    ...
}
```

The next thing is to include the value when we insert or update.

For the update code, change the SQL statement and the data array:

```
if(isset($_POST['update'])) {
    ...
    //  Process
        if(!$errors) {  //  proceed
            $sql = 'UPDATE images SET title=?, description=?,
                gallery=? WHERE id=?';
            $prepared = $pdo -> prepare($sql);
            $prepared -> execute([$title, nl2pilcrow
            ($description),
                $gallery, $id]);
        }
        else {          //  handle error
            ...
        }

    ...
}
```

We'll need to do something similar for the insert code, but first we'll need to make a change to the addImageData() function:

```
function addImageData(string $name, string $title,
    string $description, int $gallery=1) {

    ...

// Add to the Database
    $description = nl2pilcrow($description);

    $sql = 'INSERT INTO images(title, description, name, src,
    gallery)
        VALUES(?, ?, ?, ?, ?)';
    $pdoStatement = $pdo -> prepare($sql);
    $data = [$title, $description, $name, $name, $gallery];
    $pdoStatement->execute($data);

    ...
}
```

We've made the following changes:

- There's now an additional parameter variable, $gallery.

  The $gallery variable has a **default** value, which means that if you leave it out, its value will be set to the default. In this case, the default is 1, so that the function will set the gallery value to true, as before.

- The VALUES clause now has a fifth placeholder (?) instead of hard-coding the true as before.

- The data array now includes the $gallery value.

It's important to make changes to functions as unobtrusive as possible. Formerly, when you called the function, it was without the $gallery parameter, and the gallery value was set to true. By using a default value like this, you can still call it the old way and get the expected result, but now you have the option to change the value.

In the insert code, we can now send the additional parameter:

```
if(isset($_POST['insert'])) {
    ...

    //  Process
        if(!$errors) {  //  proceed
            $name = $_FILES['image']['name'];
            [$id, $src] = addImageData($name, $title,
            $description,
                $gallery);

            ...

        }
        else {            //  handle error
            ...
        }

}
```

You can now test updating the images with the gallery checkbox turned off. If you view the gallery, they should no longer appear. You can try this with new images as well.

Finishing Touches

Clearing the $id when Adding an Image

The insert event is the only one which doesn't take you back to the image list, in case you want to add more images. Part of the process fetched the id when adding the image to the database; this sets the $id variable.

One of the changes we made was to display an existing preview image when editing or deleting data. We used the $id variable to decide whether to show the image block. Unfortunately, this has the side effect that the preview for the recently added image will be visible when adding another image.

We'll need to add one variable to the cleanup for adding images:

```php
if(isset($_POST['insert'])) {
    ...

    // Process
    if(!$errors) { // proceed
        ...

        // Finish Up
        $errors = '';
        $title = $description = '';
        $id = 0;

    }
    else {           // handle error
        ...
    }

}
```

You'll often find that even simple changes to one part of the code has side effects on other parts of the code. That's the tedious part of development—checking everything again.

Fixing the Hidden Field

Remember, at the beginning, we changed the hidden id field to a text field. Once we've established that everything is working, we can change it back:

```
<input type="hidden" name="id" value="<?= $id ?>">
```

Restoring the Images

In Chapter 7, we included some code to clear out the old data and images when importing the ZIP file. This code may have been commented out to allow imports of additional data:

```
if(isset($_POST['import'])) {
/*
    $pdo -> exec('TRUNCATE TABLE images');
    $directories = ['uploads', 'images/originals',
        'images/display', 'images/thumbnails',
        'images/icons', 'images/scaled'];
    foreach($directories as $dir)
        array_map('unlink', glob("$root/$dir/*"));
 */

    ...

}
```

In testing the code for this chapter, you may have deleted or changed much of the original data. At this point, you may wish to reimport the original data.

If so, you may also wish to uncomment the preceding code to restore things as they were.

Summary

You can go a long way to developing a database management client using web technology. In particular, you can use PHP to interface between the Web and the database.

There are four main operations on a database table:

- SELECT fetches data from the table.

- INSERT adds data to the table.

- UPDATE changes data in specific rows in the table.

- DELETE deletes rows from the table.

In this chapter, we developed two pages to manage a database table: one page to list the table contents and the other to manage the content. The list page uses the SELECT statement to fetch and then display the table rows, while the edit page uses the INSERT, UPDATE, or DELETE statement to manipulate the data.

Communicating between these pages involves a series of submit buttons. Buttons from the list page prepare data for the edit page. Buttons from the edit page implement the database operations.

You can display database table contents in an HTML table. HTML tables are complex structures and are tedious to generate by hand, but are readily constructed using PHP.

HTML table cells can contain simple values, but can also contain other HTML elements such as images and buttons. In turn, the table can be part of an HTML form. This makes the table ideal for organizing a large collection of related fields or buttons.

The HTML table's contents can be generated in PHP in a similar way to generating the image gallery. Data is extracted using a SELECT statement and placed into the HTML table using string operations.

Once a single image has been selected, its id can be used to fetch the full details to populate a form for processing. To add a new image, the form is essentially empty, and the form has an id of 0. To edit or delete an image, the form is populated with existing data, and its id is added to the form.

It's possible to use one page for different tasks by making adjustments to its contents. In this case, we adjust the submit buttons, the content of the form fields, the image preview and upload elements, and whether part of the form is enabled. We do this in PHP by examining the event details and using conditional PHP blocks.

The actual changes are implemented using various SQL statements. We had already added new images using the INSERT statement, and here we edit and delete images using the UPDATE and DELETE statements.

Deleting data from the database takes a simple SQL statement, but it should also delete the related image fi les. This means iterating through an array of directories and unlinking the fi les within them.

Updating data is a little more complex. The submitted data needs to be checked as it was when inserting a new image. We have also allowed an optional replacement image, which also needs to be checked, and then copied over the original images.

There is a gallery column in the images table to determine whether the image should be included in the gallery. Originally, we defaulted to the true value. Here, we can add a checkbox to make the choice.

Processing a checkbox is different to processing text fields, since it's not always submitted with the rest of the data—only when it's selected. In PHP, we need to test whether it is present and use test as the data.

We also need to make adjustments to the code that prepares the form, to set the checkbox, as well as the code that inserts and updates the data, to include the checkbox value.

Coming Up

We've put some effort into protecting our site from email header injection as well as SQL injection. We're now going to protect our site from intruders altogether.

In the next chapter, we're going to look at restricting administration tasks, such as what we've worked on in this chapter, to specific users.

In the process, we'll learn about managing a table of users. This will include securely managing passwords.

We'll learn how to implement a login and logout for users and how to work with PHP sessions, which will be used to manage the logged in state. We'll also learn how to force visitors to log in for specific pages and how to restrict access to those pages.

CHAPTER 10

Sessions and Logging In

You'll have noticed by now that the `imagelist.php` and `editimage.` `php` pages aren't directly accessible from the site menu. That's because we're not really inviting the general public to join in and tamper with the contents of the site.

Of course, it's not enough to hide the links. What we need to do is filter who's allowed to access them in the first place.

In this chapter, we're going to look at restricting activity to acceptable users. That means limiting access to some areas to someone who's logged in and has permission to be there.

We'll begin by discussing PHP session data—short-term storage for maintaining values between PHP pages. In this case, the data we're interested in maintaining relates to a user's logging in.

We'll then discuss how passwords are managed and used in PHP. This includes what's required to keep user data as safe as possible from intruders.

From there, we'll set up a table of authorized users and consider how users are added to this table.

Once we have the table of users in place, we'll see how we manage logging in. This will involve checking the username and password against the database and, on success, saving relevant values in the session data.

© Mark Simon 2024
M. Simon, *An Introduction to PHP*, https://doi.org/10.1007/979-8-8688-0177-8_10

When user authentication is in place, we'll look at how to limit access to certain parts of the website.

First, however, we'll need to understand something about maintaining state between web pages.

Sessions

By design, HTTP is stateless. That is, every connection between the browser is forgotten as soon as it's been completed. This means that the server doesn't have to waste resources tracking connections, especially if the visitor abandons the website without telling anyone.

The problem with this is that sometimes you need to track what's going on. For example, you certainly need to remember the state of a shopping cart if you're doing some online shopping. You also need to remember whether the visitor has successfully logged in.

PHP can store temporary short-term data in **sessions**. Essentially, they are stores of data kept on the server. This may be in a file in the server's temporary folder, but it can be configured to be in a database.

Session data is well suited to remembering important values between pages on a website.

By default, session data will expire after 24 minutes of idleness. This session lifetime can be altered. The session will automatically be renewed when the user interacts with the server again, so an active user can retain session data indefinitely.

The session data is identified purely by a random string. This string is sent to the browser in a cookie and returned to the browser next time.

You can use sessions for a variety of purposes. For example, you could store a shopping cart in a session, though you might want to back it up in a database if you want the visitor to interrupt their shopping. You could also use sessions to remember what you did in one page as you move to the next.

We're going to use a session to manage a login. When you successfully log in, the session data will remember that and be used to allow access to protected pages.

Session Settings

You can vary the behavior of PHP sessions in a number of settings. The relevant settings in the .htaccess file are

```
php_value    session.name PHPSESSID

php_value    session.use_only_cookies 1

php_value    session.gc_maxlifetime 600

php_value    session.gc_probability 1
php_value    session.gc_divisor 1
```

and in the .user.ini file:

```
session.name=PHPSESSID

session.use_only_cookies=1

session.gc_maxlifetime=600

session.gc_probability=1
session.gc_divisor=1
```

1. The session.name value is the name of the browser cookie. When a session store is created, a unique identifier is generated and sent to the browser as a cookie. By default, the cookie name is PHPSESSID, but you can change it.

2. It's possible to use an alternative to cookies in the
    form of a query string, such as ?PHPSESSID=........
    That may be necessary if cookies are unavailable,
    but putting it on a query string is less secure. By
    default, it's cookies only.

3. The session.gc_maxlifetime value is the lifetime
    of an idle session, in seconds. The default value
    is 1440, which is 24 minutes. If the server doesn't
    hear from you in that time, then the session *may* be
    expired.

4. It's a little more complicated than that ...

5. The session.gc_probability and session.gc_
    divisor values are used to determine when a timed
    out session *may* expire. By default, they are 1 and
    100, respectively.

PHP has a surprising approach to expired sessions. After the session.
gc_maxlifetime has expired, PHP won't always clear out the session.
Presumably, it's too busy doing other things to worry about that. Instead,
it will *sometimes* clear it out. The definition of "sometimes" is session.
gc_probability / session.gc_divisor. That is, it's a probability factor.

By default, the probability that PHP will expire a session is 1/100. That
means you can expect the data to be expired about once every 100 page
loads. In a busy server, that's not long. However, in a development server,
that could take all day.

For development purposes, the session.gc_probability and
session.gc_divisor values should be set to 1 and 1. That means that
PHP will purge old sessions on every page load, which is wasteful on a live
server, but fine for now.

As for the other settings, the current settings are fine. The default session cookie name is PHPSESSID, so there's no change there. The default for the using sessions is with cookies only, so there's no change there either.

The settings file has, however, shortened the session time to five minutes, but you can lengthen it if you want.

Starting a Session

Managing session data is extra effort for PHP, so it won't do it unless you ask for it.

To start a session, you use the session_start() function:

```php
<?php
    session_start();
```

This doesn't have to be at the very beginning of the script, but it does have to be before you need the data. Putting it at the beginning is convenient, especially if what follows depends on the session data.

The session_start() function will handle all of the background work:

1. If this is the first time, a new session store is defined.

2. If this is a subsequent time, the data is loaded from the session store.

You'll access the session through a magic $_SESSION superglobal array:

*   What you write into the array will be saved to the session store at the end of the script.

*   When you restart a session, the array will be populated from the session store.

The $_SESSION variable is effectively a gateway to the stored data.

PHP doesn't like it if you call this function when a session is already in progress, so if you do this:

```php
<?php
    session_start();
    session_start();    // oops
```

you'll get a warning or possibly an error.

Of course, you're not likely to write code like that, but you may write code which does this indirectly. For example, suppose you have a file called something.php:

```php
    session_start();

    // etc
```

You may then include it in another file:

```php
    requre_once 'something.php';

    session_start();    // oops
```

The simplest way to avoid this is to test whether a session has already started. You can do this with the session_id() function:

```php
<?php
    if(!session_id()) session_start();

    // etc
```

The session_id() function will return the id of the current session. This will be a random string. If there is no current session, the result is an empty string, which will test false. Here, we're starting a session only if the id is empty.

Actually, the session id is a reference to the data as stored. By default, it's saved in a file, and you can see the location of these files in the php.ini file. The location where the session files are stored is in the session.save_path setting.

The value of session_id() is the value that will be stored in your session cookie on the browser. Every different visitor to the website will get a different session store, and every different visitor will get a different value for this cookie.

When you revisit the server, as you will when reloading a page or selecting another, all of the cookies from the site will be returned to the server, including the session cookie. This is the only way the server has of knowing which session store belongs to you.

If you're on a shared network, it's possible for someone to intercept all of the traffic, including cookies, including session cookies. Changing the session name may help a little in that the intervening software or human may not recognize the cookie as a session cookie. A more reliable approach is to make the value of the cookie a moving target.

The session_regenerate_id() function will change the id of the session, so even if your original cookie was intercepted, it's useless for next time:

```php
<?php
    if(!session_id()) {
        session_start();
        session_regenerate_id(true);
    }
    // etc
```

We've put the code inside the if() block, so it only gets called if we're actually starting a session. We've also added the optional parameter value true, which means that it will clear out any data associated with the old session id. This will avoid complications if we're clearing out the session data later.

We'll use this pattern at the beginning of all pages which use session data.

This is one case when you may find yourself writing to the headers without necessarily realizing it. Starting a session is enough to generate a cookie, which, of course, is added to the headers. If there's any body output before you start a session, you'll get the Headers Already Sent message, as discussed before.

This is why it's so important to organize your PHP code so that all of the processing is done at the very beginning, before anything is output.

Using Session Data

Session data is written and read using PHP's $_SESSION array. This array acts as a gateway to the external session store.

If you want to save something, you just add it to the $_SESSION array:

```php
<?php

    if(!session_id()) {
        session_start();
        session_regenerate_id(true);
    }

    $_SESSION['data'] = 'hello';
```

This data will be saved at the end of the script.

The $_SESSION array is automatically restored when the session is restarted.

The point of session data is to be able to share data between pages. Here is a simple example of passing data from the home page to another.

At the beginning of the index.php page, add the following script:

```php
<?php

    if(!session_id()) {
        session_start();
        session_regenerate_id(true);
    }

    $_SESSION['visited'] = time();
?>
<?php require_once 'includes/aside.code.php'; ?>
```

On the contact.php page, add the following:

```php
<?php
    if(!session_id()) {
        session_start();
        session_regenerate_id(true);
    }

    printf('Visited on %s', date('l, jS F Y g:i a',
        $_SESSION['visited']));
?>
```

We've used the sprintf() function many times before, but this one is different. The printf() function works the same way, but instead of saving the result in a string, it's output directly.

We've also used the date() function before, but, again, this is slightly different: instead of using the current time, we've given it a specific time, which was saved in the $_SESSION['visited'] item.

If you now load the home page, and then the contact page, you'll see the additional message. Don't worry that it's made a mess of the page.

You can now delete both blocks, and we'll start using the session data more seriously.

But first, we need to learn a little more about how to manage logins.

Managing Users

Authorized users should be stored in another database table, which we'll call users. This table will include the following:

1. A unique identifier.

2. A unique email address, used for logging in.

3. A password hash. We'll discuss what this means shortly.

4. Whether the user has permissions to administer the site.

5. Other details, such as the user's name.

The unique identifier is known as the **primary key**. In theory, any unique value, such as the email address, could be used as the primary key, but the email address can change, so it's better to rely on an arbitrary unchanging value. In this case, it will be a simple sequence number.

At some point, you'll be asking for a password, and you'll need to check this. However, it's very risky to store passwords in a table. You will have heard of cases where user data has been hijacked, and this includes their usernames and passwords. It gets worse if the user has reused their password on other sites.[1]

Encryption and Hashing

You will, of course, need to store something in the database if you're going to check passwords. One thing is clear, and that is the password shouldn't be clear. It should be scrambled.

There are two processes which appear to do the same job, but there's a fundamental difference.

Encryption scrambles text in such a way that it can be **decrypted** later on. It comes from a Greek word meaning hidden. The word "crypt" is used to refer to a hidden room used as a tomb.

Encryption involves using a secret key. When you communicate with a web server using https, you're using one of a pair of keys. There is a public key which is used to encrypt your data, while the server uses a private key to decrypt it. A similar process involves encrypting the server response and decrypting at the browser.

Hashing scrambles text so that it *cannot* be unscrambled. This may seem counterproductive, since you will have lost the original text. However, that's not how it's used.

---

[1] Which, of course, you should never never do …

The real benefit of hashing is when you hash another text which is supposed to be the same as the original, such as a password. It doesn't matter whether we know what the original password is: if hashing one string gives the same result as hashing another, then you can conclude that they're the same.[2]

Because hashing is one way, knowing the hash isn't going to let an intruder in. That's because any attempt to log in will always rehash the submitted password and end up with a completely different, and completely wrong, result.

There are many hashing methods available, some very bad, some very good. PHP has a built-in function called password_hash() which uses a choice of hashing methods. The current default method is called **BCRYPT** which is very good.

To make things even more difficult, the hashing function uses the following:

1. A **salt** is an additional string used to further mix up the data.

2. There is a deliberate delay which is implemented by running the hashing function many times. You won't notice the delay for a single login, but it will drastically slow down brute-force attacks which work by trying out millions of passwords.

---

[2] Hashing is a destructive process, and it's theoretically possible for two different strings to have the same hash by pure coincidence. That's called a hashing collision. However, it's very unlikely for normal strings, even more unlikely for the sort of strings you would use as a password, and even more unlikely with newer hashing methods.

Password Hashing in PHP

To get a password hashed, you use something like the following code:

```php
<?php
    $password = 'Test@321';
    $hash = password_hash($password, PASSWORD_DEFAULT);
?>
```

The second parameter selects which hashing method to use. Unless you have a technical reason to choose otherwise, you should use PASSWORD_DEFAULT. The result will be something like this:

```
$2y$10$PG4P.8HXxk/OfBCfzxvmA.nqpAakypFBZi57cIpO1aOjrxmlwSO7K
```

but not quite. Every time you run this function, you'll get a different value. That's because the salt used to hash the password will be randomly generated when you run the function, so the result will be different.

When you want to test a password, you use password_verify():

```php
<?php
    $password = 'Test@321';
    $hash =
      '$2y$10$PG4P.8HXxk/OfBCfzxvmA.
      nqpAakypFBZi57cIpO1aOjrxmlwSO7K';
    if(password_verify($password, $hash)) {
        print 'Password OK';
    }
    else {
        print 'Unsuccessful';
    }
```

As you'll see, it doesn't matter exactly what the hash is, as the $hash string also contains enough of the salt to compare it successfully.

351

The User Table

Potentially, we might want a number of site administrators, as well as some other registered users. We'll manage that in a table.

User information will be stored in a user table. The structure of the table will be as follows:

Column	Notes
id	Primary key
email	Also used as a username
givenname	Given name
familyname	Family name
hash	Hashed password
admin	Whether an administrator

The SQL to create the table in MySQL is

```
USE australia;
DROP TABLE IF EXISTS users;
CREATE TABLE users (
    id INT UNSIGNED AUTO_INCREMENT PRIMARY KEY,
    email VARCHAR(60) NOT NULL UNIQUE,
    familyname VARCHAR(40) NOT NULL,
    givenname VARCHAR(40) NOT NULL,
    hash VARCHAR(255) NOT NULL, -- use with PHP password
    functions
    admin BOOLEAN NOT NULL DEFAULT FALSE
) CHARACTER SET utf8mb4 COLLATE utf8mb4_unicode_520_ci
ENGINE = INNODB;
```

1. The id is the primary key and is simply a number.

2. The email address will be used as a login.

3. The familyname and givenname aren't strictly necessary, but nice to have.

4. You'll notice that we've allowed 255 characters for the password hash. That's far too much, but it doesn't hurt to leave room for the future, and the space won't be used up unless necessary.

5. The admin value will distinguish between administrators and other users.

This code is in setup/mysql/users.sql. You can use this in the SQL tab in PHPMyAdmin. Make sure that you first select the australia database.

Alternatively, you can use the setup shortcut:

http://australia.example.com/setup?action=users

We can now add one or more administrative users.

Adding a User

You have a choice of three methods to add a user:

1. You can run the SQL directly.

2. You can add a user using PHPMyAdmin.

3. You can add a user using the setup page.

In principle, all methods amount to the same thing, as all methods need to run the SQL code one way or the other.

In this book, we're going to use the password Test@321 for our sample password. For such a naïve password, it passes a surprising number of typical password tests:

1.   It has mixed upper and lower case.

2.   There is at least one special character.

3.   It's at least eight characters long.

4.   It doesn't have a long sequence of characters.

Hopefully, it goes without saying that you shouldn't use Test@321 or any other published password in real life. Just saying.

Method 1: Running the SQL Directly

The SQL to add a user is

```
INSERT INTO users(email, familyname, givenname, hash, admin)
VALUES ('...', '...', '...', '...', ...) ;
```

We can run this code directly in the SQL tab in PHPMyAdmin, but there will be a technical problem we will need to solve.

We need to store the *hash*, not the password, in the table. Working out the actual hash requires running the password_hash() function before we add the user.

The setup page includes a simple password hashing form, as in Figure 10-1.

Figure 10-1. *The Password Form*

If you enter a password, say Test@321, you can then click the title. A new hash will appear below it, as in Figure 10-2.

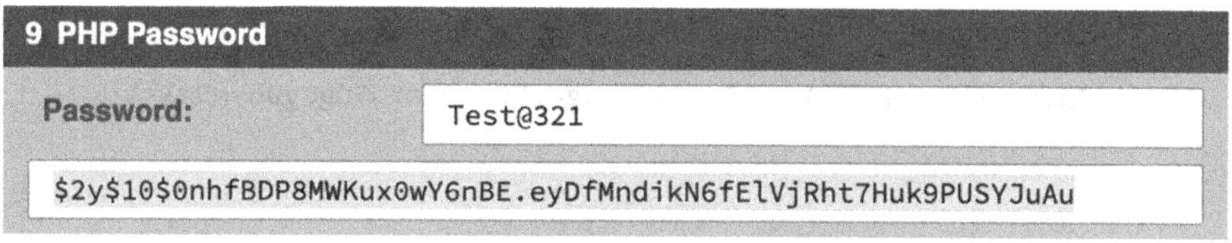

Figure 10-2. *The Password Form Filled In*

Alternatively, you can use the password_hash() function in the PHP Runner tab in the Virtual Hosts application, shown in Figure 10-3.

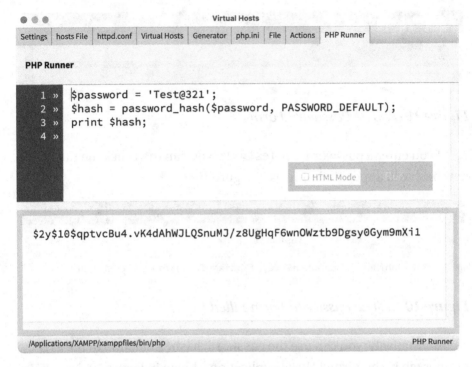

Figure 10-3. *Password Hashing with PHP Runner*

Once you have the hash, you can add the following in SQL:

```
INSERT INTO users(email, familyname, givenname, hash, admin)
VALUES (
    'Fred', 'Nurke',
    'fred.nuke@example.net',
    '$2y$10$PG4P.8HXxk/OfBCfzxvmA.
    nqpAakypFBZi57cIpO1aOjrxmlwSO7K',
    1
);
```

Of course, you can use your own name and other details here. Just make sure that you use 1 or true for the admin value and that the hash is valid.

Method 2: Adding a Password Using PHPMyAdmin

You can use PHPMyAdmin to insert into any table. We could have done that with the images before, but you'll find that it's rather clumsy, and you don't get the chance to do anything else, such as upload files or process any of the data.

Of course, you can create your own form to add a user, and, in the future, that might be a good idea, especially if you want new users to register themselves. However, for just one or two users, we can take advantage of PHPMyAdmin.

To add a user

1. Select the users table in the australia database on the left panel.

2. Select the Insert tab on the top.

You'll see a form similar to Figure 10-4.

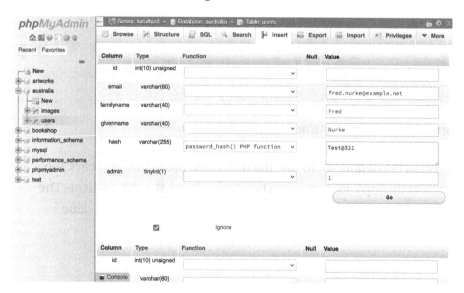

Figure 10-4. Add User with PHPMyAdmin

You'll notice that there's more of the form below to add a second user, but the Ignore checkbox is selected, as it should be for now.

Fill in the details, making sure that you *don't* fill in the id—that will be automatically generated by the database. Again, make sure that the admin value is set to 1.

The important part is the drop-down menu for the hash value. At the bottom, you'll find the password_hash() PHP function item, which will be used on the value in the text box on the right.

After you've entered the details, click the **Go** button.

Method 3: Adding an Admin User with the Setup Page

The setup page includes a simple form to add an admin user which looks like Figure 10-5.

8 Create Admin User	
Given Name:	Fred
Family Name:	Nurke
Email:	fred.nurke@example.com
Password:	Test@321

Figure 10-5. *Create Admin User with Setup*

Fill in the details, including the unhashed password, and click the button at the top which acts as a heading—8 Create Admin User. The PHP code behind it will hash the password and set the admin value.

Logging In

To a large extent, logging in is an illusion—we don't magically enter a new world full of wonders. All that's really happening is that we have authenticated ourselves once, that authentication is remembered (for a while), and we are allowed access to certain parts of the site which are otherwise restricted.

To do this, we'll work through a number of steps:

- The user enters a username and a password in a login form. In this case, the username is the email address.

- If the username and password check out, PHP will store some data in the $_SESSION array.

- For some pages, PHP will check the $_SESSION array to decide what the visitor can and can't do.

Remember, the PHP session has a limited idle time, so eventually the user will no longer be logged in.

The administration page, admin.php, has two sections:

```
<!-- if not logged in -->
    <form id="login" method="post" action="">
        <?=$errors?>
        <p><label>Email Address:<br>
            <input type="text" name="email"></label></p>
        <p><label>Password:<br>
                <input type="password" name="password"
                id="password">
                <button type="button" name="show-password">
                👀</button>
            </label>
        </p>
```

```
    <p><button type="submit" name="login">Login
    </button></p>
  </form>
<!-- else -->
  <ul id="admin-links">
    <li><a href="imagelist.php">Manage Images</a></li>
    <li><a href="bloglist.php">Manage Blog</a></li>
  </ul>
  <form method="post" action="">
    <button type="submit" name="logout">Logout</button>
  </form>
<!-- endif -->
```

Currently, you'll see both sections:

1. The first section is a login form.

2. The second section is a collection of buttons, as well as a logout form.

When we've finished, you'll see only the second section after you've logged in, and you'll see only the first section if you haven't.

Processing Login

The login form, abbreviated, is as follows:

```
<form method="post" action="">
  <p><label>Email Address:<br>
    <input type="text" name="email"></label></p>
  <p><label>Password:<br>
    <input type="password" name="password"></label></p>
  <p><button type="submit" name="login">Login</button></p>
</form>
```

The names of the three elements (login, email, and password) will be used in the PHP script.

Unlike the previous forms we have processed, we won't reprint old values in the form elements, and we won't offer any detail as to why login failed. A login form is an obvious target for any one trying to break in, and we should be as unhelpful as possible.

As with the other pages, we'll start by creating a new file in the includes folder called admin.code.php.

At the beginning of the admin.php page, add the include:

```php
<?php require_once 'includes/admin.code.php'; ?>
<?php
    $pagetitle = 'Administration';
    $pageheading = 'Administration';

    require_once 'includes/head.inc.php';
?>
```

In the new admin.code.php file, we'll have a single PHP block. In the block, we'll need to

1. Start the session

2. Connect to the database

3. Process the login and logout forms

We can set up the preliminary code:

```php
<?php
    if(!session_id()) {
        session_start();
        session_regenerate_id(true);
    }
```

```
$root = str_replace($_SERVER['SCRIPT_NAME'], '',
    $_SERVER['SCRIPT_FILENAME']);
$pdo = require_once "$root/includes/db.php";

$errors = '';

if(isset($_POST['login'])) {

}

if(isset($_POST['logout'])) {

}
```

Most of this can, of course, be copied from previous code. What follows will be much simpler than in previous code, because there's not so much to do.

To log in, we'll need to extract the form data:

```
if(isset($_POST['login'])) {
    $email = $_POST['email'];
    $password = $_POST['password'];

}
```

Actually, we don't really need to do this either, but it will make the code more manageable if we use simple variables. We won't trim the data, and we won't even check for missing data. This is no time to allow for user sloppiness.

We now need to check against the database. To do that, we'll need to extract the password hash from the database. While we're doing that, we'll get the rest of the details in case it's successful.

We'll use a prepared statement and extract the first and only row:

```
if(isset($_POST['login'])) {
    $email = $_POST['email'];
    $password = $_POST['password'];
```

```
$sql = 'SELECT id, givenname, familyname, hash, admin
    FROM users WHERE email=?';
$pds = $pdo->prepare($sql);
$pds -> execute([$email]);
$row = $pds->fetch();
}
```

There are three possibilities:

1. The email address doesn't match. In this case, $row
    will be null, and login should fail.
    If the email address matches, we can fetch the
    hash value.

2. The hashed $password doesn't match the stored
    hash value. Again, login should fail.

3. The hashed $password *does* match, in which case
    login should succeed.

We can test for the possibilities using the short-circuited && expression:

```
if(isset($_POST['login'])) {
    ...

    $sql = 'SELECT id, givenname, familyname, hash, admin
        FROM users WHERE email=?';
    $pds = $pdo->prepare($sql);
    $pds -> execute([$email]);
    $row = $pds->fetch();

    if($row && password_verify($password, $row['hash'])) {
        // success
    }
```

```
    else {
        // failure
    }
}
```

The test will only succeed if $row is not null, and then the password_
verify() function succeeds.

If the test fails, we can set up a simple error message:

```
if($row && password_verify($password, $row['hash'])) {
    // success
}
else {
    $errors = '<p class="errors">Unsuccessful Login</p>';
}
```

Note that we don't go into any detail as to *why* login failed. There
are only two things which might have gone wrong, so it's not hard for a
legitimate user to work out which. However, an intruder might be guessing,
and we shouldn't offer any help.

Successful Login

A successful login is a matter of remembering. In this case, we'll store the
relevant details in the $_SESSION array.

To begin with, the $_SESSION array is empty, since nothing's been
saved. Here, we'll populate it with data from the $email variable, as well as
data from the $row array:

```
if($row && password_verify($password,$row['hash'])) {
    $_SESSION['user'] = $row['id'];
    $_SESSION['givenname'] = $row['givenname'];
    $_SESSION['familyname'] = $row['familyname'];
```

```
    $_SESSION['email'] = $email;
    $_SESSION['admin'] = $row['admin'];
}
else {
    $errors = '<p class="errors">Unsuccessful Login</p>';
}
```

Note that the email value comes from the login. Also, note that we don't remember the hash value—it's only used to check the password.

Technically, we don't really need all of this, but we'll use this data as follows:

1. $_SESSION['user'] will be used to check whether the user has logged in at all.

2. $_SESSION['admin'] will then be used to check whether the user is an administrator.
   At this stage, we don't have a role for a non-administrative user, but we may in the future.

3. The $_SESSION['givenname'] and $_SESSION['familyname'] will simply be there as a courtesy to the logged-in user.

4. We probably don't need $_SESSION['email'], but it doesn't hurt to have it.

Switching Between Content

The first thing we'll do is switch between sections of the form. We could have set this part up before, but it will be easier to check once we've handled the login.

Briefly, the two parts of the form are as follows:

```
<!-- if not logged in -->
    <form id="login" method="post" action="">
        Login Form
    </form>
<!-- else -->
    <ul id="admin-links">
        Links
    </ul>
    <form method="post" action="">
        Logout Form
    </form>
<!-- endif -->
```

Since we don't have any role for a non-administrative user, we'll test whether the user has logged in and whether they're an administrator at the same time. In the admin.php page, add the following code to switch blocks:

```php
<?php if(!isset($_SESSION['user']) || !$_SESSION['admin']): ?>
    <form id="login" method="post" action="">
        Login Form
    </form>
<?php else: ?>
    <ul id="admin-links">
        Links
    </ul>
    <form method="post" action="">
        Logout Form
    </form>
<?php endif; ?>
```

This means if you're not logged in, or you're not an administrator, you'll have to log in first.

A Crash Course in Negative Logic. To pass as an administrator, you need to satisfy *both* tests: `logged in AND admin`. To fail, you negate the test: `not(logged in AND admin)`. This can be expanded as `not logged in OR not admin`. When you negate a logical expression, you negate the contents and change the AND to OR.

If you think about it, this is what you'd expect if you were to express this in English.

Once you've logged in, you should now only see the administrative links.

Showing the User's Name

After a user has logged in, it would be useful to see their name somewhere. It's not only friendlier, but it helps to confirm that they're logged in.

We're going to add the user's name to the main menu, in place of the `Administration` text. That means making a few changes to the navigation block.

To add the user's name, we'll need to check the `$_SESSION` array. There's going to be a logistic problem here, because we can't start a session in the `nav.inc.php`. That's because it's too late. This code is loaded *after* the other PHP includes, such as the header and the aside, and they will have already started to add content to the body. Starting a session will attempt to write a cookie, which is in the header.

Instead, we'll add the following code to the head.inc.php file. This is included before all other output:

```php
<?php
    if(!session_id()) {
        session_start();
        session_regenerate_id(true);
    }

    $date = date('l, jS F Y g:i a');
    $timezone = date_default_timezone_get();
?>
```

It's quite possible that some other PHP code has already started a session, but the if(!session_id()) test at the beginning ensures that it doesn't happen twice.

Note that we already have some other PHP code at the beginning.

If you reopen the nav.inc.php file, you'll recall that there's a PHP block at the beginning.

We have a set of hard-coded links, including one for the admin page. First, we can remove the last link for administration, so that we can add it dynamically:

```php
<?php
    $current=basename($_SERVER['SCRIPT_FILENAME']);

    $links = [
        'Home' => 'index.php',
        'About Oz' => 'about.php',
        'Contact Us' => 'contact.php',
        'Oz Blog' => 'blog.php',
        'Animals' => 'gallery.php'
    ];

    ...
?>
```

We can now add the last link, using the $_SESSION data to change the text of the link:

```php
<?php
    ...

    $links = [
        ...
    ];

    if(isset($_SESSION['user']) && $_SESSION['admin'])
        $text = "{$_SESSION['givenname']}
        {$_SESSION['familyname']}";
    else $text = 'Administration';

    $links[$text] = 'admin.php';

    ...
?>
```

1. The text is the reverse of the one used for the login form: if the user has logged in *and* the user is an administrator.

2. We've generated the text from the user's names using string interpolation. We needed to use the braces because the keys are strings.

•   Once we have a value for the text, we add the final link.

We could also simply have joined the names with a space:

```php
$text = $_SESSION['givenname'] . ' ' . $_SESSION['familyname'];
```

369

Joining strings this way is called **concatenation**, and, in PHP, you do this with a dot (.).[3]

You should now see your name instead of the Administration text for the last link on the menu. It's still a link to the admin.php page, however.

Logging Out

When you log in, data is saved in the PHP session, and a cookie is set to link to the data. Logging out is basically the reverse of this process.

We'll do this in three steps:

1. session_unset() will clear the $_SESSION array in memory. It's the equivalent of $_SESSION = [] which will set the $_SESSION variable to an empty array.

2. session_destroy() will clear any session data still saved on the system.

    We can also destroy the browser cookie which tracks the session. In principle, the cookie name can vary, so we use session_name() to fetch the current name. PHP can't really destroy a cookie, but it can set the value to nothing and set the use-by date to 0 (the beginning of time).

3. setcookie(session_name(), '', 0) will clear the browser cookie.

---

[3] This is *very* confusing if you work with other programming languages, where the dot usually means a property of a member of some value.

We can do all of this in the logout script:

```php
<?php
    if(isset($_POST['logout'])) {
        session_unset();
        session_destroy();
        setcookie(session_name(), '', 0);
    }
```

You can now test logging in and logging out.

Restricting Access

The whole point of logging in and out is to identify the user and to control what the user is permitted to do.

We've done that a little by hiding the buttons to the administration links, but that's hardly secure. You can always visit a page if you know the URL or, at least, if you can guess it.

What we'll do now is restrict access to the admin-only pages. We'll do that by testing whether the visitor is logged in as an administrator; if not, we'll send them to the login page.

The two administrative pages we've worked on so far are `imagelist.php` and `editimage.php` pages.

For both pages, we need to start and test the session data. If the test fails, we can redirect.

The code for the `editimage.php` page is in the `includes/manage-images.code.php` file. There, we can first start the session:

```php
<?php
    if(!session_id()) {
        session_start();
        session_regenerate_id(true);
    }
```

```php
$root = str_replace($_SERVER['SCRIPT_NAME'], '',
    $_SERVER['SCRIPT_FILENAME']);
$host = $_SERVER['HTTP_HOST'];
$protocol = isset($_SERVER['HTTPS'])
&& $_SERVER['HTTPS'] == 'on'
    ? 'https'
    : 'http';
```

We can use the same test as we did for the login form:

```php
<?php
if(!session_id()) {
    session_start();
    session_regenerate_id(true);
}

$root = ... ;
$host = ... ;

if(!isset($_SESSION['user']) || !$_SESSION['admin']) {
    // go to login
}
```

From there, we can redirect to the admin.php page:

```php
<?php
if(!session_id()) {
    session_start();
    session_regenerate_id(true);
}

...
```

```php
if(!isset($_SESSION['user']) || !$_SESSION['admin']) {
    header("Location: $protocol://$host/admin.php");
    exit;
}
```

The code for the imagelist.php page is in the includes/imagelist. code.php file. We can do the same for that file, but note that we haven't yet included the code for the $host and $protocol variables, so we'll need to add that as well:

```php
<?php
    if(!session_id()) {
        session_start();
        session_regenerate_id(true);
    }

    $root = str_replace($_SERVER['SCRIPT_NAME'], '',
        $_SERVER['SCRIPT_FILENAME']);
    $host = $_SERVER['HTTP_HOST'];
    $protocol = isset($_SERVER['HTTPS']) && $_
SERVER['HTTPS'] == 'on'
        ? 'https'
        : 'http';

    if(!isset($_SESSION['user']) || !$_SESSION['admin']) {
        header("Location: $protocol://$host/admin.php");
        exit;
    }
```

We've now made our site a little more secure by restricting who can do what.

Summary

Although we've been using a database to store data, PHP can also store small amounts of data for more immediate use. This is in the form of PHP sessions.

Sessions can be used to maintain state in the current user's activity. In this chapter, we used session data to manage user authentication by maintaining a user's logged-in state.

There are a number of session settings which can be set in the .htaccess or .user.ini settings files. This includes session timeout and when the session data is likely to be cleared, as well as how the session is identified for the user.

PHP handles session data automatically, but, because of the extra work required, it needs to be initiated deliberately.

The session_start() function initiates a PHP session, while the session_regenerate_id() function can be used to make the session data more difficult to intercept.

When a session is first started, some storage is allocated on the server, and a cookie is generated so that the browser is able to identify the particular session.

Session data is added to by setting data in the $_SESSION superglobal array. This is automatically saved.

When a session is restarted, using the session cookie from the browser, the $_SESSION array is populated from the stored data and can be read from that point. This way, data can be saved and restored between PHP pages.

To manage authentication, we first create a table of users and their details, including their administrative status.

The users table does not, however, store the user's password—instead, it stores a hash of the password. This is to protect the user data in case the data is compromised: the hash can't be reversed to regenerate the password.

PHP has the password_hash() function to generate a password hash for storage. When the time comes, we use the password_verify() function to check whether the submitted password has the same hash value and so matches the user's password.

The login form includes the user's email address for identification and the password to be hashed. After submitting, the email address is used to fetch the user's data from the database, including the password hash. If the password and hash don't match, then we generate a simple error message.

If the password and hash do match, then we save some data in the $_SESSION array. This data is used in a number of ways:

1. To switch between a login form and a logout form with administrative links

2. To replace the administration link with the user's name.

3. To decide whether the user has access to certain restricted pages.

The $_SESSION array, with its data, is dependent on being able to identify the session data. We can log the user out by emptying the $_SESSION array, deleting the stored data, and expiring the session cookie.

We can also wait, of course, until the session has timed out.

Coming Up

By now, we have covered a number of important principles in maintaining a dynamic website in PHP:

1. Using PHP code to manipulate parts of a web page

2. Managing uploaded data

3. Storing and maintaining data in a database

4.   Using PHP to read from and write to the database

5.   Securing parts of the website

In the next chapter, we'll put all of this together in developing a basic content management system. In the final part of the project, you'll develop a simple blog, in which you can upload blogging text and images, maintain the database, and present the blog to visitors.

CHAPTER 11

A Configuration System

A number of pages we've developed so far include arbitrary values, such as the dimensions of the images. Because they're not part of the logic, we put them in an array called $CONFIG near the top of the code, promising to do something with them later. Now, this is later.

Many packages use a special file format for configuration options. This includes PHP's default settings, php.ini, and the site's .user.ini file. This format is known as an **ini file**.

We're going to develop our own ini file with our site configuration options. We'll be able to use this file to change some of the arbitrary settings. This will replace the settings we put in individual files.

We'll also write a web page to make configuration easier and use the configuration file to replace the individual configuration data in the other pages. We'll then add this to our collection of administrative pages.

Using a configuration system like this, you can make your website more customizable.

The ini File Contents

We'll begin by creating an ini file for our settings. In the site root, create a file called config.ini.php.

M. Simon, *An Introduction to PHP*, https://doi.org/10.1007/979-8-8688-0177-8_11

Normally, the file would be something like config.ini, but we're going to use a special technique to hide the file from inquisitive visitors. The .php extension won't interfere with the way we use it. The .ini extension is unnecessary, but helps us to organize our code.

In theory, files like the site's .htaccess or .user.ini files should also be hidden from prying eyes. However, the web server already knows not to display them.

We can add the following to the config.ini.php files:

```
title = Australia Down Under
contact = Support <info@australia.example.com>

[images]
    directory = images
    display-size = 480 x 360
    thumbnail-size = 240 x 180
    icon-size = 40 x 30
    scaled = 50

[gallery]
    page-size = 3

[imagelist]
    page-size = 6
```

The ini file contains all of the $CONFIG array data from some of the previous pages that we worked on:

- contact.code.php
- gallery.code.php
- aside.code.php

- `imagelist.code.php`

- `manage-images.code.php`

all in one convenient location. When we've finished, we'll go back to those pages and get them to reference the new ini file.

At the beginning are two settings:

```
title = Australia Down Under
contact = Support <info@australia.example.com>
```

We won't need the `title` setting; it's only there as an example. We will, however, use the `contact` setting when we update the `contact.php` page.

Each item takes the following form:

```
item = value
```

After that, we have a number of sections, which are labeled in square brackets:

```
[section]
    item = value
    item = value
```

Not all ini files make use of sections, but they do make it easier to manage more complex collections of settings. This way, we can reuse the item name for different sections.

The first two settings (`title` and `contact`) aren't specifically in any section; you could say that they're in a global section. How you organize this is a matter of taste—you could also have created another section for the global settings or, on the other hand, dispense with sections altogether and name the items more distinctly.

The items in each section don't have to be indented. The indentation will be ignored. Indentation is only there to make the file more readable. The same with blank lines, which are also ignored.

In a moment, we'll read the data in the file, but first, we're going to protect the file from intruders.

Remember that the file has a `.php` extension. That means that if you open the file directly, it will first be processed by PHP. We can take advantage of that by adding a self-destruct statement at the beginning:

```
;<?php die("Nothing to see here ..."); ?>
...
```

The ini file is now a sort of hybrid file. Any line starting with a semicolon in an ini file is a comment—it will be ignored as ini data.

However, if you attempt to load the file directly, PHP will look inside the PHP block and see the `die` statement, which will immediately terminate the script with the message.

Making changes to the file isn't difficult, and it's easy enough to understand. In fact, we've been looking at that sort of thing when discussing PHP settings files. However, we can create a form to make it easier.

Reading an ini File

There is a file called `config.php`. There's not much in it at the moment. We're going to write some code to read the ini file and generate a table full of input elements. When we've finished, it will look like Figure 11-1.

Figure 11-1. *The Configuration Form*

All we have so far is this form:

```
<form method="post" action="">
    <table>
        <?= $table ?>
    </table>
    <button name="save">Save</button>
</form>
```

There's also a PHP block at the beginning which initializes the $table variable to an empty string.

First, we'll need to prepare the code. Create a new file in the includes directory called config.code.php. Then cut the PHP block from the config.php file to the new file. We can also include the code to calculate the $root variable:

```php
<?php
    $root = str_replace($_SERVER['SCRIPT_NAME'], '',
        $_SERVER['SCRIPT_FILENAME']);

    $table = '';
```

Don't forget to remove the closing PHP tag.

In the config.php file, add an include:

```php
<?php require_once 'includes/config.code.php'; ?>
<?php
    $pagetitle = 'Config';
    $pageheading = 'Configuration';

    require_once 'includes/head.inc.php';
?>
```

To read the ini file, we use the parse_ini_file() function:

```php
<?php
    $root = str_replace($_SERVER['SCRIPT_NAME'], '',
        $_SERVER['SCRIPT_FILENAME']);

    $CONFIG = parse_ini_file("$root/config.ini.php", true);

    $table = '';
```

The parse_ini_file() function has two values. The first is, of course, the location of the file. The second optional value is to enable sections. If it's left out, it defaults to false, which means the sections will be ignored. The items will still be set, but they won't be in sections. If a name appears twice in the same section, or the global section, the newer value will replace the older value.

If you were to print the $CONFIG array, you would see something like the following nested array:

```
Array
(
    [title] => Australia Down Under
    [contact] => Support <info@australia.example.com>
    [images] => Array
        (
            [directory] => images
            [display-size] => 480 x 360
            [thumbnail-size] => 240 x 180
            [icon-size] => 40 x 30
            [scaled] => 50
        )

    [gallery] => Array
        (
            [page-size] => 3
        )

    [imagelist] => Array
        (
            [page-size] => 6
        )

)
```

You can print this sort of result with the print_r() function:

```php
<?php
    $root = str_replace($_SERVER['SCRIPT_NAME'], '',
        $_SERVER['SCRIPT_FILENAME']);

    $CONFIG = parse_ini_file("$root/config.ini.php", true);
    print_r($CONFIG);

    $table = '';
```

The print_r() function is used to print the contents of a structure such as an array. You may need to view that page source to see the same layout, as an HTML page doesn't care much for line breaks. It may also make a mess of the page, but you can delete the statement as soon as you've finished checking it.

We now need to separate the global settings from the sectioned settings. In the following section, we'll need to treat them differently.

Each item in the array will either be a string, as for the global settings, or an array, as for the sectioned settings. In the arrays, there will, of course, be strings for the other settings.

To test for a string, you can use the is_string() function, while an array can be tested with the is_array() function. Both functions will either return true or false and so can be used as a filter.

In Chapters 7 and 9, we used the array_map() function to apply a function over the items in an array. There is another function called array_filter() which can be used to filter items in an array, resulting in a new array. We can use this to generate two arrays from the original:

```php
<?php
    $root = str_replace($_SERVER['SCRIPT_NAME'], '',
        $_SERVER['SCRIPT_FILENAME']);
```

```
$CONFIG = parse_ini_file("$root/config.ini.php", true);
$global = array_filter($CONFIG, 'is_string');
$sections = array_filter($CONFIG, 'is_array');

$table = '';
```

Just as with the array_map() function, the function is applied to every item in the array. In the array_map() function, the result is a new array with the changed values. In the array_filter() function, however, the result is a new array with only the items which tested true.

Also, *unlike* the array_map() function, the parameters are reversed: array_filter(array, function). Nobody knows why.

Generating the Configuration Form

When we finish, the form will contain a table with something like this:

item	value
item	value
Section	
item	value
item	value
Section	
item	value
item	value

The HTML will look something like this:

```
<table>
    <thead><tr><th colspan="2"></th></tr></thead>
    <tbody>
        <tr><td>item</td><td><input name="..."
        value="value"></tr>
        <tr><td>item</td><td><input name="..."
        value="value"></tr>
    </tbody>
    <thead><tr><th colspan="2">Section</th></tr></thead>
    <tbody>
        <tr><td>item</td><td><input name="..."
        value="value"></tr>
        <tr><td>item</td><td><input name="..."
        value="value"></tr>
    </tbody>
    <thead><tr><th colspan="2">Section</th></tr></thead>
    <tbody>
        <tr><td>item</td><td><input name="..."
        value="value"></tr>
        <tr><td>item</td><td><input name="..."
        value="value"></tr>
    </tbody>
</table>
```

The thead elements will be for the ini sections, while the tbody
elements will contain one or more tr row for each item within the section.

Each row in the tbody elements will include

- The name of the item

- An input element

The input element has a name and a value. The name will be one of two forms:

- The global items have a simple name such as name="contact".

- The sectioned items have an array name such as name="images[display-size]".

We've used array names for the edit and remove buttons, but with numbered keys. PHP will also accept associative keys and build an array accordingly.

Generating the Config Table

To generate the table, we'll begin with two template strings:

```php
<?php
    $root = str_replace($_SERVER['SCRIPT_NAME'], '',
        $_SERVER['SCRIPT_FILENAME']);

    $CONFIG = parse_ini_file("$root/config.ini.php", true);

    $thead = '<thead><tr><th colspan="2">%s</th></tr></thead>';
    $tr = '<tr><td>%s</td><td><input name="%s"
value="%s"></tr>';

    $table = '';
```

The colspan="2" in the first row will allow a single cell to span two columns, which, in this case, will be the entire row.

We'll use the same technique that we've used to populate tables in other code. This means initializing an empty $table array and imploding it afterward. We'll use the foreach() statement to iterate through the arrays:

```php
<?php
    $root = str_replace($_SERVER['SCRIPT_NAME'], '',
        $_SERVER['SCRIPT_FILENAME']);

    $CONFIG = parse_ini_file("$root/config.ini.php", true);

    $thead = '<thead><tr><th colspan="2">%s</th></tr></thead>';
    $tr = '<tr><td>%s</td><td><input name="%s"
    value="%s"></tr>';

    $table = [];

    foreach($global as $name => $value) {

    }

    foreach($sections as $section => $items) {

    }

    $table = implode($table);
```

Here, we have *two* foreach() statements, one for each part of the original $CONFIG array. The first foreach() uses the variables $name and $value, because the items will be simple. The second foreach() uses the variables $section and $items. In turn, we'll use another foreach() for the nested $items array.

We don't need the $table = ''; statement anymore, since imploding an empty array will give you an empty string anyway. Of course, it won't be empty when we've finished with it.

We need to begin our table with a section for the global settings. We can do this by adding a thead row with an empty value. We'll also need to wrap the items in a tbody section:

```php
<?php
    ...
    $table = [];
    $table[] = sprintf($thead, '');
    $table[] = '<tbody>';
    ...
    $table = implode($table);
```

The thead sections have a weird behavior. Originally, you were expected to put the thead *after* the tbody, and it would hoist itself to the top. You'll see the same behavior if you have a tbody before a thead—the thead would creep before it. That's why we have a thead with empty content, just to stop the next thead from moving up.

For the global items, we can now add the table rows, using the sprintf() function and the $tr template string:

```php
<?php
    ...
    $table = [];

    $table[] = sprintf($thead, '');
    $table[] = '<tbody>';
    foreach($global as $name => $value) {
        $table[] = sprintf($tr, $name, $name, $value);
    }
    $table[] = '</tbody>';

    ...
```

The $name variable is used twice: once for the label and once for the name attribute of the input. The $value is used for the current value of the input.

For the sectioned settings, it's a little more complicated:

- Each section will need an additional thead element.

- Each item is a nested array which also needs to be iterated.

- The name property will be more complicated.

We can add a new thead section in the foreach() block. At the same time, we can add the tbody tags for the nested item:

```php
<?php
    ...

    foreach($sections as $section => $items) {
        $table[] = sprintf($thead, $section);
        $table[] = '<tbody>';

        $table[] = '</tbody>';
    }

    $table = implode($table);
```

Inside the foreach() block, we can add another foreach() block to iterate through the $items nested array:

```php
<?php
    ...

    foreach($sections as $section => $items) {
        $table[] = sprintf($thead, $section);
        $table[] = '<tbody>';
        foreach($global as $name => $value) {
```

```
        $table[] = sprintf($tr, $name, $name, $value);
    }
    $table[] = '</tbody>';
}

$table = implode($table);
```

The foreach() block is basically a copy of the previous one for the global settings, except that we iterate through the $items array.

The name, however, will not be quite right.

Because this is a nested array, we'll need the name to be in the form section[name]. The first instance of the $name variable is just a label and can stay as it is. The second should be replaced with "{$section} [$name]". The double-quoted string allows the variable to be interpolated:

```
foreach($sections as $section => $items) {
    $table[] = sprintf($thead, $section);
    $table[] = '<tbody>';
    foreach($global as $name => $value) {
        $table[] = sprintf($tr, $name, "$section[$name]"`,
        $value);
    }
    $table[] = '</tbody>';
}
```

We had to wrap the $section variable inside braces. Otherwise, the following square brackets would fool PHP into thinking it's another PHP array.

We can now load the configuration data into the form.

Saving the Configuration

PHP does not include a function for writing an ini file, so we'll need to do this ourselves.

First, we'll look out for the submit button:

```php
<?php
    $root = str_replace($_SERVER['SCRIPT_NAME'], '',
        $_SERVER['SCRIPT_FILENAME']);

    $CONFIG = parse_ini_file("$root/config.ini.php", true);

    if(isset($_POST['save'])) {

    }

    $global = array_filter($CONFIG, 'is_string');
    $sections = array_filter($CONFIG, 'is_array');
```

The $_POST array should have all the configuration, but it also includes the save button. In theory, it might also include some other unwanted data. It's also possible that some incoming data is missing.

Reading the New Values

We're going to create a new array to store the values we want to save, but we also need to make sure to save only the right data. What we need to do is include missing values, but exclude extra values. We can do this in two steps.

First, only include items whose keys are in *both* the $_POST array and the preexisting $CONFIG array. We can do this with the array_intersect_ key() function, which returns a new array with only the keys in both:

```php
$settings = array_intersect_key($_POST, $CONFIG);
```

Only the keys which are in both arrays will be copied into the new $settings array. At the same time, values will be copied from the *first* array ($_POST) to the *second* array ($CONFIG), which is, of course, the whole point.

If, somehow, the $_POST array was missing some of the keys from the original, the $settings array will also be missing them. To fix that, we can use the array_replace_recursive() function:

```
$settings = array_replace_recursive($CONFIG, $settings);
```

This will copy items from the *second* array to the *first* array, including the missing ones. Notice that, again, the order of parameters works differently to the previous function. This is PHP.[1]

We can now add the code:

```
<?php
    $root = str_replace($_SERVER['SCRIPT_NAME'], '',
        $_SERVER['SCRIPT_FILENAME']);

·   $CONFIG = parse_ini_file("$root/config.ini.php", true);

    if(isset($_POST['save'])) {
        $settings = array_intersect_key($_POST, $CONFIG);
        $settings = array_replace_recursive($CONFIG,
        $settings);
    }

    $global = array_filter($CONFIG, 'is_string');
    $sections = array_filter($CONFIG, 'is_array');
```

Once we have the $settings array, we'll need to write it to the file.

---

[1] Seriously, PHP has a reputation for unexpected parameter order.

Writing the ini File

Writing out the PHP file is simply a matter of iterating through the $settings array. We're going to overwrite the original file completely.

We'll begin by initializing a new array variable, which we'll implode at the end:

```
if(isset($_POST['save'])) {
    $settings = array_intersect_key($_POST, $CONFIG);
    $settings = array_replace_recursive($CONFIG, $settings);

    $ini = [];

    $ini = implode("\r\n", $ini);
}
```

This time, we've joined the items with a line break in between ("\r\n" for good measure).

The $settings array has global items and nested items. We can test which type with the in_array() function. If it fails, it's a global item:

```
if(isset($_POST['save'])) {
    $settings = array_intersect_key($_POST, $CONFIG);
    $settings = array_replace_recursive($CONFIG, $settings);

    $ini = [];
    foreach($settings AS $name => $value) {
        if(!is_array($value)) $ini[] = "$name = $value";
        else {
            // section
        }
    }
    $ini = implode("\r\n", $ini);
}
```

For a global item, we add a simple name = value string.

For a section, we'll add the section heading and then iterate through the items:

```
foreach($settings AS $name => $value) {
    if(!is_array($value)) $ini[] = "$name = $value";
    else {
        $ini[] = "[$name]";
        foreach($value as $name => $value)
            $ini[] = "\t$name = $value";
    }
}
```

The section string is simply the section name in square brackets. For each section, we have a foreach() statement. It doesn't need braces, since it's a simple statement.

You'll notice the foreach() statement:

```
foreach($value as $name => $value) ... ;
```

The $value variable is being replaced with other values through the iteration. That's OK, since its original value has already been read and isn't needed anymore. If it makes you feel uncomfortable, you might use something like this:

```
foreach($value as $n => $v) $ini[] = "\t$n = $v"; ;
```

To write the file, we can use the file_put_contents() function:

```
if(isset($_POST['save'])) {
    ...

    $ini = implode("\r\n", $ini);

    file_put_contents("$root/config.ini.php", $ini);
}
```

Finally, you can reassign the $CONFIG variable to the new value of the array:

```
if(isset($_POST['save'])) {
    ...

    $ini = implode("\r\n", $ini);

    file_put_contents("$root/config.ini.php", $ini);
    $CONFIG = $settings;
}
```

You can now save changes to your ini file. Of course, it won't make any difference because the existing pages still use their own settings. We'll now have to modify those pages to use the new settings.

When writing out the file, we first assembled what needs to be written and then wrote it out in one statement. PHP also has the ability to write out one line at a time, but it's more complicated and involves more disk activity. If possible, it's usually better to minimize reading and writing to disk storage.

Using the Configuration Settings

As we saw, there are five pages that use arbitrary values, which we put into a hard-coded $CONFIG variable:

- contact.code.php
- gallery.code.php
- aside.code.php
- imagelist.code.php
- manage-images.code.php

We'll start with the contact page code. At the top of the code, you'll see something like

```php
<?php
    // Configuration
    $CONFIG['contact']['to']
        = 'Support <info@australia.example.com>';
```

We'll need to make a few changes to this file. First, we'll add the $root variable to the top, something we've been using for other code:

```php
<?php
    $root = str_replace($_SERVER['SCRIPT_NAME'], '',
        $_SERVER['SCRIPT_FILENAME']);

    // Configuration
    $CONFIG['contact']['to']
        = 'Support <info@australia.example.com>';
```

We'll now replace the configuration code with a statement to load the ini file. There's no need to keep the comment.

```php
<?php
    $root = str_replace($_SERVER['SCRIPT_NAME'], '',
        $_SERVER['SCRIPT_FILENAME']);

    $CONFIG = parse_ini_file("$root/config.ini.php", true);
```

The other change is to note that the to address is a global setting, not a sectioned setting. There's no technical requirement for it to be one or the other, and this is a simple change to handle.

In the code which sends the email, change the $to variable to the new settings:

```php
if(!$errors) {          // If no errors, Send Email
    $to = $CONFIG['contact'];
    ...
}
else {                  //  Else, Report Errors
    ...
}
```

We'll now do something similar for the other files: gallery.code.php, aside.code.php, imagelist.code.php, and manage-images.code.php.

At the beginning of these files, add the $root variable. In some cases, it's already there, so don't bother with those:

```php
<?php
    $root = str_replace($_SERVER['SCRIPT_NAME'], '',
        $_SERVER['SCRIPT_FILENAME']);

    ...
```

Rewrite any includes to use the $root variable. Again, in some cases, it's already there:

```php
<?php
    $root = str_replace($_SERVER['SCRIPT_NAME'], '',
        $_SERVER['SCRIPT_FILENAME']);

    $pdo = require_once "$root/includes/pdo.php";
    require_once "$root/includes/default-library.php";
    require_once "$root/includes/library.php";

    ...
```

Now replace the $CONFIG array assignments with the statement to load the ini file. Again, you can remove the comment:

```php
<?php
    $root = str_replace($_SERVER['SCRIPT_NAME'], '',
        $_SERVER['SCRIPT_FILENAME']);

    $pdo = require_once "$root/includes/pdo.php";
    require_once "$root/includes/default-library.php";
    require_once "$root/includes/library.php";

    $CONFIG = parse_ini_file("$root/config.ini.php", true);

    ...
```

You won't need to change anything else in these files. They're now ready to use the new configuration.

Resizing Images

Some of the settings include image dimensions. We made use of these dimensions when uploading or importing the images, so changing these dimensions really ought to include an update in the saved images.

To resize the images, we'll need to access the database to get a list of images and the default library to resize them. At the beginning of the code, make sure you have the following includes:

```php
<?php
    $root = str_replace($_SERVER['SCRIPT_NAME'], '',
        $_SERVER['SCRIPT_FILENAME']);

    require_once "$root/includes/pdo.php";
    require_once "$root/includes/default-library.php";
```

Just before the **Save** button is a checkbox:

```
<label><input type="checkbox" name="resize"> Resize Images
</label>
```

If selected, this input will be included with the rest of the submitted form. We'll use that to decide whether we want to resize the images.

At the end of the save code, add a test for the checkbox:

```
if(isset($_POST['save'])) {

    ...

    file_put_contents("$root/config.ini.php", $ini);

    if(isset($_POST['resize'])) {

    }

    $CONFIG = $settings;
}
```

The code is *before* the reassignment to the $CONFIG variable. We'll need the original shortly.

To resize the images, we'll do something similar to what we did when importing the images. But first, we'll need a list of images. Since we're not going to make any other changes, we only need the src value of all of the images.

To get the src of all the images, we can use

```
SELECT src FROM images;
```

Since there's no user data, we can use the query() method directly, and since the SQL is simple, we can use a literal string:

```
$pdo -> query('SELECT src FROM images');
```

We can iterate through the result directly with a foreach():

```
foreach($pdo -> query('SELECT src FROM images') as $row) {
    ... ;
}
```

Remember that the $row variable will be an array of values. We can destructure the row with

```
[$src] = $row;
```

However, you can also do that directly in the foreach():

```
foreach($pdo -> query('SELECT src FROM images') as [$src]) {
    ...
}
```

In the manage-images.code.php file is the addImageFile() function. We can copy the resizeImage() calls to the current code:

```
if(isset($_POST['resize'])) {
    foreach($pdo -> query('SELECT src FROM images') as
    [$src]) {
        resizeImage(
            "$root/{$CONFIG['images']['directory']}/
            originals/$src",
            "$root/{$CONFIG['images']['directory']}/
            display/$src",
            $CONFIG['images']['display-size']
        );
        resizeImage(
            "$root/{$CONFIG['images']['directory']}/
            originals/$src",
            "$root/{$CONFIG['images']['directory']}/
            thumbnails/$src",
```

```php
        $CONFIG['images']['thumbnail-size']
    );
    resizeImage(
        "$root/{$CONFIG['images']['directory']}/
        originals/$src",
        "$root/{$CONFIG['images']['directory']}/
        icons/$src",
        $CONFIG['images']['icon-size']
    );
    resizeImage(
        "$root/{$CONFIG['images']['directory']}/
        originals/$src",
        "$root/{$CONFIG['images']['directory']}/
        scaled/$src",
        $CONFIG['images']['scaled'], ['method'=>'scale']
    );
  }
}
```

You may find that resizing all of the images takes a long time, depending on the speed of your machine, the number of images, and the size of the originals. In fact, you may find the PHP times out after 30 seconds. If you need more time, you can *temporarily* adjust the timeout settings.

At the beginning of the script, add the following statement:

```php
<?php
    ini_set('max_execution_time', 60);
```

When you've finished your resizing, you can delete the statement or, at least, comment it out:

```php
<?php
    // ini_set('max_execution_time', 60);
```

Still, this can be a waste of resources if only one of the settings has been changed. You can prepend the resizeImage() function with a comparison between the new $settings variable and the original $CONFIG variable:

```
if($settings['images']['display-size']
    != $CONFIG['images']['display-size'])
resizeImage(
    ...
);
if($settings['images']['thumbnail-size']
    != $CONFIG['images']['thumbnail-size'])
resizeImage(
    ...
);
if($settings['images']['icon-size']
    != $CONFIG['images']['icon-size'])
resizeImage(
    ...
);
if($settings['images']['scaled']
    != $CONFIG['images']['scaled'])
resizeImage(
    ...
);
```

If you really need to redo all of the images regardless, you can comment out the line with the if() statements. (If you wrote the if statements on two lines, as in the preceding example, don't forget to comment out *both* lines.)

Adding Configuration to Administration

The final step is to add the configuration page to the administration section. This means

- Adding a link in the admin.php page
- Checking whether the user is a logged-in administrator

In the admin.php page, add the following link:

```
<ul id="admin-links">
    <li><a href="imagelist.php">Manage Images</a></li>
    <li><a href="bloglist.php">Manage Blog</a></li>
    <li><a href="config.php">Configuration</a></li>
</ul>
```

You'll now see an additional link, styled to look like a big button. In the config.code.php file, add the following to check for the user:

```
//  ini_set('max_execution_time', 60);
if(!session_id()) {
    session_start();
    session_regenerate_id(true);
}

$root = str_replace($_SERVER['SCRIPT_NAME'], '',
    $_SERVER['SCRIPT_FILENAME']);
$host = $_SERVER['HTTP_HOST'];
$protocol = isset($_SERVER['HTTPS']) && $_
SERVER['HTTPS'] == 'on'
    ? 'https'
    : 'http';
```

```php
if(!isset($_SESSION['user']) || !$_SESSION['admin']) {
    header("Location: $protocol://$host/admin.php");
    exit;
}
```

We've already added the $root variable.

We have now extended the administration to include configuration.

Summary

It's important to be able to separate the logic and fundamental values of your code from arbitrary values, such as image dimensions.

A good way of defining arbitrary values is to put them in a configuration file. A common format is the ini file, a format which is used for many other applications.

The ini file format can be a simple flat format, or it can include sections for more complex structures. PHP has a parse_ini_file() format which can read the file into an array, optionally with sections as nested arrays.

In order to protect the ini file from casual browsing, you can make the file a hybrid PHP file by adding the .php extension and including a self-destruct statement as a comment line.

Although you can easily configure an ini file by hand, you can make it easier by developing a form and letting PHP manage the file that way. You can also use the opportunity to check the data.

When you submit the form, you can read the new configuration settings into an array and check it against the original array.

PHP doesn't include a file to write out an ini file, but you can take the new array, implode it, and write it out to a single text file with the file_put_contents() function.

Reconfiguration may involve resizing the copies of the image. This is easily done, but resizing a large number of images may take a little while and may exceed the normal time limit for PHP processes. It's possible to extend the time allowed using the `ini_set()` function, but this shouldn't be a permanent change. It's also possible to limit what needs resizing by checking the new settings against the old.

Finally, it's important to protect the configuration page by restricting it to logged-in administrators. It's also useful to add a link to the page to the administration page.

Coming Up

By now, we have covered a number of important principles in maintaining a dynamic website in PHP:

- Using PHP code to manipulate parts of a web page

- Managing uploaded data

- Storing and maintaining data in a database

- Using PHP to read from and write to the database

- Securing parts of the website

In the next chapter, we'll put all of this together in developing a basic content manage system. In the final part of the project, you'll develop a simple blog, in which you can upload blogging text and images, maintain the database, and present the blog to visitors.

CHAPTER 12

A Content Management System

In this chapter, we consolidate the skills developed in this book and work with a practical example of working with data in a database.

In this chapter, we'll create a blog management system. This will be similar to the work we did for working with the images, so much of the code will be copied and pasted from existing code.

The word "blog" comes from a "web log." Possibly, someone read that as "we blog" and turned that last part into a distinct word, or possibly someone was in too much of a hurry to use the full term and shortened it, as one does. Best not to get blogged down in that.

This chapter combines the techniques developed in managing, navigating, and viewing the images in the database, as well as in using the configuration and security we developed.

In this chapter, we'll be working on the following tasks, based largely on the work covered in previous chapters:

- Uploading a new article

- Attaching an image to the uploaded article

- Bulk uploading of articles and images

© Mark Simon 2024
M. Simon, *An Introduction to PHP*, https://doi.org/10.1007/979-8-8688-0177-8_12

- Viewing an article with an image

- Developing a list page of articles

- Editing and deleting selected articles

We'll also use the work done in previous chapters to

- Secure the administration pages

- Extend the configuration settings

By the end, we'll have a fairly comprehensive system to manage data in a database.

The Blog Pages

We'll be working on four pages, two for administration and two for the visitor:

- For the administrator, we'll have a list page of articles to be edited and a page for editing the articles.

  This is similar to the list and edit pages for the images.

- For the visitor, there'll be a list page of articles to be read and a page with the individual article.

  For the images, the list page is combined with a single image. These two will be separate for the blog articles, as they are potentially quite long.

The administration pages are

- `admin-bloglist.php`: The list of articles to be edited

- `edit-blog.php`: The generic page to insert a new article or to update or delete an existing article.

As with the image management pages, there will be a system of events between the pages, as you see in Figure 12-1.

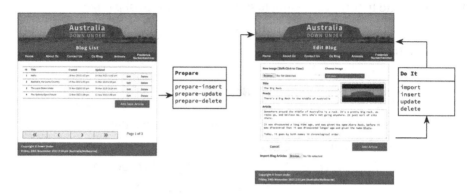

Figure 12-1. *Administration List and Edit Pages*

For the visitor, the pages are

- `bloglist.php`: The list of articles to be read

- `blogarticle.php`: The individual article for reading

The list page will contain links to view the individual articles as in Figure 12-2.

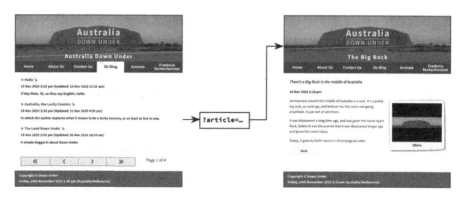

Figure 12-2. *Visitor List and Read Pages*

409

Although logically you would expect to see the article list first, it won't be populated until we have at least one article. For this reason, we will begin with the Insert processing first on the editblog.php page.

Just to help you keep track of the many files we'll be working with, here is a list of them:

Existing Files	New Files
blogarticle.php	manage-blog.code.php
bloglist.php	blog.code.php
config.ini.php	admin-bloglist.code.php
	bloglist.code.php

The Blog Table

The blog articles will be stored, of course, in a separate database table. The table will have the following columns:

Column	Purpose	Data Type
id	ID (primary key)	auto_increment int
imageid	Reference to an image	int
title	Entry title	varchar(255)
precis	Summary of article	varchar(1024)
article	Article contents	text
created	Created date	timestamp (date)
updated	Updated date	timestamp (date)

- The id will be an auto-incremented integer, similar to
  the id in the images table.

- The imageid will be a reference to an id in the images
  table. This is referred to as a **foreign key**.

  The image will be optional, which is to say that
  imageid may be null. If it's not null, then it *must*
  match one of the IDs in the images table.

- The title is just a title for the article.

  If you add a new image for the blog article, the title
  will be used for the image as well.

- The article is the article itself, while the precis is a
  brief summary of the article. The data type text is sort
  of unlimited in size.

  If you add a new image for the blog article, the
  precis will be used for the image description.

- The created and updated columns are the date and
  time the article was created and, later, when it was
  updated.

To create the blog table, you can use the code from the /setup/mysql/
createblog.sql file. It looks like this:

```
USE australia;
DROP TABLE IF EXISTS blog;
CREATE TABLE blog (
    id INT UNSIGNED AUTO_INCREMENT PRIMARY KEY,
    imageid INT UNSIGNED REFERENCES images(id) ON DELETE SET NULL,
    title varchar(255) NOT NULL,
    precis varchar(1024) NOT NULL,
    article text NOT NULL,
```

```
    created timestamp NOT NULL default CURRENT_TIMESTAMP,
    updated timestamp NOT NULL default CURRENT_TIMESTAMP
) CHARACTER SET utf8mb4 COLLATE utf8mb4_unicode_520_ci
ENGINE=INNODB;
```

You'll notice that all of the values are NOT NULL except for the imageid, which is optional, and the id which is a primary key and, therefore, never NULL.

In principle, you could set the updated column to NULL when the row is first inserted and set a new value when the row is updated. That would be a perfectly satisfactory approach.

We've taken the view here that the column will be set to the same as the created column when the row is inserted, and updated later as necessary. This would allow us to search the updated column alone if we just want the dates.

The imageid column has two special features related to its role as a foreign key. First is the REFERENCES images(id) clause which is what defines it as a foreign key. Second is the ON DELETE SET NULL clause, which means that if an image is deleted from the images table, the matching imageid in the blog table would be set to NULL. This guarantees that a blog article cannot reference a non-existing image.

As usual, you can create the table by entering the code directly into the SQL tab of PHPMyAdmin—don't forget to first select the australia database.

Alternatively, you can click the **Create Blog Table** link on the setup page or go directly to

```
http://australia.example.com/setup?action=blogcreate
```

We can now start writing the code to add an article.

Preparatory Blog Code

The first page to work on is the `editblog.php` page. When it's finished, it should look something like Figure 12-3.

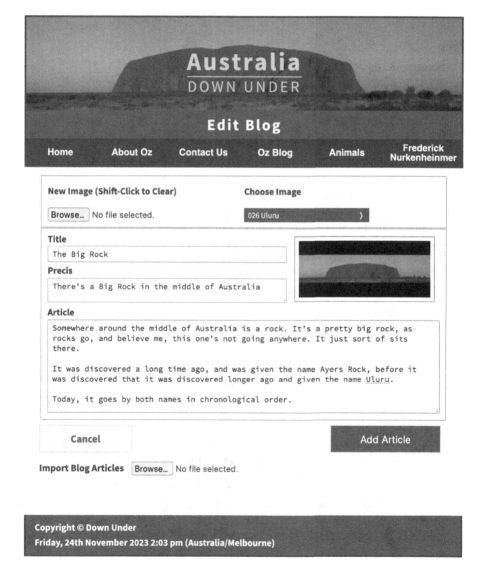

Figure 12-3. *Edit Blog Page*

First, create a file in the includes directory called manage-blog.code.
php. We can copy much of the introductory code from manage-images.
code.php to add the following.

We've included a comment in the beginning identifying the file name,
since it's easy to get lost when working with multiple files:

```php
<?php
#    manage-blog.code.php

    if(!session_id()) {
        session_start();
        session_regenerate_id(true);
    }

    $root = str_replace($_SERVER['SCRIPT_NAME'], '',
        $_SERVER['SCRIPT_FILENAME']);

    $host = $_SERVER['HTTP_HOST'];
    $protocol = isset($_SERVER['HTTPS']) && $_
SERVER['HTTPS'] == 'on'
        ? 'https'
        : 'http';

    if(!isset($_SESSION['user']) || !$_SESSION['admin']) {
        header("Location: $protocol://$host/admin.php");
        exit;
    }

    require_once "$root/includes/pdo.php";
    require_once "$root/includes/default-library.php";
    require_once "$root/includes/library.php";

    $CONFIG = parse_ini_file("$root/config.ini.php",true);
```

We can also initialize variables. These come directly from the current editblog.php page, so you can cut them from there and paste into the new file:

```php
<?php
#   manage-blog.code.php

    ...

    // Initialise
    $title = $precis = $article = '';
    $id = 0;
    $errors = '';
    $disabled = '';
    $chooseImage = $previewImage = '';

    $pagetitle = 'Edit Blog';
    $pageheading = 'Edit Blog';
```

- The $title, $precis, and $article variables will constitute the text data for the blog article, similar to the $title and $description for the images.

- The $id will be used to identify an existing article; it will be 0 for a new article.

- The $errors variable is for error handling.

- The $disabled variable is to disable a fieldset if the article is to be deleted.

- The $chooseImage variable will be used for a list of existing images which may be included.

- The $previewImage variable will be used later to preview an existing image.

- The $pagetitle and $pageheading variables will be set dynamically, as we did for the Edit Image page.

In the editblog.php file, you can replace the opening PHP block with an include:

```php
<?php require_once 'includes/manage-blog.code.php'; ?>
<?php require_once 'includes/head.inc.php'; ?>
```

In the main form part are some comments for conditional blocks:

```
    <form ... id="editblog-form">
        <input type="hidden" name="id" value="<?= $id ?>">
        <?= $errors ?>
<!-- if not delete -->
        <fieldset id="new-image" <?= $disabled ?>>

            ...

        </fieldset>
<!-- endif -->
        <fieldset id="content" <?= $disabled ?>>

            ...

        </fieldset>
        <p id="control">
            <a class="button" href="/admin-bloglist.php">
            Cancel</a>
<!-- if edit -->
            <button type="submit" name="update">
                Submit Changes</button>
<!-- elseif remove -->
            <button type="submit" name="delete">
                Delete this Article</button>
<!-- else -->
            <button type="submit" name="insert">Add Article
            </button>
<!-- endif -->
        </p>
    </form>
```

```
<!-- if not $id -->
    <form id="editblog-import" method="post"
    enctype="multipart/form-data">
        ...
    </form>
<!-- endif -->
```

You'll notice that they already have PHP output blocks. The conditional sections will work the same way as for the editimages.php page, so we can replace the comments with PHP blocks:

```
<form method="post" action="" id="editblog-form">
    <input type="hidden" name="id" value="<?= $id ?>">
    <?= $errors ?>
<?php if(!isset($_POST['prepare-delete'])): ?>
    <fieldset id="new-image" <?= $disabled ?>>
        ...
    </fieldset>
<?php endif; ?>
    <fieldset id="content" <?= $disabled ?>>
        ...
    </fieldset>
    <p id="control">
        <a class="button" href="/admin-bloglist.php">
        Cancel</a>
<?php if(isset($_POST['prepare-update'])): ?>
        <button type="submit" name="update">
            Submit Changes</button>
<?php elseif(isset($_POST['prepare-delete'])): ?>
        <button type="submit" name="delete">
            Delete this Article</button>
```

```php
<?php else: ?>
            <button type="submit" name="insert">Add Article
            </button>
<?php endif; ?>
        </p>
    </form>
<?php if(!$id): ?>
    <form id="editblog-import" ...>
        ...
    </form>
<?php endif; ?>
```

We can now write the code for adding blog articles.

Adding a Single Blog Article

The page to add or edit a blog article is called editblog.php. Similar to the editimage.php page, this page will come from the previous admin-bloglist. php page. In turn, that will come from the previous admin.php page:

admin.php ➤ admin-bloglist.php ➤ editblog.php

Of course, you'll need to log in to get there.

Much of the code we write here will be used in other sections, so we'll write much of that code in reusable functions.

First, we can write the preparatory code adding an article. In the manage-blog.code.php file, we can write some code to prepare for inserting a new article:

```php
<?php
#   manage-blog.code.php
    ...
    // Initialise
        ...
```

```
//  Prepare Page
    if(isset($_POST['prepare-insert'])) {
        $pagetitle = 'Upload Article';
        $pageheading = 'Upload Article';
    }
```

This, of course, presupposes that you've come from the admin-bloglist.php page. While we're developing the code, that won't always be true, so we can temporarily change the code to

```
<?php
#   manage-blog.code.php

    ...
    //  Prepare Page
    if(empty($_POST) || isset($_POST['prepare-insert'])) {
        $pagetitle = 'Upload Article';
        $pageheading = 'Upload Article';
    }
```

The empty() function will test whether the $_POST array is empty, as it would be if you just loaded the page directly. Later, we can remove this test.

After that, we can write the test to actually insert the article:

```
<?php
#   manage-blog.code.php

    ...
    //  Initialise
        ...
    //  Prepare Page
        ...
    //  Process
    if(isset($_POST['insert'])) {
    }
```

Both the insert and update events will need to read the submitted data and to check it for errors. The data we're looking for is

- The $id of the submitted data as an integer. It will be 0 for a new article.

- The $title, $precis, and the $article, all of which will be from text fields.

- The $image to be included, if any.

- The $errors array.

We'll write a function called getBlogData() to do that:

```php
<?php
#    manage-blog.code.php
    ...

    //  Get Submitted Data
        function getBlogData() {
        }

    //  Process
        if(isset($_POST['insert'])) {
        }
```

The function will return an array with the checked data.

We'll begin with fetching four pieces of data from the $_POST array, the id, title, precis, and article data. We'll also set a fifth piece of data, the $image variable, to null as a placeholder for later:

```php
function getBlogData() {
    $id = intval($_POST['id']);
    $title = trim($_POST['title']);
    $precis = trim($_POST['precis']);
```

```
    $article = trim($_POST['article']);
    $image = null;
}
```

The $id is an integer, while the rest are strings. If we're inserting a new article, the $id will be a 0, which we'll be ignoring. It's more important when we're updating.

Next, check for errors. This means initializing an empty $errors array and testing for missing values. After that, we can return an array with the values as well as the $errors array:

```
function getBlogData() {
    $id = intval($_POST['id']);
    $title = trim($_POST['title']);
    $precis = trim($_POST['precis']);
    $article = trim($_POST['article']);
    $image = null;

    $errors = [];

    //  Check Text
        if(!$title) $errors[] = 'Missing Title';
        if(!$precis) $errors[] = 'Missing Précis';
        if(!$article) $errors[] = 'Missing Article';

    return [$id, $title, $precis, $article, $image, $errors];
}
```

This time, not including an image isn't an error. We'll handle the uploaded image in the next section. For now, we'll set it to null.

Back to the insert article code, we can first fetch the data using getBlogData() and test the $errors array:

```
if(isset($_POST['insert'])) {
    [$id, $title, $precis, $article, $image, $errors] =
    getBlogData();
```

```
if(!$errors) {  //  proceed

}
else {            //  handle error
    $errors = sprintf('<p class="errors">%s</p>',
        implode('<br>',$errors));
}
}
```

If there are no errors, we'll want to add the result to the database. Since we'll also be importing blog articles from a CSV later, we'll write a separate function to do that.

After the getBlogData() function, we can start another function called addBlogData():

```
<?php
#   manage-blog.code.php
    ...

    //  Get Submitted Data
    function getBlogData() {

        ...

    }

    //  Add Blog Data
    function addBlogData(string $title, string $precis,
        string $article) {
        global $pdo, $root, $CONFIG;

        return $id;
    }

    //  Process
    if(isset($_POST['insert'])) {

        ...

    }
```

This function will accept the title, precis, and article as parameters and return the id of the new article. It includes a global statement to access the $pdo variable, as well as the $root and $CONFIG variables, which we'll be needing later.

You'll have noticed that we haven't needed a global statement for the $_POST array. That's why it's called a superglobal variable—it, as well as the other superglobals, is always available inside functions.

Unfortunately, you can't create your own superglobals. You can, however, access outside variables using the $GLOBALS array, such as $GLOBALS['pdo'].

The précis and article may include line breaks, so we'll run them both through the nl2pilcrow() function:

```
function addBlogData(string $title, string $precis, string
$article) {
    global $pdo, $root, $CONFIG;

    $precis = nl2pilcrow($precis);
    $article = nl2pilcrow($article);

    return $id;
}
```

The data can now be added to the database:

```
function addBlogData(string $title, string $precis, string
$article) {
    global $pdo;

    $precis = nl2pilcrow($precis);
    $article = nl2pilcrow($article);
```

```
$sql = 'INSERT INTO blog(title, precis, article, created,
updated)
    VALUES(?, ?, ?, ?, ?)';
$pdoStatement = $pdo -> prepare($sql);
$data = [$title, $precis, $article,
    date('Y-m-d H:i:s'), date('Y-m-d H:i:s')];
$pdoStatement->execute($data);

    return $id;
}
```

Although we're really only adding the title, precis, and article for now, we also need to set the date and time the article was created and updated. We could have used MySQL's now() function instead of one of the placeholder values, but later we'll want to set different dates.[1]

Here, we face a language problem: we want to default a missing date to the current date and time. However, PHP's equivalent of now(), such as the time() function, gives us a number (the number of seconds since January 1970), which doesn't work with MySQL. We'll have to convert the current date and time to a string. We can do that with the date() function:

```
date('Y-m-d H:i:s')
```

This will give us a date format like 1969-07-20 20:17:40 (which is the date and time of the moon landing). Without specifying a particular time, the date() function uses the current date and time.

---

[1] Australia did play an important role in the moon landing, but we weren't writing blog articles about it, or about anything else, at the time.

Next, we can fetch the id of the new article so that it can be returned:

```
function addBlogData(string $title, string $precis, string
$article) {

    ...

    $id = $pdo -> lastInsertId();

    return $id;
}
```

Back again to the Insert code, we can use the addBlogData() function to add the result of the getBlogData() function. We'll also clear the variables when that's done:

```
if(isset($_POST['insert'])) {
    [$id, $title, $precis, $article, $image, $errors] =
    getBlogData();

        if(!$errors) {  //  proceed
            $id = addBlogData($title, $precis, $article);

            //  Finish Up (temporary)
                $errors = '';
                $title = $precis = $article = '';
                $id = 0;
        }
        else {            //  handle error
            $errors = sprintf('<p class="errors">%s</p>',
                implode('<br>',$errors));
        }
}
```

The Finish Up code clears the variables, but that's temporary. When we've finished the code, we'll redirect to the `admin-bloglist.php` page. For now, we'll stay on the page while we continue developing and testing.

This code is much simpler than for adding an image, because we've ignored the image.

You can test the page now, but for now you'll only see the results if you browse the table in PHPMyAdmin.

Uploading the Optional Image

We have allowed for an optional image. When we add it, we'll take a similar approach to adding a new image for the gallery, but there will be some changes:

- Since the image is optional, it's not an error if it's missing—only if it's the wrong type or too big. We'll use similar code to that for replacing an image.

- We won't have the adjusted image file name yet, since it isn't part of the previous code. We'll need to work it out separately.

- The blog data will need to be updated with the `id` of the newly added image.

We'll also have the option of including an image that's already in our `images` table.

Again, we'll want to add an image while we're updating the article, so we'll write a separate function for that too, called `addBlogImage()`.

First, we'll make a small adjustment to the `addBlogData()` function to accept an optional image. In turn, the `addBlogData()` function will call the `addBlogImage()` function:

```
function addBlogData(string $title, string $precis, string
$article,
    array|string $image=null) {
    ...
    $id = $pdo -> lastInsertId();

    return $id;
}
```

You'll notice that the parameter variable $image has two types
separated with the or symbol (|). This is referred to as a **union** type. In
a moment, we'll send an array to the variable, but later it will be a string.
Assigning null makes it optional.

Union types are only available as of PHP 8. If you're running an earlier
version of PHP, you should just leave out the data type for that last
parameter and just use $image=null.

In the insert code, add the following to include the $image parameter:

```
if(isset($_POST['insert'])) {
    [$id, $title, $precis, $article, $image, $errors] =
    getBlogData();

    //  Process
        if(!$errors) {  //  proceed
            $id = addBlogData($title, $precis, $article,
            $image);

            ...

        }
```

```
    else {              // handle error
        ...
    }
}
```

The $image variable is initialized to null, which is acceptable as any data type.

Checking for an Optional Image

We can now check to see whether an image has been included and whether it's OK. We'll adapt the code for checking a replaced image in manage-images.code.php. You'll find it in the if(isset($_POST['update'])) code.

```
function getBlogData() {
    ...

    $errors = [];

    // From manage-images.code.php:if(isset($_POST['update']))
    // Optional Image
        if(isset($_FILES['image']) && $_FILES['image']['error']
            != UPLOAD_ERR_NO_FILE) {
            $imagetypes = ['image/gif', 'image/jpeg',
            'image/png',
                'image/webp'];
            switch($_FILES['image']['error']) {
                case UPLOAD_ERR_OK:
                    if(!in_array($_FILES['image']['type'],
                    $imagetypes))
                            $errors[] = 'Not a suitable
                            image file';

                    if(!is_uploaded_file($_FILES['image']
                    ['tmp_name']))
```

```
                        $errors[] = 'Not an uploaded file';
                break;
              case UPLOAD_ERR_INI_SIZE:
              case UPLOAD_ERR_FORM_SIZE:
                $errors = 'File too big';
                break;
              default:
                $errors = 'Problem with file upload';
          }
          if(!$errors) {
              //  set $images variable
          }
        }
    //  Check Text
        ...
    return [$id, $title, $precis, $article, $image, $errors];
}
```

This code is the same as for the manage-images.code.php code, except that we won't immediately upload the new image yet.

Note that we've added the code *before* the Check Text code. That's because it uses the $errors variable, which we're checking for image errors. We don't want that to include text errors until after we've finished the image check.

If there are no errors, we'll simply set the $images variable with the data needed to add the image later. All we need is the name of the uploaded file and its location. We can put that into an associative array:

```
if(isset($_FILES['image']) && $_FILES['image']['error']
        != UPLOAD_ERR_NO_FILE) {

    ...

    if(!$errors) {
        $image = [
```

```
            'imageName' => $_FILES['image']['name'],
            'imageFile' => $_FILES['image']['tmp_name']
        ];
    }
}
```

If you haven't uploaded a new image, the $image variable will still be null.

Keeping the Optional Image

For the most part, keeping the optional image will be similar to what we did when we uploaded images in the manage-images.code.php code. However, we'll also need to reference that image in the new article.

All of this will be in a new function called addBlogImage():

```php
<?php
#   manage-blog.code.php

    ...
    // Add Blog Data
        function addBlogData(string $title, string $precis,
        string $article) {
            global $pdo, $root, $CONFIG;

            return $id;
        }

    // Add Blog Image
        function addBlogImage(int $id, array|string $image,
          string $title, string $precis) {
            global $pdo, $root, $CONFIG;

            return $id;
```

```
    }

//  Process
    if(isset($_POST['insert'])) {
        ...
    }
```

The function receives the $id of the article to which we're adding an image, the $image variable for the image data, and the $title and the $precis, which will become the title and description of the new image. It also includes the $pdo, $root, and $CONFIG global variables.

Again, the $image variable can be an array or a string. If you're using PHP before version 8, you should leave the array|string union type out.

If the $image variable has an array, we'll take it to be the file name and location of a new image to be added. Later, we'll interpret a different type of value as a reference to an existing image.

We'll begin by testing whether there's an image to be processed:

```
function addBlogImage(int $id, array|string $image,
  string $title, string $precis) {
    global $pdo, $root, $CONFIG;

    if(is_array($image)) {

    }

    return $id;
}
```

Remember, if there's a new image to be processed, the $image variable will have an array of the image name and location.

If there is an image array, we'll need the two items. For convenience, we can copy them into simple variables, using the extended array destructuring:

```
function addBlogImage(int $id, array|string $image,
```

431

```
  string $title, string $precis) {
    ...
    if(is_array($image)) {
        ['imageName'=>$name, 'imageFile'=>$file] = $image;
    }
}
```

This is equivalent to

```
$name = $image['imageName'];
$file = $image['imageFile'];
```

We can now add the image as we would in the addImageData()
function in the manage-images.code.php code:

```
if(is_array($image)) {
    ['imageName'=>$name, 'imageFile'=>$file] = $image;

    $name = strtolower($name);
    $name = str_replace(' ', '-', $name);

    // $description = nl2pilcrow($description);
    // ** Deleted

    $sql = 'INSERT INTO images(title, description, name,
    src, gallery)
        VALUES(?, ?, ?, ?,
        false)';                        // ** Changed
    $pdoStatement = $pdo -> prepare($sql);
    $data = [$title, $precis, $name, $name];
    // ** Changed
    $pdoStatement->execute($data);

    $imageid = $pdo -> lastInsertId();
```

432

```
$src = sprintf('%06s-%s', $imageid, $name);
// **  Changed

$sql = 'UPDATE images SET src=? WHERE id=?';
$pdoStatement = $pdo->prepare($sql);
$pdoStatement->execute([$src, $imageid]);
// **  Changed
}
```

We have the following adjustments:

- We're going to use the $precis for the description, so we delete the line which sets the $description variable. Here, it's only commented out; you can see what's happening.

- The value for gallery is hard-coded to false. If you want to add the new image to the gallery, you can always do that later through the image editing form.

- The $data array uses the $precis variable instead of the $description variable. It also loses the last value which has been hard-coded to false previously.

- The $src variable uses the $imageid for the numeric part; the $id variable refers to the article's ID.

- We don't really need the $data variable for the last statement, since there are only two values. We've put the array directly in the execute() function. We can also do that with the previous execute(), of course.

There's one more thing to do, which is to update the article with the new image ID. We already have the image ID in the $imageid variable and the article's ID in the $id variable. With this, we can add the update code:

```
if(is_array($image)) {
    ['imageName'=>$name, 'imageFile'=>$file] = $image;

    ...

    $sql = 'UPDATE images SET src=? WHERE id=?';
    $pdoStatement = $pdo->prepare($sql);
    $pdoStatement->execute([$src, $id]);

    $sql = 'UPDATE blog SET imageid=? WHERE id=?';
    $pdoStatement = $pdo->prepare($sql);
    $pdoStatement->execute([$imageid, $id]);
}
```

Deciding on variable names is one of the biggest challenges in any programming language, so it's important to try to develop your own pattern.

Here, the $id variable is the ID of the current item, which is the new article. The $imageid variable is a reference to a different item.

You may prefer a different pattern. That's OK, as long as you stick to it.

However, we have only added the database data. We haven't actually saved the new image itself. To do that, we can copy more code from the manage-images.code.php file, this time from the addImageFile() function. This goes straight after the database additions:

```
//  Optional Image
    if(is_array($image)) {
        ['imageName'=>$name, 'imageFile'=>$file] = $image;

        ...

        $sql = 'UPDATE blog SET imageid=? WHERE id=?';
        $pdoStatement = $pdo->prepare($sql);
        $pdoStatement->execute([$imageid, $id]);

    copy($file,
        "$root/{$CONFIG['images']['directory']}/
        originals/$src");

    resizeImage(
        "$root/{$CONFIG['images']['directory']}/
        originals/$src",
        "$root/{$CONFIG['images']['directory']}/
        display/$src",
        $CONFIG['images']['display-size']
    );
    resizeImage(
        "$root/{$CONFIG['images']['directory']}/
        originals/$src",
        "$root/{$CONFIG['images']['directory']}/
        thumbnails/$src",
        $CONFIG['images']['thumbnail-size']
    );
    resizeImage(
        "$root/{$CONFIG['images']['directory']}/
        originals/$src",
        "$root/{$CONFIG['images']['directory']}/
        icons/$src",
        $CONFIG['images']['icon-size']
```

```
    );
    resizeImage(
        "$root/{$CONFIG['images']['directory']}/
        originals/$src",
        "$root/{$CONFIG['images']['directory']}/
        scaled/$src",
        $CONFIG['images']['scaled'], ['method'=>'scale']
    );
}
```

We've put quite a lot of code in one place, but we're not planning on reusing any of it for other operations, so there's no need to write additional functions.

Functions sometimes simplify coding, but they can also make coding more complicated.

First, every call to a function is extra work for the processor, as it also has to keep track of where the code was before the function was called, and it has to manage passing data between the two sections of code. Second, it's harder for you to see what's going on if you find yourself searching another part of the script to see what's happening next.

This is part of the Fine Art of programming—deciding when it makes more sense to break your code into smaller functions and when it makes more sense to keep it in one place.

There's one final, but crucial, step. That's to incorporate the addBlogImage() function into the addBlogData() function. We'll do that near the end, after we've got the article ID:

```
function addBlogData(string $title, string $precis, string
$article,
```

436

```
array|string $image=null, string $created=null, string
$updated=null) {

...

$id = $pdo -> lastInsertId();

if($image) addBlogImage($id, $image, $title, $precis);

return $id;
}
```

We've included the if($image) test to ensure that the function is only called when needed.

We can now add images to new blog articles.

Previewing the Image

You'll notice that there's a space beside the Title and Precis fields. That's to show a preview of the uploaded image. You can't do that in PHP, so there's actually some JavaScript attached to do that.

What you can do in PHP is to generate the img element which will display the selected image.

In the initialization section, remove the assignment to $previewImage as an empty string. After that, assign the variable with what will be a template string:

```
// Initialise
$title = $precis = $article = '';
$id = 0;
$errors = '';
$disabled = '';
```

```
$chooseImage = '';                    // Modified
$previewImage = '<img src="%s" width="%s" height="%s"
alt="%s"
    id="preview-new-image">';   // New

$pagetitle = 'Edit Blog';
$pageheading = 'Edit Blog';
```

The fact that its id is preview-new-image is enough for JavaScript to find it and to populate the preview when the time comes.

That will work, but it's better to fill in the placeholders, which we'll do in the Prepare Insert code:

```
if(empty($_POST) || isset($_POST['prepare-insert'])) {
    $pagetitle = 'Upload Article';
    $pageheading = 'Upload Article';

    [$width, $height]
        = splitSize($CONFIG['images']['thumbnail-size']);
    $previewImage = sprintf(
        $previewImage,
        '', $width, $height, 'No Image'
    );
}
```

The size of the preview will be the same as for the thumbnail images.

When you reload the page, you'll see a blank image with the alt text of No Image. If you now add an image, its preview will be displayed. Shift-clicking the **File** button will restore the blank image.

438

Selecting an Existing Image

It's possible that there's already an image which you want to include for your blog article. We can add an option to select one.

If you have a very large number of images, what follows may not be practical. We'll proceed, assuming that you don't have too many images. This section includes an image-free alternative, so that might be a useful compromise.

The first thing is that you'll need some way of choosing one of many. In HTML, there are two ways of doing this.

First, there is the select form element. It would look something like this:

```
<select name="use-image">
    <option value="">[No Image]</option>
    <option value="1">Image 1</option>
    <option value="2">Image 2</option>
    <option value="3">Image 3</option>
</select>
```

By default, the select appears as a drop-down menu. You can turn it into an open list with the size attribute, which is the number of option elements permanently visible:

```
<select name="use-image" size="6">
    <option value="">[No Image]</option>
    ...
</select>
```

It's good practice to have the first item as a dummy or no-value option, especially if the drop-down box is closed.

The downside is that the option elements are text only—you can't include an image preview. On the other hand, it's not too heavy on bandwidth.

The alternative is a collection of radio buttons. HTML has rather an odd way of managing radio buttons. A collection would look like this:

```
<label><input name="use-image" value="">[No Image]</label>
<label><input name="use-image" value="1">Image 1</label>
<label><input name="use-image" value="2">Image 2</label>
<label><input name="use-image" value="3">Image 3</label>
```

The important part is that they all have the same name attribute. This results in a radio group, where selecting one would deselect the others.

The wrapping label element is used to associate the text with the input element: clicking the text activates the radio button.

You can go either way. We'll look at coding both. Fortunately, processing the submitted form will be exactly the same either way.

Selecting an Image from a Menu

The simplest approach is to generate a drop-down menu. In HTML, this is a select element full of option elements. The select element has a name attribute which is what will be submitted with the form. In this case, the name will be use-image.

For simplicity, we can write the code in a simple function, called getImageSelect(), which we'll add before the initialization section:

```
<?php
#   manage-blog.code.php
    ...

    // Initialise
       ...
```

```
//  Functions
    function getImageSelect() {

    }
```

The function will pull in data from the database, so we'll need to import the $pdo variable:

```
function getImageSelect() {
    global $pdo;
}
```

As usual, the simplest way to build the menu is to add items to an array and then implode it afterward. That's the value we'll be returning:

```
function getImageSelect() {
    global $pdo;

    $select = [];

    $select = implode($select);

    return $select;
}
```

The select element will be filled with option elements. For that, we'll use the following template string:

```
function getImageSelect() {
    global $pdo;

    $option = '<option value="%s" %s>%03s %s</option>';
    $select = [];

    $select = implode($select);

    return $select;
}
```

There are three placeholders:

- The first is the value of the selected option. It will be the id of the image.

- The second placeholder will be used later. It's to allow you to preselect one option. For now, it will be an empty string.

- The third and fourth placeholders are what you see on the items. They will be the id again, padded to three digits, and the title of the image.

We then start and finish the array with the select tags. The opening tag includes the name attribute, which will be important when submitting the form. We'll also want the first option to be hard-coded to something which means no image has been selected yet.

```php
function getImageSelect() {
    global $pdo;

    $option = '<option value="%s" %s>%03s %s</option>';

    $select = [];

    $select[] = '<span>';
    $select[] = '<select name="use-image">';
    $select[] = sprintf($option, 0, '', '   ', '[No Image]');

    $select[] = '</select>';
    $select[] = '</span>';

    $select = implode($select);

    return $select;
}
```

The first option element has a value of 0, which is no image, since the ids start at 1. The second placeholder gets an empty string for now.

The text of the option element includes spaces where the ID should go and the dummy text [No Image]. There are three spaces to stop the zero-padding. The use of square brackets is nothing special—it's just to make it stand out.

Note that the select element is wrapped inside a span element. You don't normally do that, but it's there for a special trick in CSS. It's very difficult to style a select drop-down in CSS, so some of the styling has been applied to the span element.

There's a lot of trickery involved when trying to make form elements look right. Because they have been traditionally tied to the operating system version, they have resisted appearance changes. The situation is slowly improving, but, for now, we still need to do some strange things if we want our form elements to look nice.

We'll want to get a list of images from the database. We can use the following SQL:

```
SELECT id, title FROM images;
```

Using the $pdo variable, we can fetch the data:

```
$pdo -> query('SELECT id, title FROM images')
```

We can then put this directly into a foreach() statement, at the same time destructuring the rows into two variables:

```
function getImageSelect() {
    global $pdo;

    $select = [];
```

```
    $select[] = '<span>';
    $select[] = '<select name="use-image">';
    $select[] = sprintf($option, 0, '', '    ', '[No Image]');

    foreach($pdo -> query('SELECT id, title FROM images')
      as [$id, $title]) {

    }

    $select[] = '</select>';
    $select[] = '</span>';
    $select = implode($select);

    return $select;
}
```

Finally, we can use the data to generate the option elements. The $id will be used as the value of each option, while both the $id and the $title will form the text of the option. The $id will be zero-padded for neatness:

```
function getImageSelect() {
    ...

    foreach($pdo -> query('SELECT id, title FROM images')
      as [$id, $title]) {
        $select[] =sprintf($option, $id, '', $id, $title);
    }

    ...
}
```

Now that we have the function in place, we can call it as part of the prepare insert code:

```
if(empty($_POST) || isset($_POST['prepare-insert'])) {
    ...

    $chooseImage = getImageSelect();
}
```

You'll now see a drop-down menu when you next reload the page.

Processing the Selected Image

It's much easier to accept a preexisting image than it is to upload a new one. The only thing to worry about is the case when the user has decided to submit both.

The new image and the preexisting image are in two separate parts of the form. It would make sense to prioritize the new image, since that takes more effort to have included.

In the getBlogData() function, we can include an alternative to the image test:

```
function getBlogData() {
    ...

    // Optional Image
        if(isset($_FILES['image']) && ...) {
            ...
        }
        else $image = $_POST['use-image'];

    // Check Text
    ...
}
```

You'll see that the alternative is only processed if the $_FILES test fails, giving the new file priority.

With a select element, one option is always selected. By default, the selected item is the first one, which has an empty value attribute. Otherwise, it's a *string* containing a numeral.

In the addBlogImage() function, we can now process the alternative value for $image.

First, we'll add the test:

```
function addBlogImage( ... ) {

    ...

    //  Optional Image
        if(is_array($image) ) {
            ...
            switch() {
                ...
            }
            if(!$errors) {
            }
        }
        elseif(is_numeric($image)) {

        }

    return $id;
}
```

The is_numeric() function tests whether a string can be interpreted as a number. An empty string can't, so the function would fail.

It's now just a matter of adding the blog article to include the ID of the image. If the user has used the form correctly, there shouldn't be a problem, but we should always be on the lookout for trickery, so we're going to take a slightly more careful approach.

Suppose you have a number, and you're not sure whether it matches one of the image ids. You can try the following:

```
SELECT id FROM images WHERE id= ... ;
```

If the id matches, you'll just get the id again. If, however, it doesn't, you'll get nothing.

If you incorporate the preceding query into the UPDATE statement, you get something like

```
UPDATE blog SET imageid=(select id from images where id=?)
WHERE id=?
```

The SELECT statement in parentheses is called a **subquery**. In this case, if the id doesn't match, the result would be NULL, and you'd be setting the imageid to NULL, which means that there isn't a matching image.

We can include that in the code:

```
function addBlogData(...) {
    ...

    // Optional Image
    if(is_array($image) ) {
        ...
    }
    elseif(is_numeric($image)) {
        $sql = 'UPDATE blog
            SET imageid=(select id from images where id=?)
            WHERE id=?';
        $pdoStatement = $pdo->prepare($sql);
        $pdoStatement->execute([$image, $id]);
    }

    return $id;
}
```

Here, the $image variable is the image ID we're attempting to add, and the $id variable is the ID of the new blog article.

You can now test adding a preexisting image to a new blog article.

Previewing the Selected Image

We can preview a new image, but it would be nice to be able to preview the selected image, especially since you can't see them in the select menu. To do that, we'll make a few changes to the getImageSelect() function.

The first step is to add a data-preview attribute to the option template string:

```
function getImageSelect() {
    global $pdo;

    $option = '<option value="%s" data-preview="%s" %s>
        %03s %s</option>';
    ...
```

Note that the string has been split over two lines to fit in the book. If possible, you should try to keep on one line:

```
$option = '<option value="%s" data-preview="%s" %s>%03s %s
</option>';
```

Any attribute starting with data- is a custom attribute, and it's up to either CSS or JavaScript to deal with it. In this case, the data-preview attribute has a reference to a thumbnail copy of the image, and the JavaScript will use it to display the preview.

The next step is to include it with the first option element:

```
function getImageSelect() {
    global $pdo;

    $option = '<option value="%s" data-preview="%s" %s>
```

```
    %03s %s</option>';
$select = [];

$select[] = '<span>';
$select[] = '<select name="use-image">';
$select[] = sprintf(
    $option, 0, '/images/blank.png',
    '', '   ', '[No Image]'
);

...
}
```

Note that the data-preview attribute is now the second placeholder.

There's an image in the images directory which is actually a one-pixel blank image. It will be used to populate the preview with a blank if you select the [No Image] option.

For the other options, we'll include the reference to the actual thumbnail image. That means that the SELECT statement will also need to include the src value, and we'll need to include it in the destructure:

```
function getImageSelect() {
    ...

    foreach($pdo -> query('SELECT id, title, src FROM images')
        as [$id, $title, $src]) {
        $select[] = sprintf(
            $option, $id,
            "/images/thumbnails/$src", '', $id, $title
        );
    }
    ...
}
```

The JavaScript handles the rest. You can now reload the page and see the preview of the image.

Selecting an Image from a Radio Group

The trouble with the select element is that it's limited: you can't add images, and you have practically no control over the appearance of the option elements. You can change the appearance of the closed menu, but that's a lot of work, as you'll see if you examine the CSS for the menu.

An alternative would be to create a group of radio buttons. Radio buttons can also appear quite boring, but CSS can do more with them.

We're going to build a collection of input elements similar to the following:

```
<p id="use-image">
    <label><input type="radio" name="use-image" value=""
    checked>
        <span>[No Image]</span></label>
    <label><input type="radio" name="use-image" value="1">
        <img ...></label>
    <label><input type="radio" name="use-image" value="2">
        <img ...></label>
</p>
```

- The type is radio, and the name for all of them is the same: use-image. Having the same name is what causes the buttons to act as a radio group, in that selecting one will deselect the others in the group.

- The label element wraps the contents. It's there to associate the rest of the content with the input element. That is, clicking the content is the same as clicking the input element itself.

- The first element is the empty choice. The text [No
  Image] is in a span element simply so that CSS can
  style it.

We'll also add a data-preview attribute so we can preview the selected
image, as we did with the select menu.

Note that when we finish the job, you won't actually see the radio
buttons. CSS will have hidden them for aesthetic reasons. It will still work,
since the image is part of the label element, and can still be used to select
one of the buttons. The CSS will also handle highlighting the selection.

The name for the group is the same as the name we used for the
select element, which means that we have already got the code to process
the element.

For convenience, we can create a new function called function
getImageButtons():

```php
<?php
#    manage-blog.code.php

    ...

    // Functions
    function function getImageSelect() {

        ...
    }

    function function getImageButtons() {

    }
```

The process will be very similar to the getImageSelect() function, and
we can write much of the code the same way:

```php
function getImageButtons() {
    global $pdo, $CONFIG;

    $buttons = [];
```

```
    foreach($pdo -> query('SELECT id, title, src FROM images')
        as [$id, $title, $src]) {

    }
    $buttons = implode($buttons);

    return $buttons;
}
```

The most obvious difference is that the array is called $buttons. We've also included the global $CONFIG array.

We'll add a template string for the buttons:

```
function getImageButtons() {
    global $pdo, $CONFIG;

    $button = '<label>
        <input type="radio" name="use-image" value="%s" %s>
        <img src="%s" alt="%s" title="%s" width="%s"
        height="%s"
            data-preview="%s">
        </label>';

    ...
}
```

This is a long template string, so we've written it over multiple lines to fit on the page. The thing about img elements is that there are typically five attributes or more. Of course, you don't have to write your code that way. Note that the template also includes the data-preview attribute.

There is also what looks like an anonymous second placeholder. It's there to take a possible value of checked for a preselected button, similar to the selected attribute for the select menu.

Unlike a select menu, there's no preselected radio button. We'll preselect the first one by setting the checked attribute on that one. For the rest, we'll set the attribute to an empty string for now.

We're going to use images from the icons directory, so we'll need to extract the dimensions from the $CONFIG array. We can also set up the first radio button:

```
function getImageButtons() {
    global $pdo, $PDO;

    $button = ' ... ';
    [$width, $height] = splitSize($CONFIG['images']
    ['icon-size']);

    $buttons = [];

    $buttons[] = sprintf(
        $button,
        0,                          //  id
        'checked',                  //  checked
        '/images/blank.png',        //  src
        'none',                     //  alt
        '',                         //  title
        $width, $height,            //  width, height
        '/images/blank.png'         //  data-preview
    );

    ...
}
```

The sprintf() function is spread over many lines simply to allow for comments to explain the many values. Of course, you don't need to be so verbose:

```
$buttons[] = sprintf(
    $button, 0, 'checked', '/images/blank.png', 'none',
    '', $width, $height, '/images/blank.png'
);
```

From here, we can fill in the rest of the buttons:

```
function getImageButtons() {
    ...

    foreach($pdo -> query('SELECT id, title, src FROM images')
      as [$id, $title, $src]) {
        $buttons[] = sprintf(
            $button, $id, '', "/images/icons/$src", $title,
            $title, $width, $height, "/images/thumbnails/$src"
        );
    }

    ...
}
```

If you want to test it, you'll have to make a small change to the Prepare Insert code:

```
if(empty($_POST) || isset($_POST['prepare-insert'])) {
    ...
    // $chooseImage = getImageSelect();
    $chooseImage = getImageButtons();

    ...
}
```

The previous line has been commented out rather than deleted, since we're leaving it there as an option.

Choosing Between Buttons and the Menu

Leaving the option there as a comment is a little hidden. We can set the option using the configuration file instead.

In the config.ini.php file, add the following:

```
title = Australia Down Under
contact = Support <info@australia.example.com>
...
[blogedit]
    use-image = buttons
```

You can now make a change to the Prepare Insert code to use this configuration value:

```
if(empty($_POST) || isset($_POST['prepare-insert'])) {
    $pagetitle = 'Upload Article';
    $pageheading = 'Upload Article';

    switch($CONFIG['blogedit']['use-image']) {
        case 'buttons':
            $chooseImage = getImageButtons();
            break;
        case 'select':
        default:
            $chooseImage = getImageSelect();
            break;
    }

    ...
}
```

Using the switch statement makes it easy to choose alternatives, especially if you can think of more ways of selecting an image later.

Redirecting to the Blog List Page

Once you're sure that your insert article code is working, we don't need to hang around. We can finish the job by redirecting to the admin-bloglist. php page.

In the insert section, replace the temporary finish up code with the following redirect code:

```
if(isset($_POST['insert'])) {
    [$id, $title, $precis, $article, $image, $errors] =
    getBlogData();

    if(!$errors) {  //  proceed
        $id = addBlogData($title, $precis, $article, $image);

        // Move On
        header("Location: $protocol://$host/admin-
        bloglist.php");
        exit;
    }
    else {          //  handle error
        $errors = sprintf('<p class="errors">%s</p>',
            implode('<br>',$errors));
    }
}
```

Of course, at this point, there's nothing to see on the admin-bloglist. php page, until we write the code to populate it later.

Importing Blog Articles

As with the images, it would be handy to be able to import the blog articles in bulk. Unlike the images, there may not be any actual images, so we don't necessarily need a zipped folder. We'll have to bear that in mind when checking the MIME type.

If you're uploading a ZIP file, then it should expand to something like this:

```
@blog.csv
bathing-boxes.jpg
opera-house.jpg
uluru.jpg
```

or whatever you like. The CSV file, however, should be called @blog. csv; again, the @ sign at the beginning is just to lift the file name to the top.

If you're uploading a CSV file without images, you can call it anything you like.

You'll find a file called blog.zip in the setup directory, as well as a simple @blog.csv file.

The CSV file will have six columns:

```
title,precis,article,created,updated,image
...
```

That's more than the CSV for the images, but it will largely work the same way.

Changes to the Insert Code

When importing blog articles, some of the articles may have been created or updated earlier. That means we shouldn't hard-code those dates to the current date/time. We'll need to make a change to the addBlogData() function accordingly.

Change the function to the following:

```
function addBlogData(string $title, string $precis, string
$article,
    array|string $image=null, string $created=null,
    string $updated=null) {

}
```

We've added two more parameters for the created and updated dates:

- PHP doesn't really have a proper date type, so we use a string.

- It's always important to try to maintain existing behavior when making changes to a function. We've added the default nulls to the new parameters to allow you to leave them out as before.

The next thing is to change the values for the INSERT statement to include the new parameter variables.

There's always the possibility that these new values will still be null, so we'll need to default them to the current date/time. We can use the short ternary operator for that:

```
$sql = 'INSERT INTO blog(title, precis, article, created,
updated)
    VALUES(?, ?, ?, ?, ?)';
$pdoStatement = $pdo -> prepare($sql);
$data = [$title, $precis, $article,
    $created?:date('Y-m-d H:i:s'), $updated?:date('Y-m-d H:i:s')];
$pdoStatement->execute($data);
```

Remember the short ternary operator will use the first value if it's not null or fall through to the second value if it is null.

We can now use this function to add articles with different created and updated dates. However, when adding a single article manually, the dates will still default to the current date/time.

Starting the Import Code

First, we'll start off the code for the import event:

```
// Process
    if(isset($_POST['insert'])) {
        ...
    }

    if(isset($_POST['import'])) {
        $pdo -> exec('TRUNCATE TABLE blog');
        $pdo -> exec('DELETE FROM images WHERE NOT gallery');
    }
```

We've included the TRUNCATE statement, which will reset the blog table. That's because we'll probably be testing this many times. We've also included a statement to delete the non-gallery images, which shouldn't be any so far, unless you've been experimenting.

In the end, once you've got everything working you'll probably want to comment out both of these statements, so we can import additional articles without losing the others.

Handling the Import File

We can largely copy the code from the import part of the manage-images. code.php file, but we'll need to make a number of changes.

First, we'll check whether anything's been uploaded and whether there are other errors. This is copied directly from the image code:

```
if(isset($_POST['import'])) {
    $pdo -> exec('TRUNCATE TABLE blog');
    $pdo -> exec('DELETE FROM images WHERE NOT gallery');

    if(!isset($_FILES['import-file'])) $errors =
    'Missing File';
    else switch($_FILES['import-file']['error']) {
        case UPLOAD_ERR_OK:
            if($_FILES['import-file']['type'] !=
            'application/zip')
                $errors = 'Not a suitable ZIP file';
            break;
        case UPLOAD_ERR_INI_SIZE:
        case UPLOAD_ERR_FORM_SIZE:
            $errors = 'File too big';
            break;
        case UPLOAD_ERR_NO_FILE:
            $errors = 'Missing File';
            break;
        default:
            $errors = 'Problem with file upload';
    }
}
```

However, we'll need to allow for two different MIME types. It may be a ZIP file, complete with images and a CSV file. However, it may simply be a CSV file without images.

To make it easier, we'll wrap the switch statement inside braces after the else. That will allow us to do a little more work before testing the file:

```
if(isset($_POST['import'])) {
    $pdo -> exec('TRUNCATE TABLE blog');

    if(!isset($_FILES['import-file'])) $errors =
    'Missing File';
    else {
        switch($_FILES['import-file']['error']) {
            ...
        }
    }
}
```

It also makes sense to further indent the switch statement, since now it's part of a nested block.

The next thing is to get the MIME type of the image before actually testing for the other errors:

```
if(isset($_POST['import'])) {
    $pdo -> exec('TRUNCATE TABLE blog');

    if(!isset($_FILES['import-file'])) $errors = 'Missing
    File';
    else {
        $mime = MimeType($_FILES['import-file']['tmp_name']);
        switch($_FILES['import-file']['error']) {
            ...
        }
    }
}
```

Again, we've used the MimeType library function rather than the
$_FILES['import-file']['type'] because of complications with the
CSV file.

We can now adapt the file type test to test for both MIME types:

```
if(isset($_POST['import'])) {
    $pdo -> exec('TRUNCATE TABLE blog');

    if(!isset($_FILES['import-file'])) $errors = 'Missing
    File';
    else {
        $mime = MimeType($_FILES['import-file']['tmp_name']);
        switch($_FILES['import-file']['error']) {
            case UPLOAD_ERR_OK:
                if($mime != 'application/zip' && $mime
                != 'text/csv')
                    $errors = 'Not a suitable ZIP or CSV file';
                break;

            ...

        }
    }
}
```

We've also modified the error message to include the CSV file.

We'll need the $mime variable again when we process the file.

Copying the Blog Import Files

If we're happy with the file, one way or the other, we can extract the ZIP file
or simply copy the CSV file. That means testing the $mime variable again:

```
if(isset($_POST['import'])) {
    $pdo -> exec('TRUNCATE TABLE blog');
```

```
if(!isset($_FILES['import-file'])) $errors = 'Missing
File';
else {
    ...
}

if(!$errors) {
    if($mime == 'application/zip') {    //  extract Zip

    }
    else copy( ... , ... );                          //  copy CSV
}
}
```

The extract ZIP code is copied from manage-images.code.php; the copy is simply the copy() function from the file's temporary location to the uploads directory:

```
if(isset($_POST['import'])) {
    ...
    if(!$errors) {
        if($mime != 'application/zip') {
            ['files'=>$files, 'names'=>$names]
                = unzip($_FILES['import-file']['tmp_name'],
                    "$root/uploads");
            if(
                !file_exists("$root/uploads/@blog.csv")
                || MimeType("$root/uploads/@blog.csv") !=
                'text/csv'
            ) $errors = 'No valid @blog.csv file';
        }
```

```
      else copy($_FILES['import-file']['tmp_name'],
          "$root/uploads/@blog.csv");
  }
}
```

Now we should have a CSV file called @blog.csv, with or without images in the uploads directory. If you uploaded the ZIP file, then the included CSV file must be called @blog.csv; if you uploaded just a CSV file, it will be renamed in the copy() function.

Importing the Blog Data

We may, of course, have picked up some new errors on the way, but, if we haven't, we can now begin the process of adding the articles:

```
if(isset($_POST['import'])) {

    ...

    if(!$errors) {
        if($mime != 'application/zip') {

            ...

        }
        else ...;
    }
    if(!$errors) {
        // Add articles
    }
    else {
        $errors = sprintf('<p class="errors">%s</p>', $errors);
    }
}
```

We've also prepared the error message if there are any errors.

Adding the articles is similar to adding the images and starts off by reading the CSV file:

```
if(isset($_POST['import'])) {
    ...

    if(!$errors) {
        if($mime != 'application/zip') {

            ...
        }
        else ...;
    }

    if(!$errors) {
        $file = "$root/uploads/@blog.csv";
        $data = file($file, FILE_IGNORE_NEW_LINES |
            FILE_SKIP_EMPTY_LINES);
        $header = array_shift($data);
        $data = array_map('str_getcsv', $data);
    }
    else {
        $errors = sprintf('<p class="errors">%s</p>', $errors);
    }
}
```

We'll now iterate through the CSV data. As we do, however, we'll also want to check whether there's an image to be included. For that

```
if(!$errors) {
    $file = "$root/uploads/@blog.csv";
    $data = file($file, FILE_IGNORE_NEW_LINES |
        FILE_SKIP_EMPTY_LINES);
```

```php
$header = array_shift($data);
$data = array_map('str_getcsv', $data);

$imagetypes = ['image/gif', 'image/jpeg', 'image/png',
    'image/webp'];

foreach($data as $row) {

}
}
else {
    $errors = sprintf('<p class="errors">%s</p>', $errors);
}
```

For importing the images, we only had three items per row to deal with, so it wasn't a hardship to reference the items by their index number. With six, however, we might use a different approach and use an associative array to make it easier to identify the items.

We can construct an associative array on the fly by combining two arrays: one with the names of the keys and one with the numbered items. You then use the array_combine() function to do the work. For example:

```php
$keys = ['a', 'b', 'c'];
$values = ['apple', 'banana', 'cherry'];
$array = array_combine($keys, $values);
print_r($array);
```

You'll end up with something like this:

```
Array
(
    [a] => apple
    [b] => banana
    [c] => cherry
)
```

Writing out an array is somewhat tedious, so it's often convenient to write a string and use the explode() function, which will split a string into an array, using whatever separator you like:

```
$keys = explode(' ', 'a b c');
```

We'll use the same approach with each row of the CSV file:

```
if(!$errors) {
    ...

    $imagetypes = ['image/gif', 'image/jpeg', 'image/png',
        'image/webp'];

    $keys = explode(' ','title precis article created updated
    image');

    foreach($data as $row) {
        $row = array_combine($keys, $row);
    }
}
else {
    $errors = sprintf('<p class="errors">%s</p>', $errors);
}
```

Here, we've defined the $keys array and combined it with each $row.

As we iterate through the rows, we'll eventually want to call the addBlogData() function to add individual articles. First, we'll need to test whether there's a valid image to be included; otherwise, we'll set the image to null:

```
foreach($data as $row) {
    $row = array_combine($keys, $row);
    $image = null;
```

```
    // Check for an image

    // addBlogData()
}
```

To include an image, there are three conditions:

1. It must be listed in the CSV file.

2. The image file must be in the uploads directory.

3. The file must be a valid image file.

You can test that with a compound if() statement:

```
if($row['image']
  && file_exists("$root/uploads/{$row['image']}")
  && in_array(MimeType("$root/uploads/{$row['image']}"),
  $imagetypes)
) ... ;
```

We've now got the row in associative array, so we can reference the image item with $row['image']. However, when interpolating an associative array item, PHP gets confused with the quotes inside, so we needed to wrap the expression in braces {$row['image']}.

Note the power of the short-circuited && operator. Since all terms need to evaluate to true, as soon as there's one false, it will give up on the rest. If there's no image item, it won't look for a file; if there's no file, it won't attempt to test the file. In both cases, if we'd proceeded with the next test, it would have resulted in an error.

If the test succeeds, we'll want to prepare the image data for uploading. Otherwise, we'll set it to null:

```
if($row['image']
  && file_exists("$root/uploads/{$row['image']}")
  && in_array(MimeType("$root/uploads/{$row['image']}"),
  $imagetypes)
```

```
) $row['image'] = [
    'imageName' => $row['image'],
    'imageFile' => "$root/uploads/{$row['image']}"
];
else $row['image'] = null;
```

We can now add that to the code:

```
foreach($data as $row) {
    $row = array_combine($keys, $row);
    $image = null;

    //  Check for an image
        if($row['image']
          && file_exists("$root/uploads/{$row['image']}")
          && in_array(MimeType("$root/uploads/
          {$row['image']}"),
            $imagetypes)
        ) $row['image'] = [
            'imageName' => $row['image'],
            'imageFile' => "$root/uploads/{$row['image']}"
        ];
        else $row['image'] = null;

    //  addBlogData()
}
```

The data is now ready to send to the addBlogData() function.

Calling a Function with an Array of Parameters

When we call the function, we'll have to add all of the data from the $row array. If you really want to do it the long way, you can write

```
addBlogData($row['title'], $row['precis'], $row[article],
    $row[created], $row[updated], $row[image]);
```

which will work. However, if you have more current versions of PHP, you can use a much simpler notation. In PHP 8, you can use

```
addBlogData(...$row);
```

The ... operator is used to pack or, in this case, unpack a collection. The array $row is unpacked to individual items for the function parameter. The PHP website doesn't have much detail on this operator and tends to avoid even naming it. If anything, you'll see it referred to as the **ellipsis** operator. Other languages call it something like the **spread** or even the **splat** operator.

Note that the $row array is an associative array with the same keys as the names of the parameters in the addBlogData() function. If the keys don't match, this won't work.

In PHP 7.2, you can't use the ... (or ellipsis or spread or splat) operator with an associative array. If you're working with an older version, you can do one of two things:

- Don't bother with the $row = array_combine($keys, $row); statement, and leave the $row as a numbered array.

    However, every reference to $row['image'] needs to be replaced with $row[5] (remember, arrays are numbered from zero). That's not a friendly approach.

- Alternatively, you can extract the values as a numbered array using the array_values() function:
  addBlogData(...array_values($row));

If you're stuck with an older version of PHP, you will indeed need to spread the items yourself.

We can now finish the job (obviously, choose one method):

```
foreach($data as $row) {
    $row = array_combine($keys, $row);
    $image = null;

    // Check for an image
        if($row['image']

            ...

        ) ... ;
        else $row['image'] = null;

    addBlogData(...$row);                          // PHP >= 8
    // addBlogData(...array_values($row));         // PHP >= 7.2
    // addBlogData($row['title'], $row['precis'],
        $row[article],
    //   $row[created], $row[updated], $row[image]);
        // Any  PHP
}
```

Well, not quite finished yet.

Finishing the Import

There are two more things you need to do to really finish the job.

First, you'll want to clear out the uploads directory. Then, you should redirect to the admin-bloglist.php page:

```php
if(isset($_POST['import'])) {

    ...

    if(!$errors) {

        ...

    array_map('unlink', glob("$root/uploads/*"));

        //  Move On
            header("Location: $protocol://$host/admin-
            bloglist.php");
            exit;
    }
    else {
        $errors = sprintf('<p class="errors">%s</p>', $errors);
    }
}
```

When you test this again, you'll find that you've been directed to an empty blog list page.

After you've tested the import one last time, comment out the lines which clear the old data:

```php
//  Import Blog Articles
    if(isset($_POST['import'])) {
```

```
//  $pdo -> exec('TRUNCATE TABLE blog');
//  $pdo -> exec('DELETE FROM images WHERE NOT
    gallery');

    ...

}
```

We'll work on the blog list page a little, later, but first it would be nice to see what one of the blog articles looks like. For that, we'll work on the visitor's blog article page next.

If you've been experimenting, you might find that the id of the added blog images is very much higher than those of the gallery images. That's because though you've deleted the unused images, auto-incremented values don't get recycled and so there will be gaps.

That's OK, as the id hasn't any other special meaning. If you feel you want the ids to look better, you can first reimport the images, making sure that you have the TRUNCATE TABLE images statement enabled. The TRUNCATE statement will reset the auto-incremented counter. You can then reimport the blog articles.

Reading a Blog Article

We haven't prepared the visitor's blog list page yet, but for now, we'll work on viewing an individual blog article. When finished, it will look like Figure 12-4.

There's a Big Rock in the middle of Australia

24 Nov 2023 2:18 pm

Somewhere around the middle of Australia is a rock. It's a pretty big rock, as rocks go, and believe me, this one's not going anywhere. It just sort of sits there.

It was discovered a long time ago, and was given the name Ayers Rock, before it was discovered that it was discovered longer ago and given the name Uluru.

Today, it goes by both names in chronological order.

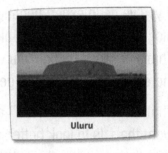

Uluru

Back

Copyright © Down Under
Friday, 24th November 2023 2:19 pm (Australia/Melbourne)

Figure 12-4. *Read Blog Article*

There is a page called `blogarticle.php`. At the beginning is a PHP block, which we'll move now.

Create a file called `blog.code.php` in the `includes` directory.

Preliminary Code

Cut the PHP block from the beginning of the `blogarticle.php` page and paste it into the `blog.code.php` page:

```php
<?php
#    blog.code.php

    $title = $precis = $created = $updated = $article =
    $figure = '';

    $pagetitle = 'Blog';
    $pageheading = 'Blog';
```

Don't forget to remove the closing PHP tag. In the blogarticle.plhp
page, replace the cut code with an include:

```php
<?php require_once 'includes/blog.code.php'; ?>
<?php require_once 'includes/head.inc.php'; ?>
<body>
    ...
</body>
</html>
```

You'll notice that the $pagetitle and $pageheading variables have
also been moved to the included file, unlike most other pages. That's to
allow us to change the heading or title according to the selected article.

At the beginning of the blog.code.php file, we can add some
preliminary code:

```php
<?php
#    blog.code.php

    $CONFIG=parse_ini_file('config.ini.php',true);
    require_once 'includes/db.php';
    require_once 'includes/default-library.php';
    require_once 'includes/library.php';
```

```
$root = str_replace($_SERVER['SCRIPT_NAME'], '',
    $_SERVER['SCRIPT_FILENAME']);
$host = $_SERVER['HTTP_HOST'];
$protocol = isset($_SERVER['HTTPS']) && $_SERVER
['HTTPS'] == 'on'
    ? 'https'
    : 'http';

$title = $precis = $created = $updated = $article =
$figure = '';

$pagetitle = 'Blog';
$pageheading = 'Blog';
```

Getting the Selected Article ID

We'll use a technique which is similar to the techniques for fetching
a selected image and loading a selected page. We'll assume that the
requested article is in a query string:

blogarticle.php?article=5

To interpret this, we can use the $_GET array or fall back to a cookie
using the null coalescing operator:

```
<?php
#   blog.code.php

    ...

    $title = $precis = $created = $updated = $article =
    $figure = '';

    $id = intval($_GET['article'] ?? $_COOKIE['article']);

    $pagetitle = 'Blog';
    $pageheading = 'Blog';
```

If both of them fail, then the intval() will give us a 0, which is invalid, but workable.

An ID of 0 isn't the only invalid one. You may have asked for a non-existing or deleted article. We can test for that in the next part.

If the article ID is valid, we should be able to fetch the data from the blog table:

```php
<?php
#   blog.code.php
    ...

    $id = intval($_GET['article'] ?? $_COOKIE['article']);

    $sql = "SELECT title, precis, created, updated,
    article, imageid
        FROM blog WHERE id=$id";
    $row = $pdo -> query($sql) -> fetch();

    $pagetitle = 'Blog';
    $pageheading = 'Blog';
```

If the ID is invalid, then the $row variable will be a null, and we can use that to send the visitor back to the bloglist.php list page:

```php
<?php
#   blog.code.php
    ...

    $sql = "SELECT title, precis, created, updated,
    article, imageid
        FROM blog WHERE id=$id";
```

```php
$row = $pdo -> query($sql) -> fetch();
if(!$row) {
    header("Location: $protocol://$host/bloglist.php");
    exit;
}

$pagetitle = 'Blog';
$pageheading = 'Blog';
```

Otherwise, we can keep the article in a cookie:

```php
<?php
#   blog.code.php

    ...

    if(!$row) {
        header("Location: $protocol://$host/bloglist.php");
        exit;
    }
    setcookie('article', $id, strtotime('+ 1 hour'));

    $pagetitle = 'Blog';
    $pageheading = 'Blog';
```

Again, you'll really want to set the cookie for much longer than one hour, but this is good enough for testing.

Fetching the Article

We've already got the article data in the $row variable. We can now destructure that in convenient variables:

```php
<?php
#   blog.code.php

    ...
```

```
setcookie('article', $id, strtotime('+ 1 hour'));

[$pagetitle, $precis, $created, $updated, $article,
$imageid]
    = $row;
$pageheading = $pagetitle;


//   $pagetitle = 'Blog';           //   Delete
//   $pageheading = 'Blog';         //   Delete
```

Do you remember the $pagetitle and $pageheading variables we moved from the blogarticle.php file to here? Remember also that the $pagetitle variable is used for the title attribute of the page, which appears on the browser tab or title bar and in bookmarks, while the $pageheading appears in the h1 element on the page itself.

You should, of course, delete the older assignments to these variables.

With the other pages, they were static enough to stick to a single value. Here, we're setting them to the title of the blog article.

We'll need to make a few adjustments to the data for presentation.

The dates coming from the database aren't always very user-friendly. We'll run them through *two* functions to fix that.

First, because the date will be extracted to a string, we'll need to convert it to PHP's own time format using the strtotime() function:

```
strtotime($created)
```

The strtotime() function is flexible enough to take a variety of strings and convert it to a PHP time. Then, we run it through the date() function, which takes an optional time and converts it to a formatted string:

```
$created = date('d M Y g:i a', strtotime($created));
```

We'll do that with the $updated variable, but we can add a little more magic: only display it if it's different to the $created value. We can start with an sprintf() function, using an expression similar to the one for the $created variable for the value:

```
$updated = sprintf(' Updated: %s', date('d M Y g:i a',
strtotime($updated));
```

Note the space at the beginning of the string.

However, we only want this if it's not the same as the $created value:

```
$updated = $updated != $created
    ? sprintf(' Updated: %s', date('d M Y g:i
    a',strtotime($updated)))
    : '';
```

We can now add this to our code:

```
<?php
#    blog.code.php
    ...

    [$pagetitle, $precis, $created, $updated, $article,
    $imageid]
        = $row;
    $pageheading = $pagetitle;

    $updated = $updated != $created
        ? sprintf(' Updated: %s',
            date('d M Y g:i a', strtotime($updated)))
        : '';
    $created = date('d M Y g:i a', strtotime($created));
```

Note that we've put the $created variable *after* the $updated variable. That's because we needed to compare the original values of the variables.

Fixing the Article Line Breaks

Earlier, we mentioned that we'll use two line breaks for a paragraph and a single line break for a non-paragraph break. The ns2pilcrow() function will have converted them to pilcrows, so now we'll need to reinterpret the pilcrows.

In the library.php file, we have the pilcrow2p() function:

```
function pilcrow2p($text) {
    return sprintf('<p>%s</p>', str_replace('¶', '</p><p>',
    $text));
}
```

We'll modify that by adding another parameter:

```
function pilcrow2p($text, $double=false) {
    return sprintf('<p>%s</p>', str_replace('¶', '</p><p>',
    $text));
}
```

The $double parameter is to indicate whether we're using double pilcrows for paragraph. As usual, we set the value to false to default to the original behavior.

We can now test the variable and use an alternative return value:

```
function pilcrow2p($text, $double=false) {
    if($double) return sprintf(…);
    else return sprintf('<p>%s</p>',str_replace('¶','</p><p>',
    $text));
}
```

The else part is the original return value. The first part will use a variation of the str_replace() function.

Normally, you would use simple strings in the str_replace()
function:

```
$text = 'the cat sat on the mat';
print str_replace('e' , '?', '$text');
//  the c?t s?t on the m?t
```

If you have an array for the first value, it will replace any of the items in
the array with the second value:

```
$text = 'the cat sat on the mat';
print str_replace(['e','a'] , '?', '$text');
//  th? c?t s?t ?n th? m?t
```

If the second value is also an array, it will replace corresponding items
of the arrays:

```
$text = 'the cat sat on the mat';
print str_replace(['e','a'] , ['?','-'], '$text');
//  th- c?t s?t ?n th- m?t
```

Here, we'll replace the double pilcrows with a paragraph break and a
single pilcrow with an HTML line break (<br>):

```
function pilcrow2p($text, $double=false) {
    if($double) return sprintf(
        '<p>%s</p>',
        str_replace(['¶¶','¶'], ['</p><p>','<br>'],$text)
    );
    else return sprintf('<p>%s</p>',str_replace('¶','</p><p>',
    $text));
}
```

With the images table, we used single pilcrows, and we can keep it that way—that's the default behavior. With the blog table, we'll use the double pilcrows. We can add this:

```
...
$updated = $updated != $created
    ? sprintf(' Updated: %s', date('d M Y g:i
    a',strtotime($updated)))
    : '';
$created = date('d M Y g:i a',strtotime($created));
$article = pilcrow2p($article, true);
```

That's the article text. The next task will be to display the optional image.

Displaying the Blog Image

In the HTML, there's a place for the image:

```
<div id="article" class="markdown">
    <?= $figure ?>
    <?= $article ?>
</div>
```

We're going to use an HTML figure element. That's meant to be a container for some sort of illustrative content. It's not necessarily an image—it might, for example, be a table if it illustrates a point. Here, we'll use an image to illustrate something in the article.

The figure may in turn contain a figurecaption element. It will end up looking like this:

```
<figure>
    <img ...>
    <figcaption> ... </figcaption>
</figure>
```

We'll populate the figure with the relevant content. First, however, we need to see whether there's an image to be displayed:

```php
<?php
#   blog.code.php

    ...

    $article = pilcrow2p($article,true);

    // Optional Image
    if($imageid) {

    }
```

If there is an image, we can define the $figure variable as a template string:

```php
if($imageid) {
    $figure = '<figure>
        <a href="/images/scaled/%s">
            <img src="/images/thumbnails/%s" width="%s"
            height="%s"
                alt="%s">
        </a>
        <figcaption>%s</figcaption>
    </figure>';
}
```

As usual, the string can be written on multiple lines and needs to be to fit in this book. You can keep it all on one line if you prefer.

We'll get the image from the thumbnails directory, and so we'll need to get the image dimensions for that size. That's in the $CONFIG array. The image is wrapped in an anchor which will be used to display a larger version from the scaled directory.

The image file and text will come from the images table. To get the data, we'll use the $imageid variable to read from the database:

```
//  Optional Image
    if($imageid) {
        $figure = ... ;

        $sql = "SELECT title, src FROM images WHERE
        id=$imageid";
        [$title, $src] = $pdo -> query($sql) -> fetch();

    }
```

Again, the value in $imageid comes from a safe source—in this case, it's the blog table—so we can simply interpolate into the SQL statement without the need to prepare it. From there, we can run the query and fetch the result. We can destructure the result directly into the variables $title and $src.

The img inside the figure string incudes placeholders for the width and height of the image. We'll use the splitSize() function in the default library to split the data from the $CONFIG array:

```
//  Optional Image
    if($imageid) {
        $figure = ... ;

        $sql = "SELECT title, src FROM images WHERE
        id=$imageid";
        [$title, $src] = $pdo -> query($sql) -> fetch();
        [$width, $height]
            = splitSize($CONFIG['images']['thumbnail-size']);

    }
```

We can now use the `sprintf()` function to put the values into the `$figure` string:

```
//  Optional Image
    if($imageid) {
        $figure = ... ;
        $sql = "SELECT title, src FROM images WHERE
        id=$imageid";
        [$title, $src] = $pdo -> query($sql) -> fetch();
        [$width, $height]
            = splitSize($CONFIG['images']['thumbnail-size']);

        $figure = sprintf(
            $figure,
            $src, $src, $width, $height, $title, $title
        );
    }
```

The `$src` variable is used twice: once for the enclosing anchor and once for the image itself. The `$title` is also used twice: once for the `alt` attribute and once for the figure caption.

You can now test various article IDs, but you'll have to enter them manually:

http://australia.example.com/blogarticle.php?article=4

Some of the articles will include an image, while some won't. If you include an article ID which you know will be out of range, then you'll be redirected to the `bloglist.php` page which is supposed to be a list of blog articles for visitors; at the moment, it's empty.

We'll work on the `bloglist.php` page a little later. First, we'll work on the blog management section.

Managing the Blog Articles

You've now got a collection of blog articles, and you can now view them. Here, we'll develop the management section.

The blog management pages will work similarly to the image management pages we worked on in Chapter 9:

- There will be a list page called `admin-bloglist.php`, which will list the blog articles for editing and have buttons to edit, delete, or add articles.

- The list page will lead to an edit page called `editblog.php`, where the individual article will be edited, deleted, or added. We've already worked on the code to add an article on this page.

- Between the `admin-bloglist.php` and `editblog.php` pages, there will be various submit events, and the `editblog.php` will also have submit events to confirm changes.

The article list page will look something like Figure 12-5.

ID	Title	Created	Updated		
1	Hello	19 Nov 2023 2:32 pm	24 Nov 2023 11:32 am	Edit	Delete
2	Australia, the Lucky Country	19 Nov 2023 2:33 pm	31 Mar 2019 4:50 pm	Edit	Delete
3	The Land Down Under	19 Nov 2023 2:33 pm	30 Mar 2019 10:54 am	Edit	Delete
4	The Sydney Opera House	12 Nov 2023 1:59 pm	12 Nov 2023 1:59 pm	Edit	Delete

Add New Article

Figure 12-5. *Administration List Page*

First, we'll create another file in the includes directory called admin-bloglist.code.php. We can begin the code with the preliminaries, such as we put in the imagelist.code.php file, without, of course, closing the PHP tag:

```php
<?php
#    admin-bloglist.code.php
```

```php
if(!session_id()) {
    session_start();
    session_regenerate_id(true);
}

$root = str_replace($_SERVER['SCRIPT_NAME'], '',
    $_SERVER['SCRIPT_FILENAME']);
$host = $_SERVER['HTTP_HOST'];
$protocol = isset($_SERVER['HTTPS']) &&
$_SERVER['HTTPS'] == 'on'
    ? 'https'
    : 'http';

if(!isset($_SESSION['user']) || !$_SESSION['admin']) {
    header("Location: $protocol://$host/admin.php");
    exit;
}

$pdo = require_once "$root/includes/db.php";
require_once "$root/includes/library.php";
require_once "$root/includes/default-library.php";

$CONFIG = parse_ini_file("$root/config.ini.php",true);
```

In the admin-bloglist.php page is a PHP block which initializes two variables. We can move that code to the admin-bloglist.code.php after the rest of the code:

```php
<?php
#   admin-bloglist.code.php
    ...
    $CONFIG = parse_ini_file("$root/config.ini.php",true);

    $tbody = $paging = $displaying = '';
```

489

Meanwhile, at the beginning of the admin-bloglist.php page, replace the removed code with an include:

```php
<?php require_once 'includes/admin-bloglist.code.php'; ?>
<?php
    $pagetitle = 'Administration Blog List';
    $pageheading = 'Blog List';

    require_once 'includes/head.inc.php';
?>
...
```

The blog list page will cater for a large number of articles, the same way the image list and the gallery pages, by paging the results. As with the image list, we'll put the number of articles per page in the config.ini. php file:

```ini
...
[imagelist]
    page-size = 6
[admin-bloglist]
    page-size = 4
```

The blog list page can fit many more than four items, of course, and you can experiment with a larger number when the code is finished. It's set to such a low number simply to test the paging.

To process the page number, we can copy the code from the imagelist.code.php file:

```php
<?php
#   admin-bloglist.code.php
    ...

    $tbody = $paging = displaying = '';
```

```
$page = intval($_GET['page'] ?? $_COOKIE
['admin-bloglist-page']
    ?? 1) ?: 1;

$limit = $CONFIG['admin-bloglist']['page-size'];
$offset = ($page - 1) * $limit;

$blogCount = $pdo -> query('SELECT count(*) FROM blog')
    -> fetchColumn();
$pages = ceil($blogCount / $limit);

$page = max(1, $page);         //  $page is at least 1
$page = min($page, $pages);    //  $page is up to $pages
setcookie('admin-bloglist-page', $page, strtotime
('+ 1 hour'));

$paging = paging($page, $pages);
$displaying = "Page $page of $pages";
```

Again, we've made a number of changes (six, if you count them):

- The cookie name is admin-bloglist-page. We've changed that for the $_COOKIE array and the setcookie() function.

- The $CONFIG array references admin-bloglist.

- The SELECT statement selects from the blog table.

- The variable name for the number of rows is changed to $blogCount, both for the PDO query and the ceil() calculation on the next line.

- We've added the $displaying variable.

We can now build the table of blog articles.

Building the Article Table

The table will have the following columns:

ID	Title	Created	Updated	[Edit] [Delete]

We can begin with the template strings, copied from the imagelist. code.php page, with a few changes:

```php
<?php
#   admin-bloglist.code.php

    ...

    setcookie('admin-bloglist-page', $page, strtotime('+ 1
    hour'));

    $tr = '<tr><th>%s</th><td>%s</td><td>%s</td><td>%s</td>
        <td>%s</td><td>%s</td></tr>';

    $editButton = '<button name="prepare-update"
        value="%s">Edit</button>';
    $deleteButton = '<button name="prepare-delete"
        value="%s">Delete</button>';

    $paging = paging($page, $pages);
    $displaying = "Page $page of $pages";
```

We've made some changes, of course:

- We don't need the image strings and data which we used in the imagelist.code.php page.

- The tr string has *six* cells.

    We've also changed the first one to a th cell for good measure, but it's not necessary.

Also note that the string wraps to another line because
it doesn't quite fit in this book. If possible, you should
try to keep the string on one line.

- We've changed the text of the delete button to **Delete**
  rather than **Remove** because it reads better; we've also
  changed the name of the variable.

We can now write the SQL query and iterate through the results. As
before, we'll put the table rows into an array called $tr:

```php
<?php
#   admin-bloglist.code.php

    ...

    $editButton = '<button name="prepare-update"
        value="%s">Edit</button>';
    $deleteButton = '<button name="prepare-delete"
        value="%s">Delete</button>';

    $sql="SELECT id, title, created, updated FROM blog
        ORDER BY id LIMIT $limit OFFSET $offset";

    $tbody = [];
    foreach($pdo->query($sql) as [$id, $title, $created,
    $updated]) {

    }
    $tbody = implode($tbody);

    $paging = paging($page, $pages);
    $displaying = "Page $page of $pages";
```

The next step is to populate the table rows. This will require the
following steps:

- Format the date using a combination of the date() and
  strtotime() functions.

- The date format is d M Y g:i a which will give a date
  and time like 20 Jul 69 8:17 pm.

- Populate the $edit and $delete values using
  sprintf().

- Add a new row to the $tbody array, using the sprintf()
  function on the $tr template string.

This gives us

```php
<?php
#   admin-bloglist.code.php
    ...

    $tbody = [];
    foreach($pdo->query($sql) as [$id, $title, $created,
    $updated]) {
        $created = date('d M Y g:i a', strtotime($created));
        $updated = date('d M Y g:i a', strtotime($updated));
        $edit = sprintf($editButton, $id);
        $delete = sprintf($deleteButton, $id);
        $tbody[] = sprintf($tr, $id, $title, $created,
        $updated,
            $edit, $delete);
    }
    $tbody = implode($tbody);

    ...
```

We now have a Blog List page which will list the blog articles.

We'll now process the **Edit** and **Delete** buttons, which will prepare the editblog.php page. This is done in the manage-blog.code.php file.

Processing the Prepare Events

In the manage-blog.code.php page, we have already written the code to prepare for a new blog article. We can now remove the empty($_POST) || part, since we've tested the code and we'll now presume that we're coming from the admin-bloglist.php page, where there's a button for this:

```php
<?php
#   manage-blog.code.php

    ...


    //  Prepare Page
    if(isset($_POST['prepare-insert'])) {
        $pagetitle = 'Upload Article';
        $pageheading = 'Upload Article';

        $chooseImage = getImageSelect();
    }
```

We can begin by adding blocks to prepare for the update and delete events. This is similar to the code in the manage-images.code.php file, where we first set the title and heading for the page:

```php
<?php
#   manage-blog.code.php

    ...

    //  Prepare Page
    if(isset($_POST['prepare-insert'])) {

        ...

    }
```

```php
    if(isset($_POST['prepare-update'])) {
        $pagetitle = 'Edit Article';
        $pageheading = 'Edit Article';

    }

    if(isset($_POST['prepare-delete'])) {
        $pagetitle = 'Delete Article';
        $pageheading = 'Delete Article';

    }
```

Again, most of the following code is modelled after manage-images.
code.php file. First, we'll extract the ID from the submit button:

```php
<?php
#    manage-blog.code.php
    ...

//    Prepare Page
    if(isset($_POST['prepare-insert'])) {
        ...
    }

    if(isset($_POST['prepare-update'])) {
        $pagetitle = 'Edit Article';
        $pageheading = 'Edit Article';

        $id = intval($_POST['prepare-update'] ?? 0);
    }

    if(isset($_POST['prepare-delete'])) {
        $pagetitle = 'Delete Article';
        $pageheading = 'Delete Article';

        $id = intval($_POST['prepare-delete'] ?? 0);
    }
```

A missing id will default to 0, which is no article.

At this point, we'll need to fetch the article data and possible image for both events. It would be easier to do that in a function so we don't have to repeat the code.

In the function section of the code, add the following new function:

```
//   Functions
function getImageSelect() {

    ...
}
function getImageButtons() {

    ...
}

function getArticle(int $id) {

}
```

The only input parameter will be the article id. The return result, however, will be a whole array of data.

First, we'll get the article data from the database. Among other things, that means we'll need the $pdo object. We'll also include the $CONFIG array for the image:

```
function getArticle(int $id) {
    global $pdo, $CONFIG;

    $sql = "SELECT title, precis, created, updated,
    article, imageid
        FROM blog WHERE id=$id";
    $row = $pdo -> query($sql) -> fetch();
}
```

It's possible that the article ID, even if not zero, is invalid—possibly it refers to a deleted article. If it's invalid, then, of course, the $row variable will be null, and we can return immediately with a null. Otherwise, we can continue and extract the data into variables. We can also process the extracted article data through the pilcrow2nl() function and format the two dates:

```
function getArticle(int $id) {
    global $pdo, $CONFIG;

    $sql = "SELECT title, precis, created, updated,
    article, imageid
        FROM blog WHERE id=$id";
    $row = $pdo -> query($sql) -> fetch();

    if(!$row) return null;        //  exit if no data

    [$title, $precis, $created, $updated, $article,
    $imageid] = $row;
    $article = pilcrow2nl($article);
    $created = date('d M Y g:i a', strtotime($created));
    $updated = date('d M Y g:i a', strtotime($updated));
}
```

The dates are processed the same way as they were for the blog article.

Displaying the Image

There may also be an image for the article. We can test the $imageid variable and, if so, fetch the data from the images table. If not, we'll generate a blank image in its place.

We already have the $previewImage template string, which we'll need to import. We'll also need to get the dimensions for the thumbnail size:

```
function getArticle(int $id) {
    global $pdo, $CONFIG, $previewImage;

    ...

    $created = date('d M Y g:i a', strtotime($created));
    $updated = date('d M Y g:i a', strtotime($updated));

    [$width, $height]
        = splitSize($CONFIG['images']['thumbnail-size']);
}
```

We can now test for an image and, if so, fetch the data from the images table. Otherwise, we'll set the image to a blank image:

```
function getArticle(int $id) {
    global $pdo, $CONFIG, $previewImage;
    ...

    [$width, $height]
        = splitSize($CONFIG['images']['thumbnail-size']);

    if($imageid) {

    }
    else $previewImage = sprintf(
        $previewImage,
        '/images/blank.png', $width, $height, 'No Image'
    );
}
```

Notice that we're rewriting the $previewImage variable—we only need the original value long enough to use in the sprintf() function, and the new value actually holds the preview image.

If there is an image, we'll fetch it and test whether that was successful:

```
function getArticle(int $id) {

    ...

    if($imageid) {
        $sql = "SELECT title, src FROM images WHERE
        id=$imageid";
        $row = $pdo -> query($sql) -> fetch();
        if($row) {
            [$imagetitle, $src] = $row;
            $previewImage = sprintf(
                $previewImage,
                "images/thumbnails/$src", $width, $height,
                $imagetitle
            );
        }
    }
    else $previewImage = sprintf( ... );
}
```

Note that we've interpolated the src variable into the string to include the images directory.

Note also that we've used the variable $imagetitle for the image title, rather than just $title. That's because the $title variable is being used for the article title. We don't need the $imagetitle variable for very long, as it's only being used to generate the $previewImage value.

Finally, we can return the data and the image in an array:

```
function getArticle(int $id) {

    ...
```

```
    if($imageid) {
        ...
    }
    else $image = sprintf( ... );

    return [$title, $precis, $created, $updated, $article,
        $imageid, $previewImage];
}
```

Apart from the text data for the article, the return array also includes the ID of the image, of any, and the preview image.

We should now fetch the data into variables in the prepare update and prepare delete code:

```
if(isset($_POST['prepare-update'])) {
    ...

    $id = intval($_POST['prepare-update'] ?? 0);
    [$title, $precis, $created, $updated, $article, $imageid,
        $previewImage] = getArticle($id);
}

if(isset($_POST['prepare-delete'])) {
    ...

    $id = intval($_POST['prepare-delete'] ?? 0);
    [$title, $precis, $created, $updated, $article, $imageid,
        $previewImage] = getArticle($id);
}
```

Finishing the Preparation

There are two more tasks to finish the preparation.

First, for the prepare update, we'll include the option to select a preexisting image to replace the current image. However, we should highlight the currently selected image if there is one. The form already includes the option to select a new image.

For both the getImageSelect() and the getImageButtons() functions, add an optional parameter variable for the current image:

```
function getImageSelect($imageid=0) {

    ...

}

function getImageButtons($imageid=0) {

    ...

}
```

The default value is 0 which means that there isn't one.

In a select menu, to preselect an option element you set its selected attribute. We already have a placeholder in the template string, and currently, it's set to an empty string.

The first option will always be selected if nothing else is. However, if another one is selected, then it will replace the first option.

Inside the foreach block, we can set the value to either selected or an empty string, depending on whether the current $id matches the $imageid variable. This is where the ternary operator allows to choose one of two values:

```
function getImageSelect($imageid=0) {

    ...

    foreach($pdo -> query('SELECT id, title, src FROM images')
        AS [$id, $title, $src]) {
        $select[] =sprintf(
            $option, $id, "/images/thumbnails/$src",
            $id == $imageid ? ' selected' : '', $id, $title
        );
```

```
    }

    ...

}
```

For the image buttons, the idea is the same, except that we set the checked attribute of the selected radio button:

```
function getImageButtons($imageid=0) {

    ...

    foreach($pdo -> query('SELECT id, title, src FROM images')
        as [$id, $title, $src]) {
        $buttons[] = sprintf(
            $button, $id, $id == $imageid ? ' checked' : '',
            "/images/icons/$src", $title, $title,
            $width, $height, "/images/thumbnails/$src"
        );
    }

    ...

}
```

In the prepare update code, we can add the call to the getImageSelect() or getImageButtons() function, complete with the $imageid of the current article:

```
if(isset($_POST['prepare-update'])) {

    ...

    [$title, $precis, $created, $updated, $article, $imageid,
        $previewImage] = getArticle($id);

    $chooseImage = $CONFIG['blogedit']['use-image']=='buttons'
        ? getImageButtons($imageid)
        : getImageSelect($imageid);
}
```

503

For the prepare delete, we won't allow the user to choose an image. What we will do, however, is set the $disabled variable to disable editing on the form:

```
if(isset($_POST['prepare-delete'])) {
    ...

    $disabled = ' disabled';
}
```

We can now test the blog list. Of course, any changes you make at this point will be ignored, until we finish writing the rest of the editing code.

Updating an Article

We've already worked on the code to update an image. Updating a blog article will be similar.

To begin with, we'll add a block for the update:

```
    ...

    if(isset($_POST['insert'])) {

        ...
    }

    if(isset($_POST['update'])) {

    }

    if(isset($_POST['import'])) {
        ...
    }
    ...
```

To get the data ready for uploading, we'll use similar code for the insert to fetch the data and test for errors:

```
if(isset($_POST['update'])) {
    [$id, $title, $precis, $article, $image, $errors] =
    getBlogData();
    $precis = nl2pilcrow($precis);
    $article = nl2pilcrow($article);

    if(!$errors) {  //  proceed

        //  Move On
            header("Location: $protocol://$host/admin-
            bloglist.php");
            exit;
    }
    else {            //  handle error
        $errors = sprintf('<p class="errors">%s</p>',
            implode('<br>',$errors));
    }
}
```

Note that we've also put the $precis and $article variables through the nl2pilcrow() function. That's because we *won't* use the addBlogData() function. Instead, we can just write the necessary code directly.

To update an article, you use the UPDATE statement:

```
UPDATE blog
SET title=?, precis=?, article=?, updated=?
WHERE id=?
```

The text content is, of course, included. So is the updated column, which is why it's there. There's also the image, but we'll deal with that later.

We'll write that into the PHP code:

```
if(isset($_POST['update'])) {
    ...

    if(!$errors) {  //  proceed
        $sql = 'UPDATE blog SET title=?, precis=?, article=?,
            updated=? WHERE id=?';
        $pdoStatement = $pdo -> prepare($sql);
        $data = [$title, $precis, $article, date
        ('Y-m-d H:i:s'), $id];
        $pdoStatement->execute($data);

        //  Move On
            ...
    }
    ...
}
```

The updated column will get the formatted current date/time.

If there's an image to be included in the updated data, it should also be added. This is why it was important to select the current image in the choose image section.

To include the image, we can just call the addBlogImage() function, which does all of the hard work:

```
if(isset($_POST['update'])) {
    ...
```

```
if(!$errors) {  //  proceed
    $sql = 'UPDATE blog SET title=?, precis=?, article=?,
        updated=? WHERE id=?';
    $pdoStatement = $pdo -> prepare($sql);
    $data = [$title, $precis, $article,
    date('Y-m-d H:i:s'), $id];
    $pdoStatement->execute($data);

    addBlogImage($id, $image, $title, $precis);

    //  Move On
        ...
}
...
}
```

You can now test this by starting on the blog list page, selecting an article to edit, and making a few minor or major changes. If you revisit the article for editing, you should see all of your changes.

Deleting an Article

This one is pretty straightforward, except when it comes to images. While we're happy to add a new image to a blog article, it's not easy to guess whether we want to keep the image later, possibly as part of the image gallery. The simple solution is to leave that to the Image Management section.

We'll begin by creating the delete block:

```
...

if(isset($_POST['update'])) {
    ...
```

```php
}

if(isset($_POST['delete'])) {

}

if(isset($_POST['import'])) {
    ...
}

...
```

To delete an article, we use the DELETE statement:

```sql
DELETE FROM blog WHERE id=?
```

We have the getBlogData() function to retrieve the uploaded data, but all we really need is the ID. We can get that directly from the $_POST array:

```php
if(isset($_POST['delete'])) {
    $id = intval($_POST['id'] ?? 0);
}
```

Since the $id variable is guaranteed to be an integer, we can interpolate it into an SQL string and run it directly using the exec() method:

```php
if(isset($_POST['delete'])) {
    $id = intval($_POST['id'] ?? 0);

    $pdo -> exec("DELETE FROM images WHERE id=$id");
}
```

After that, we can move on to the blog list:

```php
if(isset($_POST['delete'])) {
    $id = intval($_POST['id'] ?? 0);

    $pdo -> exec("DELETE FROM images WHERE id=$id");
```

508

```
    //  Move On
        header("Location: $protocol://$host/admin-
        bloglist.php");
        exit;
}
```

We can now try deleting an unwanted blog article.

The Visitor Blog List

Everything is almost in place. The one thing missing is the blog list page for visitors. However, that's easily developed with the help of the code we developed for the admin blog list. It will look like Figure 12-6.

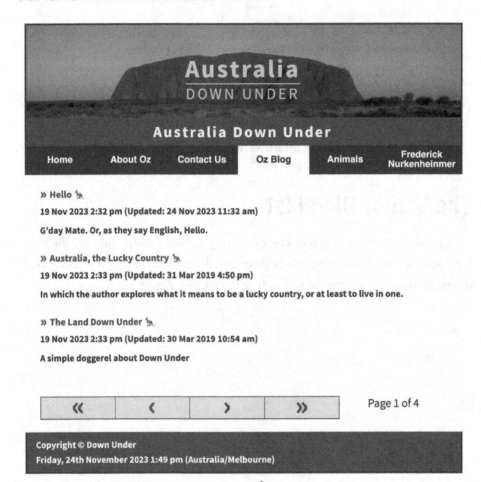

Figure 12-6. *Visitor List Page*

We'll be working with two files: the bloglist.php file and a corresponding bloglist.code.php file in the includes directory, which we haven't yet created.

- Create the bloglist.code.php file in the includes directory.

- Open the `bloglist.php` file and cut the first PHP block from there and paste it into `bloglist.code.php` file (removing the closing PHP tag).

  You should have

  ```php
  <?php
  #   bloglist.code.php

      $articles = $paging = $displaying = '';
  ```

- Replace the cut PHP block in the `bloglist.php` file with an include:

  ```php
  <?php require_once 'includes/bloglist.code.php'; ?>
  ```

We can now fill in the code.

Preparatory Code

Much of what follows can be copied from the `admin-bloglist.code.php` file. We can begin with some preliminary code to set some variables and include some files. We won't need to worry about whether the visitor's logged in, so we won't need the session code:

```php
<?php
#   bloglist.code.php

    $root = str_replace($_SERVER['SCRIPT_NAME'], '',
        $_SERVER['SCRIPT_FILENAME']);
    $host = $_SERVER['HTTP_HOST'];
    $protocol = isset($_SERVER['HTTPS']) && $_
SERVER['HTTPS'] == 'on'
        ? 'https'
        : 'http';
```

```php
$pdo = require_once "$root/includes/db.php";
require_once "$root/includes/library.php";
require_once "$root/includes/default-library.php";

$CONFIG = parse_ini_file("$root/config.ini.php",true);

$articles = $paging = $displaying = '';
```

Note the reference to the $CONFIG array. We'll need that for the number of items for page. We should add that to the config.ini.php file:

```ini
...
[images]
    ...
[gallery]
    page-size = 3
[bloglist]
    page-size = 4
[imagelist]
...
```

We'll also want to get and remember the page number and set the offset and limit for when we fetch the list of articles:

```php
<?php
#   bloglist.code.php
    ...

    $articles = $paging = $displaying = '';

    $page = intval($_GET['page'] ?? $_COOKIE['bloglist-page']
    ?? 1)
        ?: 1;

    $limit = $CONFIG['bloglist']['page-size'];
    $offset = ($page - 1) * $limit;
```

```
$blogCount = $pdo -> query('SELECT count(*) FROM blog')
    -> fetchColumn();
$pages = ceil($blogCount / $limit);

$page = max(1, $page);
$page = min($page, $pages);
setcookie('bloglist-page', $page, strtotime('+ 1 hour'));
```

We can now start generating the list of articles.

Generating the Blog Article List

We'll make the article list a little more friendly than the table we used for administration. It will basically be a collection of headings with the article precis and date—something like this:

```
<div>
    <div>
        <h2><a>[Title]</a></h2>
        <p>[Date]</h2>
        <p>[Precis]
    </div>
    <div>
        ...
    </div>
    <div>
        ...
    </div>
</div>
```

Each article preview is wrapped in a div element, and the whole collection is wrapped in another div element. That's just to make it easier for the layout and the CSS.

First, we can set up some template strings:

```php
<?php
#   bloglist.code.php

    ...

    setcookie('bloglist-page', $page, strtotime('+ 1 hour'));

    $h2 = '<h2><a href="blogarticle.php?article=%s">%s</a>
    </h2>';
    $div = '<div>%s<p class="date">%s%s</p>
        <p class="precis">%s</p></div>';
```

The string is in two parts, mainly for convenience. The $h2 string will be put into the $div string.

In the $h2 string, there's a link to the selected article in the form of ?article=%s, which is similar to the way we viewed an article previously. The link also has the title of the article.

The $div string will have the heading as well as the date and the précis. The date has two %s placeholders, one for the created date and one possibly for the updated date.

Next, we'll define the SQL and build an array of articles, which will be imploded at the end:

```php
<?php
#   bloglist.code.php

    ...

    setcookie('bloglist-page', $page, strtotime('+ 1 hour'));

    $h2 = '<h2><a href="blogarticle.php?article=%s">%s</a>
    </h2>';
    $div = '<div>%s<p class="date">%s%s</p>
        <p class="precis">%s</p></div>';
```

```
$sql="SELECT id, title, created, updated, precis FROM blog
    ORDER BY id LIMIT $limit OFFSET $offset";

$articles=[];
$articles[] = '<div>';

foreach($pdo -> query($sql) as [$id, $title, $created,
$updated,
  $precis]) {

}

$articles[] = '</div>';
$articles=implode($articles);
```

The $articles array starts and finishes with div tags to contain the entire collection.

As before, we iterate through the query results using the foreach() statement, with the columns destructured into the array of variables.

Inside the foreach(), we process the dates and then use sprintf(), first to generate a heading and then generate the item to add to the $articles array:

```
foreach($pdo -> query($sql) as [$id, $title, $created, $updated,
  $precis]) {
    $updated = $updated != $created
        ? sprintf(' (Updated: %s)', date('d M Y g:i a',
            strtotime($updated)))
        : '';
    $created = date('d M Y g:i a',strtotime($created));
    $heading=sprintf($h2, $id, $title);
    $articles[]=sprintf($div, $heading, $created,$updated,
    $precis);
}
```

Note that we've used the same technique on the $updated variable as we did for the blog article, to only display it if it's different to the $created value.

Finally, we can add the $paging and $displaying variables for the navigation block:

```php
<?php
#   bloglist.code.php

    ...


    $paging = paging($page, $pages);
    $displaying = "Page $page of $pages";
```

When you select the **Oz Blog** link, you'll see a paged list of articles, with a link to each article in the headings.

The jumping kangaroos (🦘) is just a CSS trick.

Summary

This has been quite a long chapter, but much of it has been familiar territory, though there have been a few new tricks.

There are many ways we could have worked the code for this final section, but in this chapter, we've tried to develop some solid principles in how to write reliable and maintainable code.

Here are some of the principles:

- Separate the logic from the rest of the code.

  To begin with, we have a code block in a separate file. It doesn't have to be a separate file, but it should be separated from the rest of the web page.

  Next, we developed a configuration section to allow us to set arbitrary values which are not fundamental to the logic.

Finally, we limited the PHP in the HTML part of the page to outputting results and switching between the sections. That leaves the HTML relatively maintenance free while we develop the code.

- Expect changes.

A number of times, we revisited sections of code to add more features, such as additional attributes or elements in HTML, or options to adjust the way the code works. This is also the case with a number of functions which were revisited to enhance them.

In all cases, you should try to write your changes in such a way that the original behavior is still supported. For example, when adding parameters to existing functions, we add defaults consistent with the original behavior.

Of course, it's not always possible, but you should aim to minimize disruption in your code changes.

- Write readable code.

Coding is hard enough without wading through a swamp of illegible code trying to work out what's going on. Remember that in six months' time you may have to return to the code to make changes or to fix something.

All of the code samples in this book are scrupulously indented, the variable and function names have been simple and meaningful, comments are used, and even empty lines are used to section code. All developers will have their own preferences as to how this is done, but you should always write your code with these ideas.

- Look for opportunities to reuse your code.

  Obviously, we've made use of copy and paste when writing code similar to other parts of the project. That works better if your code in different sections is organized in similar ways. However, we also made use of functions to write code which can be called from more than one place. Using functions also helps if you need to rewrite some of the behavior.

  Truly generic code can be placed in a separate library file for use in other projects. Less generic code can still be written up in functions for reuse within a script.

  Note that there are some practical limitations in writing functions. Sometimes, we need too many variations, or the code is too trivial, and the use of too many functions can make your code somewhat cryptic.

- Organize your code.

  More easily said than done, of course, but you need to avoid writing great slabs of code which don't follow any clear plan.

  Again, individual developers have personal preferences, but your code organization should include how you name your files, as well as your variables and functions. Develop a pattern for where you put your configuration and initialization code, as well as where you place your support functions and separate blocks of code.

Throughout the project, there are many places where you could have written the code differently. Indeed, some of the code in this chapter was written differently and more tightly than similar code in previous chapters. Now that you presumably know more about writing PHP than in the beginning, you can revisit the previous code and look where you might rewrite it to improve it.

The thing is you need to start developing your own patterns and, wherever possible, to stick to them. This will take time and experience, which is, of course, all part of the fun.

Adding Markdown to Your Blog Articles

You might have noticed a distinct lack of styling in your blog articles. All you have is paragraph and line breaks.

You can add some richness to your article text in a number of ways. Traditionally, this was done by adding HTML. However, that's open error and abuse. PHP has a number of functions which can filter or disable HTML, but then it starts to get very complicated. Besides, you still need the person writing the article to know some HTML.

There is a simple alternative language called **markdown**. It was proposed by John Gruber, and you can learn more about it at `https://daringfireball.net/projects/markdown/syntax`. The idea is that a few simple codes would translate into HTML, which simplifies writing a great deal.

Here, we can implement a simplified subset of markdown which is easily added to an article. Since you might not want all of your articles to be in markdown format, we'll make a few changes to the database to store the setting and a number of changes to the rest of the code to implement it.

© Mark Simon 2024
M. Simon, *An Introduction to PHP*, https://doi.org/10.1007/979-8-8688-0177-8

The Markdown Language

We're going to use a subset of the most useful features of markdown:

- Headings: `## heading`

    → `<h2>heading</h2>`

    Headings start with one or more hashes (#). The number of hashes is the heading level.

    You shouldn't include an h1 or h2 because they're supposed to be the main headings of the page. In our simple markdown interpreter, heading levels before 3 are ignored.

- Anchors: `[text](url)`

    → `<a href="url">text</a>`

    In our markdown interpreter, the links include the `target="_blank"` attribute to open them in a new window or tab.

- Strong: `__strong text__`

    → `<strong>strong text</strong>`

- Emphasis: `_emphasised text_`

    → `<em>emphasised text</em>`

- Unordered list: `- item ... etc`

    → `<ul><li> ... </li><li> ... </li></ul>`

    One item per line starting with a minus (-) and then a space.

- Ordered list: `1. item` ... etc

  → `<ol><li> ... </li><li> ... </li></ol>`

  One item per line starting with a number, a dot, then a space. The actual number doesn't matter—you don't have to write a sequence.

- Block quotes: `> quoted text`

  → `<blockquote>quoted text</blockquote>`

- Line breaks: `text(space)(space)`

  → `text<br>`

  End the text with *two* spaces, and start the next line immediately.

- Paragraphs

  All other text will be interpreted as paragraphs. The text must have double line breaks.

In the `default-library.php` file is a function called `md2html()`. This is *very* heavily inspired by a package called Slimdown (`https://github.com/jbroadway/slimdown`).

You can see a sample of a markdown text in `setup/bush-hut.md`. It's just a plain text file, but, when you've finished, it will become rich text.

Adding Markdown to the Database

We're going to add another column to the `blog` table to record whether the article uses markdown.

To make changes to a database table, we use the `ALTER TABLE` statement. This can have rather serious consequences if you make a mistake, such as dropping the wrong column. There's no undo in SQL.

Here, we'll add a column called markdown.

In PHPMyAdmin, select the australia database. In the SQL tab, run the following:

```
ALTER TABLE blog ADD COLUMN markdown BOOLEAN DEFAULT FALSE;
```

This adds another column called markdown, which defaults to false. If we want it to be true, we'll need to set it deliberately.

Adding a Checkbox to the Form

We'll add a checkbox to the editblog.php page, similar to the gallery checkbox in the editimage.pph page:

```
<fieldset id="content" <?= $disabled ?>>

    ...

    <p><label>Article<br>
        <textarea id="article" name="article">
        <?= $article ?></textarea></label>
    </p>
    <p><label>
        <input type="checkbox"
            name="markdown" <?= $markdown ?>> Markdown</label>
    </p>
</fieldset>
```

The additional field includes a variable called $markdown which will be checked or not. As before, note the two closing angle brackets on the input: <input ... <?= $markdown ?>>; one closes the PHP output tag and the other closes the HTML element.

In the manage-blog.code.php page, add the $markdown variable to the initialization section:

```
#    manage-blog.code.php
    // Initialise
        $title = $precis = $article = '';
        $id = 0;
        $errors = '';
        $disabled = '';
        $markdown = '';
```

If you load the editblog.php page, either to add a new article or to edit an existing one, you'll now see the checkbox unchecked.

Reading the Markdown Setting

The getArticle() function reads the article data from the blog table. We'll add the markdown column to what we're fetching:

```
#    manage-blog.code.php

    function getArticle(int $id) {
        global $pdo, $CONFIG, $previewImage;
        $sql = "SELECT title, precis, created, updated,
        article,
            imageid, markdown FROM blog WHERE id=$id";
        ...
        [$title, $precis, $created, $updated, $article,
          $imageid, $markdown] = $row;
        ...
        return [$title, $precis, $created, $updated, $article,
            $imageid, $previewImage, $markdown];
    }
```

We have also copied the data into an additional $marked variable and added that to the array in the return statement.

We should now include the $markdown variable in the prepare update and prepare delete code:

```
if(isset($_POST['prepare-update'])) {
    ...
    [$title, $precis, $created, $updated, $article, $imageid,
        $previewImage, $markdown] = getArticle($id);

    $markdown = $markdown ? ' checked' : '';
    ...
}

if(isset($_POST['prepare-delete'])) {
    ...
    [$title, $precis, $created, $updated, $article, $imageid,
        $previewImage, $markdown] = getArticle($id);

    $markdown = $markdown ? ' checked' : '';
    ...
}
```

We have also converted the value to either checked or an empty string.

At this point, of course, we won't see any changes because none of the current articles use markdown.

Manipulating the Markdown Setting

When an article is inserted or updated, we'll need to interpret and process the new checkbox.

First, we'll read the markdown checkbox with the other values in the getBlogData() function:

```
function getBlogData() {
    ...
    $image = null;
    $markdown = intval(isset($_POST['markdown']));

    ...
    return [$id, $title, $precis, $article,
        $image, $markdown, $errors];
}
```

We also need to return it, just before the $errors value.

The getBlogData() function is called when we insert or update an article. We'll need to add the $markdown variable to these:

```
if(isset($_POST['insert'])) {
    [$id, $title, $precis, $article, $image, $markdown,
$errors]
        = getBlogData();

    ...
}

if(isset($_POST['update'])) {
    [$id, $title, $precis, $article, $image, $markdown,
$errors]
        = getBlogData();

    ...
}
```

We have the addBlogData() function to add the data to the blog table. We'll add the $markdown parameter at the end, making it optional. This value needs to be added into the INSERT statement, both into the column list and the placeholders and into the $data array:

```
function addBlogData(string $title, string $precis,
  string $article, array|string $image=null, string
  $created=null,
  string $updated=null, int $markdown=0) {
    ...
  $sql = 'INSERT INTO blog(title, precis, article,
      created, updated, markdown)
      VALUES(?, ?, ?, ?, ?, ?)';
  $pdoStatement = $pdo -> prepare($sql);
  $data = [$title, $precis, $article, $created?:
  date('Y-m-d H:i:s'),
      $updated?:date('Y-m-d H:i:s'), $markdown];
    ...
}
```

The addBlogData() function is called from two places. First, it's called when we add an individual article. We'll need to read in the $markdown value:

```
  if(isset($_POST['insert'])) {

  [$id, $title, $precis, $article, $image, $markdown,
  $errors]
      = getBlogData();

  if(!$errors) {  // proceed
      $id = addBlogData($title, $precis, $article, $image,
          null, null, $markdown);

      ...
  }
```

```
else {           // handle error
    ...
}
...
}
```

Second, it's called when we import data. That's a little problem here in that the code originally didn't allow for the extra data, so the CSV file may still be the older style without it. We'll need to allow for that.

The first thing is to add the extra column to the $keys array string:

```
$keys
= explode(' ','title precis article created updated image
markdown');
```

If the imported row doesn't have the additional column, we can pad it with a null before combining it with the keys:

```
foreach($data as $row) {
    $row = array_pad($row, 7, null);
    $row = array_combine($keys, $row);
    ...
)
```

The array_pad() function takes the original array and pads it to a number of values, in this case to 7 values with an extra null. If the array is already the right size, the padding is ignored.

Finally, you can include it in the call to addBlogData(). You don't have to if you're using the ... operator, but you will if you're adding the parameters individually:

```
// addBlogData($row['title'], $row['precis'], $row['article'],
//     $row['created'], $row['updated'],
//     $row['image'], $row['markdown']);  // Any PHP
```

This gives us something like the following:

```php
if(isset($_POST['import'])) {
  ...
  if(!$errors) {
    ...
    $keys = explode(' ',
        'title precis article created updated image markdown');

    foreach($data as $row) {
        $row = array_combine($keys, $row);
        $row = array_pad($row, 7, null);
        ...
            addBlogData(...$row);                      //  PHP >= 8
            //  addBlogData(...array_values($row));
            // PHP >= 7.2
            //  addBlogData($row['title'], $row['precis'],
            //    $row[article], $row[created], $row[updated],
            //    $row[image], $row['markdown');   //  Any PHP
    }
    ...
  }
  else {
    ...
  }
}
```

We'll also need to include the markdown value when updating the article. We've already read the data, so it's just a matter of including it in the SQL statement and the data:

```php
if(isset($_POST['update'])) {
    [$id, $title, $precis, $article, $image, $markdown,
    $errors]
```

```
    = getBlogData();
...
if(!$errors) {  //  proceed
    $sql = 'UPDATE blog SET title=?, precis=?, article=?,
        updated=?, markdown=? WHERE id=?';
    $pdoStatement = $pdo -> prepare($sql);
    $data = [$title, $precis, $article, date
    ('Y-m-d H:i:s'),
        $markdown, $id];
    ...
}
```

We now have the markdown flag added to the database and the data.

You might try adding a new article with markdown data before the final step. You can copy the markdown from the setup/bush-hut.md file and add the image setup/bush-hut.jpg or whatever takes your fancy.

Displaying the Markdown Article

Now that we have the markdown column in the data, we'll need to read it when we're displaying the article.

In the blogarticle.php file, we'll add a variable to the article element:

```
<article id="blogarticle" <?=$markdown?>>
    ...
</article>
```

Watch out for the two closing angle brackets (>>) and the extra space before the PHP output.

This variable may contain a class attribute of class="markdown". That's so that CSS can control its appearance.

In the `blog.code.php` file, add the variable to the initialization:

```
$title = $precis = $created = $updated = $article
    = $figure = $markdown = '';
```

Then add the column to the SQL statement and to the list of variables:

```
<?php
#   blog.code.php
    ...
    $sql = "SELECT title, precis, created, updated, article,
        imageid, markdown
        FROM blog WHERE id=$id";
    $row = $pdo -> query($sql) -> fetch();
    ...

    [$pagetitle, $precis, $created, $updated, $article,
        $imageid, $markdown]  = $row;

    ...
```

Toward the end of the code, we run the article through the `pilcrow2p` function to convert the stored pilcrows to paragraphs. We'll change that to test for the $markdown variable:

```
$updated = $updated != $created
    ? sprintf(' Updated: %s',
        date('d M Y g:i a', strtotime($updated)))
    : '';
$created = date('d M Y g:i a', strtotime($created));

if(!$markdown)  $article = pilcrow2p($article, true);
else {
    //  markdown
}
```

If the $markdown variable is set, we'll convert the pilcrows to real line breaks and then convert the article itself:

```
if(!$markdown)  $article = pilcrow2p($article, true);
else {
    $article = pilcrow2nl($article);
    $article = md2html($article);
    $markdown = ' class="markdown"';
}
```

We've also set the $markdown variable to add the class to the article. You should now see something like Figure A-1.

For Sale: A little hut in the bush.

29 Nov 2023 1:54 pm Updated: 29 Nov 2023 5:07 pm

A Little Bush Hut

There's a track winding back to an old fashioned shack, but it's not on the road to Gundagai. Or any other road, for that matter, because it's in the bush and the track is about all you're likely to get in place of a road.

The misquote is from a song from the 1920s, and you can learn a little more from this **Wikipedia Article** ⌐.

Features

This little bush hut boasts the following features:

Bush Hut

- It's little. Good if you don't like it to be *too big*.
- It's in the bush. Which is to say it's not in the city or in some other *non bush* location.
- It's a hut, so if you're looking for a swimming pool or a set of saucepans this isn't for you. If you're looking for a *hut*, however, this might do the job.

How to get there

If you want to see the hut:

1. *Don't* go along the road to Gundagai, because it isn't there.
2. Find another track. Preferably the one with this little bush hut.
3. Follow the track to the hut.
4. There no step 4. If you get this far then this is as far as it gets.

That's it, really.

E & OE

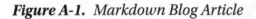

Back

Copyright © Down Under
Wednesday, 29th November 2023 5:51 pm (Australia/Melbourne)

Figure A-1. *Markdown Blog Article*

APPENDIX B

Non-PHP Tricks

Not all of the magic on the sample project comes from PHP. Obviously, there's some HTML and SQL involved, but some of the special tricks are achieved through some extra CSS and JavaScript.

If you know nothing of JavaScript or CSS, and care even less, then you can ignore the rest of this appendix. If, on the other hand, you know something about them, then you can learn a little more of how these techniques are used in the project.

Toggle Background

This isn't so much a special effect as simply an aid to troubleshooting.

You'll notice that the background is *very* busy with a vibrant repeated image. That's fine until you try to read some of the error messages or the output from troubleshooting print statements.

If you shift-click the banner image, the background will toggle off and on. That's just some JavaScript to change the state of the background and to remember this state.

The code is

```
// Background Image
   if(localStorage.getItem('debug'))
       document.body.classList.add('debug');
```

```
document.querySelector('header').onclick = event => {
    if(event.shiftKey) document.body.classList.
    toggle('debug');
    if(document.body.classList.contains('debug'))
        localStorage.setItem('debug',true);
    else localStorage.removeItem('debug');
};
```

There is a CSS class called debug. If the body has this class, the background image is hidden.

The code searches for the header element (document. querySelector('header')) and assigns a click event listener.

When you click the header element, the event listener checks whether the shift key is down. If so, the debug class is toggled.

If the toggle has set the class, the value is stored in the local storage. Otherwise, the value is removed. The local storage is maintained by the browser for each website and is useful for storing setting information.

In the initialization code, JavaScript checks the local storage for whether the debug value has been set before. It sets the class accordingly.

Visible Passwords

By default, password fields on a web form are obscured—all you see when you type is bullets instead of the characters. That's to combat so-called "shoulder-surfing"—someone looking over your shoulder as you type your password.

That's OK if you're logging in in a public place, but often you're at home or in some other private location, and all you get is the downside of obscuring your password: you can't see what you're typing. That's especially annoying if you've followed the best advice and generated a very complex password.

The login form on the sample project has a solution to that which allows you to see the password for ten seconds. It comes in three parts.

First, the HTML has an additional button beside the password field:

```
<label>Password:<br>
    <input type="password" name="password" id="password">
    <button type="button" name="show-password" title="Show
    Password">👓</button>
</label>
```

Of course, by itself it does nothing. It relies on JavaScript to do its work.

The second part is the JavaScript. First, we find the login form and attach an event listener to the show-password button. The event listener is the doShowPassword() function:

```
let form;
if(form = document.querySelector('form#login')) {
    form.elements['show-password'].onclick
        = doShowPassword.bind(null, form);
}
```

The doShowPassword() function is defined separately:

```
function doShowPassword(form, event) {
    form.elements['password'].type = 'text';
    form.elements['show-password'].setAttribute('on', true);
    window.setTimeout(() => {
        form.elements['password'].type = 'password';
        form.elements['show-password'].removeAttribute('on');
    }, 10000);
    event.preventDefault();
}
```

537

In the doShowPassword() function, all that's really necessary is that the password field has been changed to a text type, which will readily display its contents. The rest of the function sets up an attribute for CSS and reverts the field type after ten seconds.

The function adds an on attribute to the show password button. That's not a standard attribute, but neither JavaScript nor CSS cares about that. What matters is that CSS can target that attribute.

The setTimeout() function waits for 10,000 milliseconds and then restores the original state by setting the field type back to password and removing the on attribute.

The third part is the CSS, and it's only there for show. Most of the CSS for the button is to make the silly eyes look right and place the button at the end of the password field.

However, there are two important properties to give the visual effect:

```
form#login button[name="show-password"] {
    ...
    transform: scale(-1, 1);
    transition: transform 0.75s;
}
```

The transform property is technically a scale effect, but the first (horizontal) value of -1 effectively flips the image horizontally. Its natural appearance is to look stage right.

The transition property slows down the change to 0.75 of a second.

When the on attribute has been set, the following CSS is applied:

```
form#login button[name="show-password"][on] {
    transform: scale(1.6);
}
```

Both horizontal and vertical axes are scaled to 1.6 (enlarged), and the positive value flips the appearance to stage left.

Required Upload

In the `uploadimage.php/editimage.php` file, there's a form to upload a ZIP file. You'll have noticed that the submit button doesn't appear until a file has been selected.

This effect comes in two parts: the HTML which comprises the form and the CSS which toggles the submit button.

The important part of the HTML looks something like this:

```
<form id="editimage-import" ...>
    <input type="file" name="import-file" required>
    <button type="submit" name="import">Import</button>
</form>
```

The `file` input has the `required` attribute, which is an HTML5 validation attribute. Once all the form's validation requirements have been satisfied, the form is **valid**. Until then, the form is **invalid**. In this case, there's only one requirement, which is that a file must be selected.

The form also has an `id`. You don't technically need that for a form, but it's useful if you have some additional work to do in JavaScript, or you want to do something in CSS, such as hiding the button.

The relevant part of the CSS is

```
form#editimage-import input[name="import-file"]:invalid + button,
form#editblog-import input[name="import-file"]:invalid + button {
    display: none;
}
```

This selects for a button inside the form. There are three special parts of this selector:

- The [name="import"] is called an **attribute selector** and specifies an element with the name="import" attribute. It's not strictly necessary here as there's only one button in the form, but it's always best to be specific.

- The :invalid is a **pseudoclass selector**. In CSS, you use it like a class, but its value is set automatically by the state. In this case, an incomplete form would trigger the invalid state.

- The + combinator is called a **sibling** combinator and indicates a button which is adjacent but *after* the invalid input.

As you see, while the form is invalid, the button is hidden using the display: none property.

Preview Image

There are a number of places where an image is previewed. This is all done with JavaScript.

Previewing a Referenced Image

For the blog management, you have the option of choosing a selected image, either with a select menu or a radio button. In both cases, the image options are wrapped in an anchor which references a larger image.

In the JavaScript, the initialization script looks for a `div` element whose id is `use-image`:

```
if(useImage = document.querySelector('div#use-image')) {
    let previewImage
        = document.querySelector(img#preview-new-image);
    useImage.onclick = event => {
        showImage(
            previewImage, event.target.dataset.preview,
            {dw: 240, dh: 180}
        );
    };
}
```

If it finds one, it then looks for an `img` element called `preview-new-image`.

Finally, the `div` element gets a `click` event listener, which calls the `showImage()` function, with the `img` element to be populated; the `data-preview` attribute, which is a reference to a larger image; and an object with the maximum size of the preview. In JavaScript, this becomes the `dataset.preview` property.

The `showImage()` function populates the preview image with the new image:

```
function showImage(preview, src, limit) {
    preview.src = '';
    [preview.width, preview.height] = [limit.dw, limit.dh];
    let cache = new Image();
    cache.src = src;
    cache.onload = e => {
        let img = e.target;
        if(limit) {
            if(img.width/img.height < limit.dw/limit.dh)
                preview.width = limit.dh * img.width /
                img.height;
```

```
            else preview.height = limit.dw * img.height /
            img.width;
        }
        preview.src = img.src;
    };
}
```

If it were not for the need to adjust the size, the function would be much simpler. The new image needs to be scaled to fit within this limit, which is where you see the preview.width and the preview.height values being adjusted.

The problem is that you can't do anything with the image size until after it's finished loading. The cache variable is used to hold a copy of the image. When it's finished loading, it will fire the load event. Inside that event listener, the size adjustments are made, and the image is copied into the visible preview.

The File Input

The file input buttons are expected to be used to attach an image. The initialization script looks for file input buttons with the data-preview attribute:

```
if(elements
  = document.querySelectorAll('input[type="file"][data-
  preview]')) {
    elements.forEach(element => {
        doFilePreview(
            element,
            document.querySelector(img#${element.dataset.
            preview}),
            {dw: 240, dh: 180}
```

```
        );
    });
}
```

On any one page, there's only one, which will be processed by the doFilePreview() function.

The doFilePreview() is responsible for remembering the original preview image, previewing the selected image, and for restoring the original:

```
function doFilePreview(fileInput, preview, limit) {
    if(!preview) return;
    //  Remember Original
        preview.original = {
            src: preview.src,
            width: preview.width,
            height: preview.height
        };
    //  Shift-Click -> Reset to Original
        fileInput.onclick = event => {
            if(event.shiftKey) {
                fileInput.value = null;
                event.preventDefault();
                preview.src = preview.original.src;
                preview.width = preview.original.width;
                preview.height = preview.original.height;
            }
        };
    //  Preview Attached File
        fileInput.onchange = () => {
            try {
                let reader = new FileReader();
                reader.readAsDataURL(fileInput.files[0]);
```

```
        if(limit)
            [preview.width, preview.height]
            = [limit.dw, limit.dh];
        reader.onload = event => {
            showImage(preview, reader.result, limit);
        };
    }
    catch (error) {
        preview.src = '';
    }
    };
}
```

The Remember Original code simply copies the src and dimensions of the original image into a new property called original.

The Reset to Original code listens for a click event and tests for the shift key. If this happens, the src and dimension properties are copied from the original property back to the preview image. This isn't the normal behavior of a file input, of course, so the preventDefault() method is called to stop the button from attempting to upload another file.

The Preview Attached File code listens for a change to the file input, which is what happens after you select a file. It then uses a FileReader object to read contents of the file and generates a binary version using the data:// pseudo protocol. From there, it is sent to the showImage() function to be displayed.

Light Box

The pop-up image you see, especially if you click an icon in the image management, is referred to as a **light box**. The actual code is in the lightbox.js file and is much too involved to be discussed here.

The initialization script specifically looks for a container element to be used in the light box:

```
if(document.querySelector(container = 'table.manage'))
    doLightbox(container);
if(document.querySelector(container
  = 'article#blogarticle>div#article>figure'))
    doLightbox(container);
```

The light box code handles the following:

- Creates the elements for the light box: a pop-up with the image and a caption and the background to cover the screen.

- Creates the CSS to manage the appearance and disappearance of the pop-up.

- Attaches an event listener to the anchor around the image, which will show the referenced image in the pop-up.

- Attaches an event listener to the background to hide the image, as well as a key event listener for the escape key to do the same thing.

The actual zooming effect as well as the shape of the pop-up is handled in the CSS and can be adjusted in the lightbox.css file.

Paging Page Number

When you hover over a paging button, the page number appears in its place. This is pure CSS, the relevant part of which is the following:

```
p#paging a {
    position: relative;
}
```

```
p#paging a:hover:before {
    content: attr(data-page);
    position: absolute;
}
```

The rest of the CSS is there to make it look right.

The anchor element has its `display` property set to `relative`. That won't change the appearance of the anchor itself, but is to prepare for the next part.

The `a:hover:before` selector applies only when the mouse is hovered over the anchor. The `:before` is a pseudo element which refers to the content at the beginning of the element, which is normally empty. In this case, it's to be filled with the `data-page` attribute, which, as you will recall, was added to each of the paging buttons.

The `display` property `absolute` causes the new content to sit in the same position as the original content.

The Hopping Kangaroo

The hopping kangaroo is a pseudo element added to the end of the h2 element in the visitor's blog list. The relevant part of the CSS is

```
article#bloglist>div>div>h2:after {
    content: "🦘";           /* aka \1F998;*/
    display: inline-block;
    transition: transform 1s;
    position: relative;
}
article#bloglist>div>div:hover>h2:after {
    transform: scale(-1,1);
    animation: hop .5s infinite alternate;
}
```

```
@keyframes hop {
    from {
        top: 0;
    }
    to {
        top: -.5em;
    }
}
```

The :after pseudo element represents the end of the content of the h2 element. In this case, it's filled with the kangaroo icon 🦘. The CSS Unicode for that character is \1F998.

The :after pseudo element also sets a transition property. A transition is a simplified one-off animation. CSS won't transition inline elements, so the display property is set to inline-block. By itself, the transition property does nothing. However, when the listed property transform is changed, the transition will cause it to change slowly, over a time of one second.

When you hover over the div (div:hover), it will change both transform and animation properties.

The transform property is set to scale(-1,1), which reverses the direction without actually resizing the image.

Meanwhile, an animation called hop is triggered to run infinitely (or at least while the mouse is over it).

The position of the :after pseudo element is set to relative to allow adjustments. The hop animation is contained in @keyframes rule. In this case, it simply adjusts the top property, relative to the original position.

APPENDIX C

PHP Versions

PHP is, at the time of writing, at version 8 point something. All versions before version 8 are regarded as legacy versions, and you should update PHP as soon as possible.

However, that's not always readily done. Some organizations are skeptical of newer releases, some hosts are very conservative, and some third-party packages use legacy code which fails in new versions of PHP.

To be clear, none of this should be a problem. New versions of PHP sometimes do have breaking changes, but these changes have gone through a number of stages. First, old features are *deprecated*, which means they're discouraged and marked for removal. Then they start to issue warnings. Finally, the old features are removed altogether. Web administrators should try to keep up with this.

If you're working with an older version of PHP, some of the code in this book may need a few minor changes. For the most part, new versions have added features which are more convenient to use. This appendix lists the most relevant changes.

The array() and list() Language Constructs

These have been around forever.

Although these look like functions, they're not. They are called **language constructs**. You use them like functions, but on the inside they're handled differently. There are also some things you can't do with them that you can with real functions.

© Mark Simon 2024
M. Simon, *An Introduction to PHP*, https://doi.org/10.1007/979-8-8688-0177-8

The array() expression generates an array:

```
$data = array('apple', 'banana', 'cherry');
```

As of **PHP 5.4**, it's easier to use the shorter syntax:

```
$data = ['apple', 'banana', 'cherry'];
```

The list() expression assigns multiple variables from an array. For example:

```
$data = ['apple', 'banana', 'cherry'];

list($a, $b, $c) = $data;

// equivalent to:
    $a = $data[0];
    $b = $data[1];
    $c = $data[2];
```

As of **PHP 7.1,** you can use the **array destructuring** syntax:

```
$data = ['apple', 'banana', 'cherry'];

[$a, $b, $c] = $data;
```

Before **PHP 7.1**, you were limited to numeric keys, and you didn't specify them. With current versions, you can name your keys:

```
$data = ['apple', 'banana', 'cherry'];
[0 => $a, 1 => $b, 2 => $c] = $data;

$data = ['first' => 'apple', 'second' => 'banana',
    'third' => 'cherry'];
['first' => $a, 'second' => $b, 'third' => $c] = $data;
```

This is also true if you use the classic list() syntax. When using keys, you specify the key first and then the variable.

Arrays can have mixed numeric and string keys, such as the array you get from `getimagesize()`. You can also use mixed keys in `list()` or array destructuring, but you must specify all of the keys or none of them. If you specify none of them, then only the values with numeric keys will be assigned.

The ... Operator

That's what PHP calls it, which doesn't exactly roll off the tongue. If you look hard enough, you might see it called the **ellipsis** operator. In other languages, it's sometimes called the **spread** or **splat** operator. It would possibly be more helpful to call it the **packing/unpacking** operator, because that's what it does.

Introduced in **PHP 5.6**, it's used to pack or unpack an array.

If you use the operator in a function definition, it packs multiple arguments into a single array. For example:

```
function doit($thing, ...$etc) {
    // whatever
}

doit('something', 'something else', 'stuff', 'more stuff');
```

Here, the first value is sent to the $thing parameter, while the other three values are packed into the $etc array.

This type of function is called a **variadic** function as it takes a variable number of parameters. Traditionally, especially before the ... operator became available, you would call `func_get_args()` to get all of the arguments in an array.

If you use the operator when calling a function, it unpacks an array into individual parameters. For example:

```
function doit($item, $price, $quantity) {
    // whatever
}

$data = ['book', 23, 4];
doit(...$data);
```

Here, the $data array is unpacked into individual values to be sent to the function.

As of **PHP 8**, you can also unpack an associative array. However, the keys need to match the parameter names.

mail() Function Additional Headers

The mail() function includes an argument for the additional headers, which should always include the From: header.

You can set the additional headers in a string:

```
$to = '...';
$subject = '...';
$message = '...';

$headers = "Date: ...\r\nFrom: ...\r\nCc: ...";

mail($to, $subject, $message, $headers);
```

The Email Standard requires the **CRLF** line break between headers, so this is encoded in \r\n as before. This requires a double-quoted string to work—single quotes don't support most special character codes.

You also need to have a space after the colon, but not before the next header, since a space at the beginning of a line indicates continuation.

As of PHP 7.2, these headings can be in an array:

```php
$to = '...';
$subject = '...';
$message = '...';

$headers = [
    'Date' => '...',
    'From' => 'me@example.net',
    'Cc' => 'fred@example.com'
];

mail($to, $subject, $message, $headers);
```

The mail() function takes care of the rest.

If you want to use an array in an older version of PHP, you'll need to convert it to a string. Something like the following will do:

```php
$headers = [
    'Date' => '...',
    'From' => 'me@example.net',
    'Cc' => 'fred@example.com'
];

$headers = array_map(
    function($k, $v) {
        return "$k: $v";
    } , array_keys($headers), array_values($headers)
);
$headers = implode("\r\n", $headers);
```

The array_map() function will take the keys and values of the $headers array and return each item of the $headers array as a string of the form header: value. The resulting array is then imploded into a single string.

Function Data Types

Some programming languages associate variable names with data types. For example, you can declare a variable to be a string or an integer. PHP doesn't do that and probably never will—any variable can be assigned a value of any type at any time.

However, PHP does allow you to specify data types when defining a function. For example:

```
function process(int $first, int $second): string {
    $first = 'hello';
    return "Got $first and $second";
}
print process('3', 5.7);
```

This requires that the inputs be *compatible* with the particular data types. In this case, they must be compatible with integers. Note that in the example, neither of the two values sent to the function is an integer. The first is a string which can be converted to an integer, while the second is a decimal which will be truncated to an integer.

What happens inside the function is another matter: there's nothing preventing the code from changing the variable to something else, such as a string.

The return value, however, is guaranteed to be a string.

The purpose of type hinting is to provide some safety to function calls. If the inputs are guaranteed to be the correct types, then it's easy to guarantee the output.

You don't need to specify the data types for all of the parameters.

The list of acceptable data types has been growing over the years. Here are some of the changes:

- **PHP 7.1**

    - The data can be nullable, such as ?int $a.

    - The return type can be void (no return value).

- **PHP 7.2**

    - The type can be an object type.

- **PHP 8.0**

    - You can have **union** types: that is, you can specify alternative types.

There is more information at www.php.net/manual/en/language. types.declarations.php.

Named Parameters

PHP function parameters have a number of features which help to make functions more flexible:

- Parameters can be type hinted (discussed in the previous section).

- You can have optional parameters, by setting default values.

- You can use the ... to pack multiple arguments into an array (discussed in a previous section).

As of **PHP 8.0**, you can now use **named parameters**. For example:

```
function doit($a, $b, $c) {
    print $a / $b + $c;
}
```

```
doit(b: 3, a: 21, c: 20);     //   21 / 3 + 20 = 27
doit(24, 6, 10);              //   24 / 6 + 10 = 14
doit(21, c:20, b: 7);         //   21 / 7 + 20 = 23
```

This gives you a number of options:

- You specify the value of the argument after its parameter name, *without* the dollar sign ($). This can be in any order.

- You can ignore the names and specify the argument values in the traditional way. Of course, you need to get them in the correct order. If you do, they are referred to as **positional** arguments.

- You can mix positional arguments with named arguments. However, you need to dispose of the positional arguments first.

This is particularly useful when you have a function with a large number of optional parameters, and you don't want to specify them all:

```
function doit($a=12, $b=3, $c=20) {
    print $a / $b + $c;
    print "\t//\t$a / $b + $c\n";
}
```

```
doit(b: 4);                   //   12 / 4 + 20 = 23
```

Even built-in PHP functions, such as the imagecopyresampled() function, which has *ten* parameters in a mysterious order, allow you to use parameter names to make them more readable.

APPENDIX D

Default Library Functions

In the book, we've tried to concentrate on developing the core skills which you're likely to find most useful. Some of that involved using code which is useful, but on a tangent to what we're focusing on.

In this appendix, we look at some of the functions which took on some of that extra work. By now, they're mostly within your understanding, though you may have to take a little on faith.

The functions we look at are

- `resizeImage()`: The function which copies and resizes images for the image gallery and the blog. This is covered in detail, including the mathematics you need to get the scaling right.

  It also includes the `splitSize()` function which splits a dimension string into its parts.

- `unzip()`: A function which unzips a ZIP file into a directory. This is already discussed in the book, but here we add a little more detail.

- `md2html()`: A very light-duty markdown interpreter, used in Appendix A. We don't go into complete detail but discuss the use of regular expressions in interpreting the code.

© Mark Simon 2024
M. Simon, *An Introduction to PHP*, https://doi.org/10.1007/979-8-8688-0177-8

- Two minor functions which are simply wrappers for other functions. The MimeType() function is used to discover the MIME type of a file and is a convenient wrapper around a more obscure technique. The printr() function is a wrapper to make the output from the print_r() built-in function more readable.

One thing you'll learn is some more techniques, which is always a good thing.

The other thing you'll learn is that sometimes it's OK to lean on somebody else's work. You'll see that, for example, in the discussion on the md2html() function which, in turn, borrows from another party.

Resizing Images

In the sample project, you used a provided function to generate thumbnail copies of uploaded images. Here, we're going to have a look at how that function is developed.

When developing a function, there's often the question of how best to implement the input parameters. You don't want too many (you'll see an example of a PHP function with too many parameters later), but you'll want some flexibility. You may decide that the way it's done in this function could have been improved upon, and you're welcome to do so.

You can use PHP to create and manipulate images and files. This ability is not directly built into PHP itself, but is available through the GD library, one of the standard libraries which is normally part of the PHP implementation.

GD originally stood for "GIF Draw," but now informally means "Graphics Draw" (GIF support was actually dropped at one stage due to licensing reasons but has since been re-implemented after the patent expired). Officially, it's just GD.

GD has many functions for loading and saving images, transforming them, simple drawing, and writing text. Here, we won't be drawing anything, though it is possible to use GD functions, say, to superimpose a timestamp as a watermark.

Make sure that you've enabled the GD library, as described in the setup for this book.

Resizing an image in PHP is a matter of copying a larger image into a smaller copy and saving it. However, if the required copy is of a different shape from the original (i.e., the **aspect**, or the ratio of the width to the height, differs), then you will need extra work to pad the difference.

The steps required to resize images are

- Load the original.

- Later, you will need to make padding adjustments for different aspect ratios.

- Create a smaller blank image.

- Copy the original into the smaller image.

- Save the new image.

When you copy the original image into the smaller image, you'll notice that it is probably distorted. This is because the original image may not be the same shape as the copy. This will be fixed with some padding adjustments.

The resizeImage() Function

We'll start a basic function to load an image and resize it into a new image:

```
function resizeImage($source, $destination, $size='160x120',
    $options=[]) {
        // Set up
```

```
    //  Load Image
    //  Adjust Scale & Dimensions
    //  Create Blank Image
    //  Copy Original into New Image
    //  Save New Image
}
```

This function will take a source file name and save a copy to a destination file. The optional size parameter will be a string, defaulting to '160x120'. We've also included an additional $options parameter which is an array of whatever we think might be useful options.

Interpreting the Resize Dimensions

After the source and destination parameters, the next obvious parameter would be the output size. We could have used two parameter variables, such as $width and $height, and you may decide to do just that. In this case, we'll use a string of the form width x height, and we'll split it into the width and height.

For testing purposes, we can use a default string of '160x120'. You can use explode() to split a string. This function allows you to specify a separator string and will return a number array of values.

You can then use array destructuring to copy the values into two variables:

```
»    $size = '160x120';
»    [$width, $height] = explode('x', $size);
```

To be more flexible, you should allow for extra spaces in the string. The explode() function isn't flexible enough for this, but you can use the preg_match() function, which takes a regular expression and returns component parts.

If you're trying to pronounce the function name, you might try "p-reg-match." It means something like "Perl-compatible regular expression match." Perl is another programming language which features quite sophisticated regular expressions.

The regular expression we'll use is the following:

```
/^\s*(\d+)\s*[xX]\s*(\d+)\s*$/
```

If you think that's a little cryptic, you may be right. Like all regular expressions, it's pretty unreadable at a glance, but if you break it down, it makes more sense. Here's how this one works:

Code	Description
/ ... /	The whole expression is contained in the / ... / delimiters
/^ ... $/	The special characters ^ and $ represent the beginning and the end of the string. Basically, the expression needs to match the whole string
\s*	The code \s represents any spacing character (such as the space or a tab), and the * counts zero or more occurrences. Basically, we're searching for any number of possible spaces
(...)	Anything in parentheses will be stored for later. Anything outside parentheses must match, but will then be forgotten
\d+	The code \d represents any digit (0 - 9), while the + counts one or more occurrences. Here, we're looking for at least one digit. Being in parentheses, the result will be stored for later
[xX]	This represents a choice of any character in the square brackets. We're looking to match an upper or lower case x

To put this in English, we're trying to match some possible spaces, some digits, some more possible spaces, an upper or lower case x, some more possible spaces, some more digits, and some more possible spaces.

The preg_match() function takes the following form:

```
$success = preg_match($pattern, $string, $matches);
```

The function works like this:

- $pattern is the regular expression you'll use to test the string.

- $string is the string to be tested.

- If the string tests successfully, the return value is 1, which is stored in the $success variable. Otherwise, it's 0.

- If the string tests successfully, the matches are stored in an array in the $matches variable. Otherwise, the array is empty.

In this case, a successful array will contain the following items:

Index	Value
0	The whole string
1	The first number
2	The second number

We can store the pattern in a variable for easy maintenance. We'll use the return value in an `if()` statement to decide whether the match was successful. We can then write the code as follows:

```
function resizeImage($source, $destination, $size='160x120') {
    // Set up
    $pattern = '/^\s*(\d+)\s*[xX]\s*(\d+)\s*$/';
    if(preg_match($pattern, $size, $matches)) {
        // success
    }
    else {
        // failure
    }
}
```

If the match is unsuccessful, we can choose to give up immediately with a `return` statement. Alternatively, we can just use some default values, which is more friendly:

```
function resizeImage($source, $destination, $size='160x120',
  $options=[]) {
    // Set up
    $pattern = '/^\s*(\d+)\s*[xX]\s*(\d+)\s*$/';
    if(preg_match($pattern, $size, $matches)) {
        // success
    }
    else {
        [$width, $height] = [160, 120];
    }
}
```

If the match is successful, we can destructure the $matches array:

```
function resizeImage($source, $destination, $size='160x120',
  $options=[]) {
    // Set up
    $pattern = '/^\s*(\d+)\s*[xX]\s*(\d+)\s*$/';
    if(preg_match($pattern, $size, $matches)) {
        [, $width, $height] = $matches;
    }
    else {
        [$width, $height] = [160, 120];
    }
}
```

The leading comma on the left of the expression is to skip over the first value which is the entire string.

Loading the Original Image

Now that we've worked out the dimensions, we need to load the image to be resized.

Images stored on the disk, or transmitted over the Internet, are usually stored in a special format which includes compressing them to take less space, as well as other data about the image. These formats include GIF, JPEG, and PNG, which are the classic browser image formats. We'll include support for these formats in this function.

On the other hand, images in memory are uncompressed and generic. This means that you can load from one format on the disk and later save the image in another format.

While PHP has functions to do this, they are specific to individual formats. You will have to choose which of many similar functions to use to load or save images, depending on the original input format and the desired output format. There are also functions which can discover data from the images and, of course, to make changes.

Modern browsers support many other newer formats, such as APNG, WEBP, and AVIF, but not all to the same extent. PHP also supports these newer formats, though you'll have to make do with the PNG functions for the APNG format.

We won't support these formats here, but you can add support using the functions available at `www.php.net/manual/en/ref.image.php`.

Getting Information About the Original Image

To begin with, you will need to read the original image into memory. Unfortunately, GD has not one but many functions to load an image into memory, depending on the image file type. This will also involve working out the format of the original image, as well as other details.

Before loading an image, you need to know its file type. PHP has a function inaptly called `getimagesize()` which returns information about the type, as well as the image's physical dimensions.

The return from a call to getimagesize() is an array of values with the width, height, and type and a string with the dimensions for an HTML img tag, as well as other prices of data. For example, given a JPEG file whose dimensions are 640 x 480:

Key	Sample Value	Meaning
0	640	Width
1	480	Height
2	2	Image type constant
3	width="640" height="480"	Dimensions for img tag
...		
mime	image/jpeg	MIME type

Note that the image type constant will in fact be an integer (in this case, 2 is a JPEG file). PHP has a large number of built-in constants, including names for the image types, but the MIME type is preferable because it is more meaningful.

The dimension string is purely a convenience for inclusion in an img element.

Since the data comes as an array, you could read it as follows:

```
$imageInfo = getimagesize($source);

$sw = $imageInfo[0];
$sh = $imageInfo[1];
$mime = $imageInfo['mime'];
```

We're using $sw and $sh for the source image dimensions ("source width" and "source height") to distinguish these from the $width and $height parameter variables. We won't need the rest of the data from the getimagesize() function.

More practically, you could read the first two values into variables by using simple array destructuring; however, you would still need to read the nonnumeric key separately, as the simple format only supports numeric keys:

```
$imageInfo = getimagesize($source);
[$sw, $sh] = $imageInfo;
$mime = $imageInfo['mime'];
```

Even more practically, you can, if you want, include the string key using the extended array destructuring format:

```
[0=>$sw, 1=>$sh, 'mime'=>$mime] = getimagesize($source);
```

Here, we've dispensed with the imageInfo variable and done it all in one step.

We can now add it to our function:

```
function resizeImage($source, $destination, $size='160x120',
  $options=[]) {
    // Set up
      ...
    // Load Image
      [0=>$sw, 1=>$sh, 'mime'=>$mime] =
      getimagesize($source);

}
```

Now that we know the image type, we can load it into memory.

Loading the Image Data

Loading an image data is a matter of a single function call, but choosing which function to call is more involved. This will depend on the image type, which is one of the pieces of information previously gathered. You can then use a switch statement to choose the appropriate function:

```
// Load Image
   [0=>$sw, 1=>$sh, 'mime'=>$mime] = getimagesize($source);
   switch ($mime) {
       case 'image/gif':

           break;
       case 'image/jpeg':

           break;
       case 'image/png':

           break;
       default:

   }
```

Note that we've allowed for the three classic formats only. You can add others if you like.

There is all the difference between an image type and the file's extension. For example, an image saved or transmitted as the JPEG type may or may not have been saved with the traditional .jpeg or .jpg extension.

The operating system typically uses the file extension to determine the file's type. However, it may not be correct, especially when some malfeasant wants to inject something unpleasant. PHP can look beyond the extension and into the file itself.

For each image type, there is a corresponding function to load it called something like imagecreatefrom..., which returns a reference to the actual image data. You can store this in a variable called $original:

```
// Load Image
   [0=>$sw, 1=>$sh, 'mime'=>$mime] = getimagesize($source);
   switch ($mime) {
       case 'image/gif':
           $original = imagecreatefromgif($source);
           break;
       case 'image/jpeg':
           $original = imagecreatefromjpeg($source);
           break;
       case 'image/png':
           $original = imagecreatefrompng($source);
           break;
       default:

   }
```

For a default case, you can use the NULL value: default:

```
       $original = null;
```

This can be used to indicate that the image wasn't loaded.

The function now looks like this:

```
function resizeImage($source, $destination, $size='160x120',
  $options=[]) {
   // Set up
       ...
   // Load Image
       [0=>$width, 1=>$height, 'mime'=>$mime]
         = getimagesize($source);
```

```
    switch ($mime) {
        case 'image/gif':
            $original = imagecreatefromgif($source);
            break;
        case 'image/jpeg':
            $original = imagecreatefromjpeg($source);
            break;
        case 'image/png':
            $original = imagecreatefrompng($source);
            break;
        default:
            $original = null;
    }
}
```

While we're here, we'll look at how to save the result next.

Saving the Resized Image

Just as with loading an image, PHP can save an image a number of different formats, including JPEG, PNG, and GIF formats, but, again, you'll need to choose the appropriate function.

To save an image as a file, we use a function called something like imagepng(...), imagejpeg(...), or imagegif(...), depending on the file type. For example, imagejpeg($image, $filename); will save the image as a JPEG file.

If you omit the file name, PHP will output the raw image data to the
screen. Of itself, this is useless, since your browser won't interpret
it properly, being, as it were, mixed in with other data. However, in
combination with additional code to produce the appropriate HTTP
headers, this can be used to generate a live image for immediate
display. This can be used, for example, to display live graphs or
date-stamped images.

Similar to the loadImage() function, we'll use the switch() statement
to choose between image saving functions. We already have the
destination from the function parameter. We'll assume, for now, that the
image to be saved is in a variable called $copy, which we'll work on next:

```
// Save New Image
    switch ($mime) {
        case 'image/gif':
            imagegif($copy, $destination);
            break;
        case 'image/jpeg':
            imagejpeg($copy, $destination);
            break;
        case 'image/png':
            imagepng($copy, $destination);
            break;
        default:
    }
```

Here again, we use the $mime variable to choose between image saving
functions. Later, we'll see this as an opportunity to change the saved
image type.

571

The function now looks like this:

```
function resizeImage($source, $destination, $size='160x120',
$options=[]) {
    //  Set up
       ...
    //  Load Image
       ...

    ...

    //  Save New Image
       switch ($mime) {
            case 'image/gif':
                imagegif($copy, $destination);
                break;
            case 'image/jpeg':
                imagejpeg($copy, $destination);
                break;
            case 'image/png':
                imagepng($copy, $destination);
                break;
            default:

       }
}
```

The next step is to create the new image to be saved.

Creating the Blank Copy and Copying the Original

The important part of the job will be to create a new empty image of the right dimensions and to copy the original into it.

To create an empty image, we use `imagecreatetruecolor($width, $height)`. The function name reflects that we plan to allow for 24-bit color ("true color"), rather than a shallower color depth. This function requires the physical width and height of our new image. We can use the dimensions passed in the function call.

The resulting (blank) image will be stored in a variable called $copy:

```
function resizeImage($source, $destination, $size='160x120',
  $options=[]) {
    // Set up
        ...
    // Load Image
        ...
    // Adjust Scale & Dimensions

    // Create Blank Image
        $copy = imagecreatetruecolor($width, $height);
    ...

}
```

By default, the new image is actually filled in with black, which will be the background when we start adjusting the image dimensions. You can change that to another color if you like. We'll see how later on.

Copying the Original into the Image Copy

PHP has a number of functions to copy image data from one image to another. However, since you only want to create what is otherwise a simple copy of the image, the most suitable function is `imagecopyresampled()`, which will rescale and resample the copy nicely.

The `imagecopyresampled()` function has *ten parameters*, which is very flexible but somewhat overwhelming. They allow you to copy part of any image into any part of another image. This is great if you want to create a collage, but here we'll only need part of the flexibility. Nevertheless, all of the parameters must have a value.

To make the function call easier to read and maintain, we can take advantage of our ability to break a PHP statement over several lines.

Here are the ten parameters.

```
imagecopyresampled(
    destination_image, source_image,
    destination_x, destination_y, source_x, source_y,
    destination_width, destination_height, source_width,
    source_height
);
```

The function parameters specify the data of each image, the top-left corner ("origin") of each image, and the width and height of each image portion. The parameters are written in pairs for the destination and source, respectively.

When the time comes, we'll use the following code:

```
// Copy the Original into the Smaller Image

    imagecopyresampled(
        $copy, $original,        // destination image,
                                    source image
```

```
    (int) $dx, (int) $dy, (int) $sx, (int) $sy,
    // left-top corner
    (int) $dw, (int) $dh, (int) $sw, (int) $sh
    // width, height
);
```

The (int) expression before the variables *casts* the value to an integer. The imagecopyresampled() function complains if you give it decimals to work with, and we're likely to get decimals when we start scaling the copy later.

This function breaks a convention for copying data. Normally, you would copy *from* somewhere *to* somewhere else. In this function, you copy *to* the copy *from* the original. The parameters are

- The (empty) copy from the source image

- The coordinates (x,y) of the top-left corners of the copy and source images

- The dimensions (width, height) of the copy and source images

The image variables ($copy, $original) and the source image dimensions ($sw, $sh) have already been defined.

The rest of the variables will be defined in the following steps:

- We will always copy the whole of the source image. This means from the top-left corner (0, 0) and using its full width and height ($sw, $sh), as read when loaded. For the source origin, we can use

```
$sx = $sy = 0;
//  $sw and $sh already defined
```

- The destination variables will need adjusting later, but for now we'll specify the whole of blank image copy. This means using (0, 0) for the origin and ($width, $height) for the size.

We'll copy them into new variables to make the code a little more intuitive and to make adjusting them easier:

```
$tx = $ty = 0;
[$tw, $th] = [$width, $height];
```

The code now looks like this:

```
function resizeImage($source, $destination, $size='160x120',
  $options=[]) {
    ...

    // Create Blank Image
        ...

    // Adjust Scale & Dimenstions
        $sx = $sy = 0;
        // $sw and $sh already defined
        $dx = $dy = 0;
        [$dw, $dh] = [$width, $height];

    // Copy Original into New Image
        imagecopyresampled(
            $copy, $original,              // destination, source
            (int) $dx, (int) $dy, (int) $sx, (int) $sy,
            // left-top
            (int) $dw, (int) $dh, (int) $sw, (int) $sh
            // width, height
        );
```

```
// Save New Image
...
}
```

At this point, you should have a working function, and you can call the function as follows:

```
resizeImage($source, $destination, '160x120');
```

The function isn't perfect yet, as it will distort the image copies, but at least you can get it ready for testing.

Note that although there is a default copy size, it is always safe to include them anyway, making it easier to change your mind.

Padding Adjustments for Distorted Copies

If your copy shape is not the same as the original image, then you will see a distorted image as it is stretched and squeezed into the new shape, as in Figure D-1.

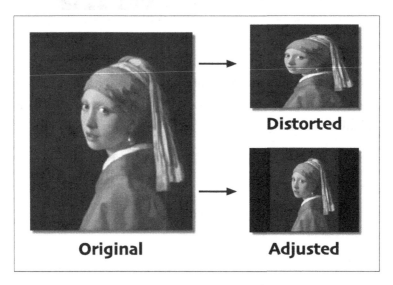

Figure D-1. Distorted Copy

Clearly, it would be better for the image to keep its shape inside the copy like the adjusted version.

To allow for a differently shaped image, you will need to adjust the part of the copy where the original will be copied into, so that the original shape is maintained. The difference in shape will be padded with the default black background or whatever color you decide on later.

You can see the idea in Figure D-2.

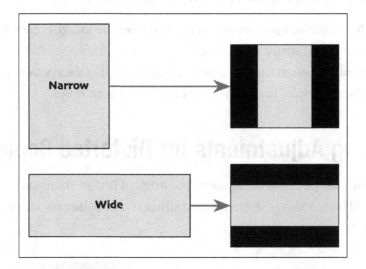

Figure D-2. *Padding Copies*

To create this padding, the destination corner point will need to be adjusted, as well as either the destination width or the destination height.

The calculation will be as follows:

- If original is thinner than copy

    - Adjust copy width

    - Adjust copy left coordinate (x)

- Else if original is wider than copy
  - Adjust copy height
  - Adjust copy top coordinate (y)
- Else (same shape)
  - Do nothing

Note that we only need to adjust *one* of the copy coordinates and *one* of the copy dimensions.

Image Shapes

At some point in your schooling, you would have learned about ratios. In case anybody is asking "why do we need to learn about ratios," you can say they help in rescaling images in PHP.

The term **aspect ratio** refers to the ratio of the width to the height of an image. You can calculate it as

$$aspect = \frac{width}{height}$$

If one image is thinner than another, then its aspect ratio will be less. If it is wider, then its aspect ratio will be greater. If the images are the same shape (even at different sizes), then the aspect ratio will be the same.

In the adjustment part of the `imageResize()` function, you can include the following:

```
// Adjust Scale & Dimenstions
  ...
  if($sw/$sh < $dw/$dh) {      // original is narrow

  }
  elseif($sw/$sh > $dw/$dh) { //  original is wide

  }
  // else do nothing
```

If the two shapes are the same, we will do nothing.

Adjusting the Size and Origin

The adjusted copy dimensions need to have the same ratio as the source dimensions:

$$\frac{dw}{dh} = \frac{sw}{sh}$$

The adjusted origin will need to start in the middle and move back *half* of the copy width.

For now, we'll focus on a narrower original image. This means adjusting the width and x-coordinate of the copy. The y-coordinate will stay at 0, and the height will be the height of the copy. Figure D-3 shows how this is going to work.

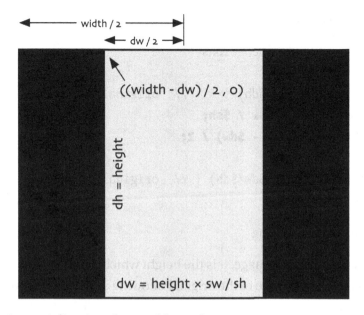

Figure D-3. *Adjusting the Width and Origin*

For the narrow version, we need to calculate the new width. This gives us

$$dw = dh \times \frac{sw}{sh}$$

In PHP, this becomes

```
$dw = $dh * $sw / $sh;
```

As for the origin, conceptually we move to the horizontal middle of the copy and move back half of the copy width:

```
$dx = $width/2 - $dw/2;
```

In practice, it's better to refactor this:

```
$dx = ($width - $dw) / 2;
```

Adding this to our function code, we get

```
// Adjust Scale & Dimenstions
    ...
    if($sw/$sh < $dw/$dh) {      // original is narrow
        $dw = $dh * $sw / $sh;
        $dx = ($width - $dw) / 2;
    }
    elseif($sw/$sh > $dw/$dh) { //  original is wide

    }
    // else do nothing
```

For a wider original image, it is the height which needs to be adjusted, as well as the y-coordinate of the origin. Following the same reasoning as before, we get

```
$dh = $sh * $width / $sw;
$dy = ($height - $dh) / 2;
```

Again, adding to our function code

```
// Adjust Scale & Dimenstions
    ...
    if($sw/$sh < $dw/$dh) {      // original is narrow
        $dw = $dh * $sw / $sh;
        $dx = ($width - $dw) / 2;
    }
    elseif($sw/$sh > $dw/$dh) { //  original is wide
        $dh = $sh * $width / $sw;
        $dy = ($height - $dh) / 2;
    }
    // else do nothing
```

If you try this now with various images, you should see padding added appropriately to maintain the shape of the copy.

The Complete resizeImage Function (So Far...)

You can view the completed code so far in a file called resizeImage-sofar.php. Here is an abbreviated version of the code, so you can compare what you've got:

```php
function resizeImage($source, $destination=null,
$size='160x120',
    $options=[]) {
        // Set up
        $pattern = '/^\s*(\d+)\s*[xX]\s*(\d+)\s*$/';
        if(preg_match($pattern, $size, $matches)) {
            [, $width, $height] = $matches;
        }
        else {
            [$width, $height] = [160, 120];
        }

    // Load Image
    [0=>$sw, 1=>$sh, 'mime'=>$mime] = getimagesize
    ($source);
    switch ($mime) {
        ...
    }

    // Adjust Scale & Dimensions
    $sx = $sy = 0;
    // $sw and $sh already defined
    $dx = $dy = 0;
    [$dw, $dh] = [$width, $height];
```

```
    if($sw/$sh < $dw/$dh) {        //  narrow
        $dw = $height * $sw / $sh;
        $dx = ($width - $dw) / 2;
    }
    else {                         //  wide
        $dh = $sh * $width / $sw;
        $dy = ($height - $dh) / 2;
    }

//  Create Blank Image
    $copy = imagecreatetruecolor($width, $height);

//  Copy Original into New Image
    imagecopyresampled(
        $copy, $original,
        (int) $dx, (int) $dy, (int) $sx, (int) $sy,
        (int) $dw, (int) $dh, (int) $sw, (int) $sh
    );

    switch ($mime) {
        ...
    }
}
```

The next job will be to handle variations.

Options

We've made a few assumptions about how the result should look, but we can add a few options to make the function more flexible. Here are some possibilities:

- Allow the destination name to be omitted.
- Change the background color.

- Change the copy image type.

- Allow a transparent background.

- Save a copy without padding.

It's easy to get carried away with flexibility so that the job is never finished, but the preceding options shouldn't be too hard to implement. Apart from the first possibility earlier, we'll use an $options array variable for the other possibilities, so as not to build an overwhelming collection of parameter variables, like the imagecopyresampled() function.

Omitting the Destination Name

You can change the function parameters to make the $destination variable optional, defaulting to null:

```
function resizeImage($source, $destination=null,
$size='160x120',
    $options=[]) {

}
```

The only problem with traditional optional parameters is that they must be specified in order. So, for example, if you want to specify your own $size value, which is very likely, you can't skip the $destination value, and you'll probably set it to null anyway.

In the section on named parameters, you'll see how this can be improved upon.

In any case, if the $destination value is null, then we can build our own destination name from the original name and the $size value.

We can add the following code to the section which saves the image:

```
//  Save New Image
    //  Missing Destination
        if(!$destinaton) {
            //  construct new name
        }
```

The new name can take the following form:

```
{directory}/{filename}-{width}x{height}.{extension}
```

where the directory, file name, and extension come from the original file name and the dimensions come from the $width and $height variables.

To get the components of the original path and name, you can use the pathinfo() function. This gives us an array with four components. You can then use array dereferencing to extract the components:

```
//  Save New Image
    if(!$destinaton) {
        ['dirname'=>$dirname, 'basename'=>$basename,
            'extension'=>$extension, 'filename'=>$filename]
        = pathinfo($source);

    }
```

We won't really need the $basename variable, since it's just a combination of the $filename and $extension values, so we can leave it out:

```
//  Save New Image
    if(!$destinaton) {
        ['dirname'=>$dirname, 'extension'=>$extension,
            'filename'=>$filename]
          = pathinfo($source);
    }
```

We can now reconstruct the name to include the dimensions:

```
// Save New Image
   if(!$destination) {
       ['dirname'=>$dirname, 'extension'=>$extension,
           'filename'=>$filename]
       = pathinfo($source);
       $destination
       = "$dirname/$filename-{$width}x{$height}.$extension";
   }
```

Note that we've wrapped the $width and $height variables in braces. In the case of the $width variable, this is to stop it from running on to the x which would have been mistaken for part of the variable name. You can do that to all of the variables, but it's only included for $height for symmetry.

Using the Options Array

The $options array might look like this:

```
$options = [
    'background' => [165,62,22],    // r,g,b
    'type' => 'png',
    'method' => 'trim',
];
```

The point of the $options array is that not all options may be present. You can take a simplistic approach and use two steps for each option:

- Test whether the option is present.

- If so, use the option.

In PHP, this would look like this:

```php
if(isset($options['...'])) {
    // use option
}
```

Another approach is to have another array of defaults and merge the two arrays. We can then go ahead and use the resulting array:

```php
$defaults = [ ... ];
$options = [...$defaults, ...$options];
```

The spread syntax (...$variable) destructures the array variables into keys and values, and the [...] expression then constructs a new array from the results. If the newer keys are the same as the previous keys, they will replace them. Prior to PHP 7.4, you would use the array_merge() function:

```php
$defaults = [ ... ];
$options = array_merge($defaults, $options);
```

At the beginning of the resizeImage() function, we can now process the options array:

```php
function resizeImage($source, $destination=null, $size='160x120',
    $options=[]) {

    // Setup
    ...

    $defaults = [
        'background' => [0,0,0],    // r,g,b (black)
        'type' => null,             // use same as source
        'method' => 'pad',          // pad copy
    ];
```

```
    $options = [...$defaults, ...$options];
    // $options = array_merge($defaults, $options);
}
```

We can now accommodate the rest of the options.

Setting a Background Color

The default background color when you create a new image is black, which is a reasonable way to start. You can set the background color to any RGB value, but it's a little complicated.

The `imagecolorallocate($image, $red, $green, $blue)` function creates an identifier for an image based on the red, green, and blue values you give it. You then use the result to fill in the created image.

The `imagefill($image, $x, $y, $colour)` function fills in the image with the color from the corner specified.

For the background color, we'll use an array of three values, each from 0 to 255. They will be the red, green, and blue values, respectively. For example:

```
resizeImage($source, $destination, $size, [
    'background' => [164, 62, 22]
]);
```

In our function, we can add the following:

```
// Create Blank Image
    $copy = imagecreatetruecolor($width, $height);

// Background Colour
    $background
        = imagecolorallocate($copy, ...$options['background']);
    imagefill($copy, 0, 0, $background);
```

Here again, we use the spread operator (...) which destructures the array into three separate values, which is what the imagecolorallocate() function requires.

You can now specify a background color or leave it at the default black.

Changing the Saved Image Type

As it stands, the resized copy will be the same type as the original, which is a reasonable assumption. It's not hard, however, to change that with one line of code.

The real problem will be with the file name. Technically, it's not necessary, but the file extension should match the MIME type—otherwise, some software will get terribly confused.

In this case, we'll do the following:

- Begin with the file extension of the $destination variable.

- If $options['type'] has been set, replace the extension with this value.

- Use the resulting extension to determine the MIME type.

First, we'll destructure the destination file name, similarly to what we did with the source name:

```
// Save New Image
  // Missing Destination
    ...
  // Check Mime Type
    ['dirname'=>$dirname, 'basename'=>$basename,
        'extension'=>$extension, 'filename'=>$filename]
      = pathinfo($destination);
```

We can then create an array of our accepted file extensions and their corresponding MIME types:

```
//  Check MIME Type
    ['dirname'=>$dirname, 'basename'=>$basename,
        'extension'=>$extension, 'filename'=>$filename]
    = pathinfo($destination);
$imageTypes = ['gif'=>'image/gif','jpeg'=>'image/jpeg',
    'jpg'=>'image/jpeg','png'=>'image/png'];
```

You'll see that the array has two file extensions for JPEG files, both of which are common; they still have the same MIME type.

Next, use the $options array to override the extension:

```
//  Check MIME Type
    ...
    if($options['type']) $extension = $options['type'];
```

We can now reconstruct the destination file name with the (possibly) adjusted extension:

```
//  Check MIME Type
    ...
    if($options['type']) $extension = $options['type'];
    $destination = "$dirname/$filename.$extension";
```

Finally, we'll use the extension to set the new MIME type:

```
//  Check MIME Type
    ...
    if($options['type']) $extension = $options['type'];
    $destination = "$dirname/$filename.$extension";
    $mime = $imageTypes[$extension];
```

Remember, PNG images take much more space than JPEG images, so you're more likely to change from PNG than the other way round. However, if you want to include transparency, then PNG is definitely the way to go.

Setting a Clear Padding Background

PNG images optionally include an alpha layer, which is a mask describing what parts of the image are solid, transparent, or anything in between. We'll use that to set a clear padding background.

We'll use the $options['method'] value to decide whether we want to do this. The three values will be

- pad: This is the default padding with a background color.

- clear: This pads the copy with a clear background; we'll implement this now.

- trim: This will trim the copy to the actual image without padding; we'll do that in the next section.

To implement a clear background, we'll need a variation on the imagecolorallocate() function we used earlier to generate the fill color. First, we'll use a switch() statement to decide whether to do this:

```
// Background Colour
switch($options['method']) {
    case 'pad':
        $background
            = imagecolorallocate($copy,
                ...$options['background']);
        imagefill($copy, 0, 0, $background);
        break;
    case 'clear':

        break;
}
```

We use a switch() in case there are more methods at some point in the future. Remember the default pad has already been set.

To implement transparency, we'll need a different function, imagecolorallocatealpha(), to set the color with alpha and to set a flag which causes the image to be saved with the alpha mask later:

```
// Background Colour
    switch($options['method']) {
        case 'pad':
            ...
        case 'clear':
            $background
              = imagecolorallocatealpha($copy, 0, 0, 0, 127);
            imagesavealpha($copy, true);
            imagefill($copy, 0, 0, $background);
            break;
    }
```

There's one more step, though. The only classic image format which supports alpha masks is the PNG format, so you'll need to override the extension, which sets the MIME type:

```
// Check MIME Type
    ...
    if($options['type']) $extension = $options['type'];
    if($options['method']=='clear') $extension = 'png';

    $destination = "$dirname/$filename.$extension";
    $mime = $imageTypes[$extension];
```

If you're building a neatly spaced gallery, it helps to have all of your copies the same shape and size. Having a clear padding background, however, allows your gallery to have whatever background you like.

Trimming the Image Copy

The code has assumed that you want your copy to be a fixed shape and size, which is why it's padded to fit the shape. You may want to dispense with the padding, so that the copy is the same shape as the original.

For this, we'll use the option

```
$option['method'] = 'trim';
```

With this option, you'll need to make two changes:

- The copy dimensions of the copy image should be those of the adjusted destination. We'll still accept both width and height and let the dimensions be the best fit.

  However, there may be a problem with the dimension values, which we'll need to allow for.

- The origin for the destination should be set to (0, 0), which is the top-left corner.

For the copy image, we can make the following change:

```
// Create Blank Image
   switch($options['method']) {
       case 'trim':
           $copy = imagecreatetruecolor((int) $dw, (int) $dh);
           break;
       case 'pad':
       case 'clear':
       default:
           $copy = imagecreatetruecolor($width, $height);
   }
```

Note that we've cast the $dw and $dh variables to integers. Again, the imagecreatetruecolor() function doesn't like decimals.

In the switch() statement, we've allowed the pad and clear options to fall through the default which is to create an empty image using the requested size.

For the destination origin coordinates, we had already set them to 0, but changed them when adjusting for the shape. We'll add a condition to only do that if the option isn't set to trim:

```
// Adjust Scale & Dimensions
    ...
    if($sw/$sh < $dw/$dh) {       // narrow
        $dw = $height * $sw / $sh;
        if($options['method'] != 'trim') $dx =
        ($width - $dw) / 2;
    }
    else {                        // wide
        $dh = $sh * $width / $sw;
        if($options['method'] != 'trim') $dy =
        ($height - $dh) / 2; }
```

You might also decide that you'd like to use a percentage instead of an enclosing rectangle if you're going to trim the result. That's not hard, but we'll leave that for some future enhancement.

Using Named Parameters (PHP 8)

You've seen that functions like imagecopyresampled() not only have an unwieldy name, but an absurd number of required parameters which must be supplied in a counterintuitive order. You'll see that in many PHP functions, but that's no reason to follow their example.

Our resizeImage() function has fewer parameters and allows options to be added in an additional array. Starting in PHP 8, there's an alternative approach.

Named parameters allow you to specify the name of the parameter variable, rather than relying on its position. For example, you can write the following alternative to the code we wrote before:

```
imagecopyresampled(
    dst_image: $copy, src_image: $original,
    dst_x: (int) $dx, dst_y: (int) $dy,
    src_x: (int) $sx, src_y: (int) $sy,
    dst_width: (int) $dw, dst_height: (int) $dh,
    src_width: (int) $sw, src_height: (int) $sh
);
```

Of course, that's not much of an improvement. However, if you want to follow the more conventional pattern of putting the source first, you can:

```
imagecopyresampled(
    src_image: $original, dst_image: $copy,
    src_x: (int) $sx, src_y: (int) $sy,
    dst_x: (int) $dx, dst_y: (int) $dy,
    src_width: (int) $sw, src_height: (int) $sh,
    dst_width: (int) $dw, dst_height: (int) $dh
);
```

Given the awkward parameter names and the fact that they're all required, it's still not so much of an improvement. However, when it comes to optional parameters, that's another story.

For example:

```
function test($a, $b=3, $c=4) {
    print $a + $b*$c;
}

test(5, c: 3);
```

Here, we have optional variables $b and $c. Using named parameters gives us the opportunity of setting $c without bothering with $b. Note that with the first parameter, $a, it's not optional. You can either set it by name in any order or by position in the first position only.

Named Parameters in the resizeImage() Function

To use named parameters in the resizeImage() function, we can make the following changes.

First, change the function definition to use separate optional parameter variables instead of the $options array:

```
function resizeImage(
    $source, $destination=null, $size='160x120',
    $background=[0,0,0], $type=null, $method='pad'
) {
    ...
}
```

Having set them here, we no longer need to bother merging arrays. You can delete or comment out the appropriate code:

```
function resizeImage(
    $source, $destination=null, $size='160x120',
    $background=[0,0,0], $type=null, $method='pad'
) {
    ...
    // Set up
        ...

/*
```

```
    $defaults = [
        'background' => [0,0,0],     // r,g,b (black)
        'type' => null,              // use same as source
        'method' => 'pad',           // pad copy
    ];
    $options = array_merge($defaults, $options);
*/

    ...

}
```

The next part is to replace all the references to the $options array with the simple variables. First, with the scale and dimensions:

```
// Adjust Scale & Dimensions
    ...

    if($sw/$sh < $dw/$dh) {        //  narrow
        $dw = $height * $sw / $sh;
        // if($options['method'] != 'trim') $dx =
        ($width - $dw) / 2;
        if($method) $dx = ($width - $dw) / 2;
    }
    else {                         // wide
        $dh = $sh * $width / $sw;
        // if($options['method'] != 'trim') $dy =
        ($height - $dh) / 2;
        if($method != 'trim') $dy = ($height - $dh) / 2;
    }
```

Next with the blank image and background color:

```php
//  Create Blank Image
    switch($method) {

        ...

    }

//  Background Colour
    switch($method) {
        case 'pad':
            $background
                = imagecolorallocate($copy, ...$background);
            imagefill($copy, 0, 0, $background);
            break;
        case 'clear':

            break;
    }
```

And finally with the MIME type:

```php
//  Check MIME Type
    ['dirname'=>$dirname, 'basename'=>$basename,
        'extension'=>$extension, 'filename'=>$filename]
      = pathinfo($destination);
    $imageTypes = ['gif'=>'image/gif','jpeg'=>'image/jpeg',
        'jpg'=>'image/jpeg','png'=>'image/png'];

    if($type) $extension = $type;
    if($method == 'clear') $extension = 'png';
```

There may be other reasons why you might prefer to keep the options in an array as before. One reason would be if you are working in an older version of PHP and don't have the option of updating it.

splitSize

The resizeImage() includes some code to split a string like 180 x 240 into two values. We'll need to do that on other occasions as well, such as deciding on the width and height attributes of an img element, so we have a stand-alone function to do that.

You have used the splitSize() function a few times. In its simplest form, you can write the function as

```
function splitSize(string $size) {
    $pattern = '/^\s*(\d+)\s*[xX]\s*(\d+)\s*$/';
    if(preg_match($pattern, $size, $matches))
        [, $width, $height] = $matches;
    else [$width, $height] = [null, null];

    return [$width, $height];
}
```

This is basically the same code as that in the resizeImage() function, except that the else part gives us a pair of nulls, rather than default dimensions.

In the actual function, there's a little more. For your convenience, you have the option of embedding those dimensions in a string like

```
width="180" height="240"
```

This makes it easier to include in the img tag later on.

The complete function looks like this:

```
function splitSize(string $size, $img=false) {
    $pattern = '/^\s*(\d+)\s*[xX]\s*(\d+)\s*$/';
    if(preg_match($pattern, $size, $matches))
        [, $width, $height] = $matches;
    else [$width, $height] = [null, null];
```

```
if($img) {
    if($width && $height)
        return sprintf('width="%s" height="%s"', $width,
        $height);
    else return '';
}
else return [$width, $height];
}
```

In this modified version

- There is an additional optional parameter $img which defaults to false. If it's not used, it will return the array with two values as before. If used, it will return the combined string instead.

- If $img is true, we also need to test whether the two dimensions have been set. If so, we can return the string using the sprintf() function. If not, we simply return an empty string.

We could have used this function in the resizeImage() function, but the code was duplicated simply to make the resizeImage() function more self-contained.

unzip Function

PHP has a ZipArchive class which allows us to work with ZIP files. In principle, it should be simple to extract files, but it's complicated by the fact that the files we want may or may not be in a folder. For that reason, we have a function to do that less simply.

We briefly described the process in Chapter 4, but here is more detail.

The function is called unzip() and broadly looks like this:

```
function unzip($source, $destination) {

}
```

The $source parameter is a reference to the ZIP file, and the $destination is the directory where the files will be going.

That should do the job, but in the process we'll be getting a list of file names. Two of them actually, and that might be useful. Or it might not. However, it doesn't hurt to make them available, which we'll do in a return statement.

To begin with, we create a ZipArchive object, open the file, and, later, close it:

```
function unzip($source, $destination) {
    $zip = new ZipArchive;
    $zip -> open($source);

    // extract files

    $zip -> close();
}
```

However, instead of using the built-in extractTo() method, we need to iterate through the contents of the ZIP file to get at the individual files. To do this, we need two things:

- The numFiles property has the number of files or directories in the archive. Note that a directory is treated as a file.

- The getNameIndex() method extracts the *name* of one of the files, by index number.

To iterate through the archive, we use a for() statement:

```
$zip = new ZipArchive;
$zip -> open($source);

for($i = 0; $i < $zip -> numFiles; $i++) {
    //   extract the file
}

$zip -> close();
```

Within each iteration, get the name of the file. The name will be the full path name including the enclosing directory, if any, so we'll need to deal with that in a moment. For now, we'll test whether it's the name of a directory by testing its last character:

```
for($i = 0; $i < $zip -> numFiles; $i++) {
    $file = $zip -> getNameIndex($i);
    if($file[-1] == '/') continue;
}
```

- We use the counter number to reference each file name, using getNameIndex().

- To get a single character from a string, we can use a notation which treats the string as an array of characters. The negative index counts from the end. Using $file[-1] means the first character from the end.

- If the last character is the forward slash (/), it's a directory name. Note that this is true even on Windows which prefers the backslash (\).

- If it's a directory, skip the rest and move on to the next one. The continue statement basically moves to the end of the block.

We'll now want to copy the file out of the archive into the real destination. For our particular case, we want to dispense with the internal path and just use the file name. We do that with the basename() function:

```
for($i = 0; $i < $zip -> numFiles; $i++) {
    $file = $zip -> getNameIndex($i);
    if($file[-1] == '/') continue;
    $name = basename($file);
}
```

Having got the base name, we'll do the copy:

```
for($i = 0; $i < $zip -> numFiles; $i++) {
    $file = $zip -> getNameIndex($i);
    if($file[-1] == '/') continue;
    $name = basename($file);
    copy("zip:// … #$file", " … /$name");
}
```

The copy(from, to) function, as the name suggests, copies the file. The special odd-looking format zip:// ... #$file copies from what was a virtual file in the ZIP archive. Here, we use the $file and $name values from the previous lines. The from part of the function references the original ZIP file; the to part of the function references where it's going.

At this point, there are two versions of the file name—the original and the simplified one. That might be useful, so we'll collect them in two arrays:

```
function unzip($source, $destination) {
    ...

    $files = [];
    $names = [];
```

```php
    for($i = 0; $i < $zip -> numFiles; $i++) {
        $file = $zip -> getNameIndex($i);
        if($file[-1] == '/') continue;
        $name = basename($file);
        copy("zip:// ... #$file", " ... /$name");

        $files[] = $file;
        $names[] = $name;
    }

    $zip -> close();
}
```

Here, we've initialized two arrays before the for() block and added the $file and $name values inside the for() block.

Functions don't need to have a return value. In PHP, a function returns null anyway, unless you return something else. That might be a wasted opportunity, so we'll return the two arrays, just in case anyone's interested:

```php
function unzip($source, $destination) {
    ...

    $files = [];
    $names = [];

    for($i = 0; $i < $zip -> numFiles; $i++) {
        ...
    }

    $zip -> close();

    return ['files' => $files, 'names' => $names];
}
```

The return value is an associative array to make it more understandable.

Markdown to HTML

The markdown language is easy enough to write in, but, in the end, it's not a web language. The next step is to convert markdown to HTML and let the CSS manage the presentation.

There are many markdown interpreters, both in JavaScript and in PHP, as well as many others in other languages. The md2html() function is a very simple interpreter written in PHP.

The code was inspired by **John de Plume**, a.k.a. **jbroadway**. You can see the original on GitHub: https://github.com/jbroadway/slimdown.

Unlike many other interpreters, this interpreter simply uses regular expressions to replace patterns, rather than a true language interpreter.

Regular expressions are special patterns used to analyze strings. Using regular expressions, you can define a pattern to be matched and how you might replace parts of the string. There's no official regular expression language, and there are variations, but most of them start off the same way.

Regular expressions are very concise and can be very powerful. They're also *very* hard to read, and we won't be going into detail here.

The most comprehensive version of regular expressions comes from the Perl programming language, and other interpreters often aim to be Perl-compatible. JavaScript has regular expressions, while PHP supports them via a library.

Regular expressions have limitations in what they can do, and this particular interpreter is not as rich or as powerful as some others. However, it's certainly good enough for our blog articles.

This is my take on the interpreter. We won't go into the full details, but enough to get a feeling for how it works and how you might modify it.

The function makes use of two PHP regular expression functions:

- `preg_replace(pattern, replacement, original)` replaces parts of the original string which match the pattern with a replacement.

- `preg_replace_callback(pattern, function, original)` does something similar, but uses a function to work out what the replacement should be.

Here are two examples, taken from the function.

Anchors

The markdown code for an anchor is `[text](reference)`, which translates to `<a href="reference">text</a>`.

The code to do the translation is

```
$text = preg_replace(
    '/\[(.+)\]\((.+)\)/',
    '<a href="$2" target="_blank">$1</a>',
    $text
);
```

The `preg_replace()` function replaces part of the text which matches a pattern.

This regular expression is complicated by the fact that the square brackets and parentheses are *both* special characters in regular expressions. To treat them as ordinary characters, you need to escape them—that is, precede them with a backslash (\).

For the first part, we're looking for something inside square brackets
(\[... \]). The backslashes treat the square brackets as literal
characters. Inside, we look for at least one character (.+?—the dot is any
character, the plus means at least one, and the question mark means don't
go too far). The result is captured as a group ((...)).

The same sort of pattern matches the second part, except that we're
looking inside parentheses (\(... \)). Again, the literal parentheses
need to be escaped.

Part of the regular expression includes what are known as **capture
groups**: references to part of the matched pattern. Those references
are $1 and $2, in the order they're found. The reason they're reversed is
that markdown puts the text before the reference, while HTML puts the
reference before the text.

The target="_blank" is a nonstandard addition for the sake of the
blog article. It causes the link to open in a new tab or window.

Headings

HTML headings are h1 to h6 to indicate the level of the heading. There are
two ways to mark a heading in markdown, but here we're using the hash
method: the line begins with one or more hash characters (#) and some
space. The number of hashes is the heading level.

Translating headings is a little more complicated than anchors
because of the varying heading level. For that reason, we use preg_
replace_callback(), which allows you to include a function rather
than a simple replacement; the return value of the function is the actual
replacement value.

The part of the code is

```
$text = preg_replace_callback(
    '/^(#{3,})(.*)/m',
    function($data) {
```

```
    [, $level, $text] = $data;
    return sprintf('<h%1$s>%2$s</h%1$s>',
        strlen($level), trim($text));
    },
    $text
);
```

The regular expression looks for a string at the beginning of the line (^) and a number of hashes. In this case, it's looking for three or more hashes #{3,}. Markdown will happily work with one or more hashes, but, for the blog, we reserve the first two levels for the web page. After that, we want the rest of the text (.*).

Putting the match expressions inside parentheses ((#{3,}) and (.*)) causes them to be captured for further use.

The second parameter is an **anonymous function**, also called a **closure**. It's a function which hasn't been defined separately and, in this case, isn't even given a name. It doesn't need to be that way. You can also use a predefined or built-in function if there's one which you find suitable.

Miscellaneous Functions

There are also a few minor functions, which basically wrap other functions into something more convenient.

The MimeType() Function

Sometimes, you need to know the type of file you're working with. Sometimes, that's for uploaded files, but it might also be for files which already exist around the place.

For uploaded files, the $_FILES array does include the type value, but that's not 100% reliable. For other files, you don't even have that.

PHP has a class called finfo. You can learn some things about the file that way, but here the interesting part is the MIME type.

Unfortunately, there's no objective way to work out what type of file you've got. The normal method is to look inside the file itself and look for certain telltale patterns. The function relies on a file called magic.mime for this. Fortunately, the finfo object will do that for you.

Using finfo isn't too difficult, but it's convenient to wrap it inside a simple function:

```
function MimeType($filename) {
    $finfo = new finfo(FILEINFO_MIME_TYPE);
    return $finfo ->    file($filename);
}
```

The $finfo object is created to specifically extract MIME type information, and the file() method does the extracting.

This is a very roundabout and counterintuitive way of getting this sort of information, which is why it's convenient to wrap it inside a more natural function.

The printr() Function

PHP has a built-in function called print_r() which can be used to output complex structures, such as an array. You don't have much control over its appearance because it's really only meant to be used while you're developing or troubleshooting.

To make the structure easier to understand, the output includes line breaks and indentation.

The only problem is that HTML ignores all line breaks and spacing, *unless* the content is inside a pre element or another element specifically designed to support the text layout.

For convenience, the library includes a function called `printr()` which simply outputs the `pre` tags around the actual `print_r()` output, so that you can see the layout within the rest of the HTML:

```
function printr($data) {
    print '<pre>';
    print_r($data);
    print '</pre>';
}
```

Index

A

Access restriction, 371–373
action attribute, 70, 71
addBlogData() function, 426,
    457, 470
addBlogImage(), 426
admin-bloglist.php, 408
Administration section, 404–406
Anchors, 607–608
Apache Web Server, 13
array_key_exists() function, 75
array_pad() function, 529
Article ID, 476–478
Aspect ratio, 579
Associative arrays, 53
Attribute selector, 540
australia, 148

B

Background colour, 589–590
BCRYPT, 350
Binary files, 199
Blog articles, 410, 521
    deleting, 507–509
    events preparation, 495–498
        image displaying, 498–501

preparation, 502–505
importing, 457
    calling a function, 470–472
    code, 459
    copying, 462–464
    data, 464–469
    finishing, 472–474
    handling, 459–462
    insert code changes,
        457–459
list, 513–516
managing, 487–492
reading, 473
    Article ID, 476–478
    article line breaks, 481–484
    displaying, 483–486
    fetching, 478–480
    preliminary code,
        474–476
table building, 492–496
updating, 504–507
Blog code, 413–419
Blog list page, redirecting, 456
bloglist.php file, 510
Blog pages, 408–410
Blog table, 410–412
Browser-side validation, 201

Printed in the United States
by Baker & Taylor Publisher Services